AMERICA'S STAKE IN EUROPEAN TELECOMMUNICATION POLICIES

America's Stake in European Telecommunication Policies

ALFRED L. THIMM

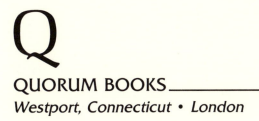

QUORUM BOOKS
Westport, Connecticut • London

Library of Congress Cataloging-in-Publication Data

Thimm, Alfred L.
America's stake in European telecommunication policies / Alfred L.
Thimm.
p. cm.
Includes index.
ISBN 0–89930–544–X (alk. paper)
1. Telecommunication policy—Europe. I. Title.
HE8085.T45 1992
384'.068—dc20 91–44111

British Library Cataloguing in Publication Data is available.

Library of Congress Catalog Card Number: 91–44111
ISBN: 0–89930–544–X

First published in 1992

Quorum Books, 88 Post Road West, Westport, CT 06881
An imprint of Greenwood Publishing Group, Inc.

Printed in the United States of America

10 9 8 7 6 5 4 3 2 1

Copyright Acknowledgment

Chapter 7 is an updated version of a paper originally published under the title, "Europe
1992: Opportunity or Threat for U.S. Business?" Copyright 1989 by The Regents of the
University of California. Reprinted from the *California Management Review*, Vol. 31, No.
2. By permission of The Regents.

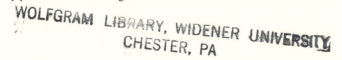

Contents

Figures and Tables

FIGURES

TABLES

Preface

The origins of this book go back to the 1985–86 academic year when I was a visiting professor at Vienna's University of Economic and Business Administration (Wirtschaftsuniversität). Before I left for Europe, several managers in the international corporate relations group of a leading American telecommunication enterprise suggested that during my year in Europe I study German and European Community (EC) telecommunication policy from a "European point of view" and present my findings on my return.

Vienna turned out to be an especially effective listening post because key executives of IBM, ITT, Philips, Siemens, and the Austrian manufacturing associates of Ericsson and Northern Telecom were sophisticated sources who could not only discuss German and EC telecommunication policy in a detached but expert manner, but also open doors to senior corporate managers in Germany and France, and to key bureaucrats in the EC.

I had already witnessed the consensus-driven nature of German telecom policies in 1975. As a visiting professor at the University of Munich, I had observed the operation of the first German government commission that had been charged with the critical assessment of the technical proficiency of the Federal Republic's telecommunication system. This commission, chaired by Eberhard Witte of the University of Munich, demonstrated the consensus nature of German politics, as well as the ability to make the sound, pragmatic recommendations that had been necessary to sustain the quality of the German infrastructure.

From my experiences in 1975 and 1985–86, it quickly became obvious that both American telecommunication managers and government officials did not understand the sociopolitical environment in which European and especially German telecommunication policy is made. The response to my subsequent presentation of the European perspective on international telecommunication issues encouraged further research on this topic over the next five years, in both Europe and North America. Abandoning the initial research approach of looking at the evolving new telecommunication order from a European viewpoint and pursuing instead as objective an analysis as possible, the initial impression was reinforced that American management and government officials had great difficulties in understanding European decision processes. The social, political, and institutional environment in which European policies have been evolving simply has not been properly analyzed. There has been misjudgment of American intentions in Brussels and Paris, Bonn and Munich, but not to the extent that even sophisticated Anglo-Americans (e.g., *The Economist*) have misinterpreted European telecommunication developments. One of the most astute, brief reports on the AT&T divestiture appeared, for instance, in German (B. Wieland, *Die Entflechtung des amerikanischen Fernmeldewesen*, Springer, 1985). No similar books on the French and German equivalent of AT&T have appeared in the United States.

The importance of telecommunication as a, or perhaps *the*, strategic industry for an emerging information society has prompted me to explore Europe's response to the technological and political changes of the last twenty years—in particular, the adaptation of hallowed institutions to the forces of creative destruction and the attempt to establish a European telecommunication system. This book—the culmination of six years of research—is directed at practicing telecommunication managers, government officials in the industrial policy areas, academics, and graduate students in management and industrial economics, but above all at the intelligent layperson whose interest in this once esoteric field has been stimulated by articles in *The Economist*, the *Financial Times*, and the *Wall Street Journal*. The discussion of telecommunication topics has been made difficult by the enormous use of acronyms and undefined technical terms that prevail in this field. I have decided to use those acronyms and technical terms that have become part of the lingua franca of telecommunication policy. I shall, of course, define each term when it appears for the first time and again if a term has not been used for a while.

A further difficulty is presented by the variation of the dollar exchange rates. Unless a European currency unit (ECU), a French franc (F), or a deutsche mark (DM) is explicitly converted at the prevailing exchange rate at a definite point of time, we will assume a general exchange rate of DM 2 : U.S. $1. The 2:1 exchange rate is a bit below the DM 2.30 : U.S. $1 purchasing power parity exchange rate that prevailed from 1988 to 1990 (2.50:1 from 1985 to 1988), but is above the average market exchange rate of about DM 1.85 : U.S. $1 that we experienced over the same 1988–90 period.

Lastly, certain words have a different meaning in the United States and in Europe. Thus European liberal parties are closer to American Republicans than to the U.S. Democrats. European liberals including French "radicals" favor a free market and free trade and have been historically anticlerical and, not infrequently, antimilitary. European conservatives have only over the past two decades committed themselves fully to a free market, as part of the Thatcher revolution; moreover, there still exists a strong mercantilistic tradition among European conservatives; Giscard d'Estaing and Franz-Josef Strauss are merely two examples of this proclivity. Whenever the terms "liberal" or "conservative" as used in this book could create a misunderstanding, I shall redefine these words.

I have received an enormous amount of help from many sources. Special thanks must be given to Eberhard Witte for his many comments and suggestions, and for his institute's hospitality. Similar thanks go to Oskar Grün at Vienna's Wirtschaftsuniversität, whose institute not only provided an excellent environment for research on three occasions, but also kept me supplied with new material even when I was in the United States. K. H. Neumann, director of Germany's superb telecom think-tank WIK (Wissenschaftliches Institut für Telekommunikation), has been of enormous help by making his monographs available to me and arranging a series of important interviews with key German telecom officials. Among managers who have helped me, and whose names I can mention, are above all Peter Flicker, director, Siemens, Austria; Heinz Hirthe, director, Siemens, Munich (now retired); Ing. Bernard Guide, Philips, Vienna; Diodato Gagliardi, director, European Telecommunication Standards Institute; my good friends Richard Schultz, director of the Institute for the Study of Regulated Industries, McGill University, Montreal; and Peter Stern, director, Teleglobe, Montreal, who provided me with the enormous amount of information only an international carrier like Teleglobe can supply. A very special acknowledgment is due to Robert Mathieson, international trade and telecommunication consultant, whose advice and criticism have been invaluable. Last, but certainly not least, thanks are due to AT&T, Northern Telecom, and NYNEX/New England Telephone, whose financial and intellectual support to the McGill University–University of Vermont telecommunication conferences provided the initial opportunity for presenting key components of the research contained in this book, and Siemens A.G., whose grant to Witte's institute provided the principal support for my research activities in Germany during the summer of 1989.

Many, many thanks to a Brussels EC technocrat who spent a year as visiting professor at the University of Vermont, but who prefers to remain anonymous. Considerable help was also obtained from other sources in France, the EC, and the United Kingdom, who expressed their beliefs freely, on the understanding that they would not be quoted. Any information received anonymously served merely as background information and enabled me to ask better informed questions from the sources cited.

We must add the usual disclaimer that none of the above mentioned is responsible for any opinion expressed in this book.

AMERICA'S STAKE IN EUROPEAN TELECOMMUNICATION POLICIES

1

European Telecommunication Policy: Creative Destruction in a Corporate Environment

European telecommunication policy is a fascinating topic that has attracted the attention of key executives in both industry and government. The *Financial Times*, *The Economist*, and the *Wall Street Journal* constantly report on European developments in the information-technology sector. These issues clearly affect economic and political interests even outside the telecommunication industry. European telecommunication policy is of interest to both intelligent laypersons and elites. It addresses four aspects of telecommunication.

- Telecommunication as a leading industry
- Telecommunication as an integral part of a common European infrastructure
- Telecommunication as a sector whose mercantilistic institutions have been exposed to the creative destruction of technological change that has destroyed the economic and technical foundations of monopolistic telecommunication administrations (the government-owned post, telegram, and telephone administrations [PTTs])
- Telecommunication as a key example of the globalization of the world economy

A leading industry, according to Joseph A. Schumpeter, not only determines a country's economic growth during a significant period, but also defines its geopolitical importance in the concert of nations.[1] Telecommunication and information technology (IT) have replaced steel and railroads as the leading industries of the last quarter of the twentieth century, and have therefore attracted the attention of politicians and bureaucrats committed to the development of industrial policies designed to support these national champions. The European Community (EC), in particular, has been committed for the past twenty years to support the development of a European computer and telecommunication industry that would be competitive with Japanese and North American multinational enterprises in the information-technology sector and thus guarantee Europe's survival as an economic and technological world power. "Telecommunications are at a meeting place of services and high technology. The advanced tele-communication network that has started to develop will be as strong a driving force for change in the 21st century as the electricity network and the motorway system have been for the twentieth."[2]

By the 1970s Europe's highly fragmented telecommunication and computer industries lagged behind their North American and Japanese competitors in both new technology and economies of scale and scope.[3] France, Germany, Great Britain, and especially the EC embarked on various industrial strategies in order to catch up with their global competitors. In this book we shall examine especially the nature, effectiveness, and political implications of these policies and America's economic and political responses.

Telecommunication as an integral part of a common European infrastructure provides a focus for analyzing the conflicting goals of protecting national champions and creating a European telecommunication-information industry. In particular we shall examine how Europe's largest telecom-electronic enterprises—Alcatel, Bull, GEC (General Electric Company of Great Britain), Philips, and Siemens—responded to EC pressures to cooperate as European enterprises. The EC policy of encouraging alliances among the major technology enterprises clashed with their aspirations to strengthen their respective positions as global competitors. Furthermore, the emergence of European telecommunication standards as a strategic device to establish a European infrastructure has provided, on one hand, a potential continental market for the European subsidiaries of American firms; on the other hand Europe-wide mandatory standards have created obstacles for entering this market to enterprises dedicated to proprietary standards or to U.S. firms without European manufacturing locations. The conflict between U.S. and European policies concerning mandatory standards and regulatory "harmonization" will be thoroughly explored in various contexts.

Telecommunication as a sector experiencing the destabilizing impact of the creative destruction of new technologies, products, and markets will be examined especially in its European context in this book in accordance with Schumpeter's observations: "The fundamental impulse that sets and keeps the capitalist engine in motion comes from the new consumers goods, the new method of production, or transportation, the new markets, the new forms of industrial organisation that capitalist enterprise creates."[4]

The established agencies that have administered the European telecommunication system, the PTTs, represent particularly deeply rooted institutions, with strong ties to political parties, the public, and the industry. The adaptation of the PTTs to the changing technical, political, and market forces gives us an excellent opportunity to study firsthand the creative destruction process over a long period of time. We are interested in the changing nature of the PTTs throughout Europe, and hence, we shall examine the restructuring of telecommunication throughout Europe. We shall pay particular attention to Germany, however, since the consensus-driven nature of the German political process makes the reform of the German PTT, the Deutsche Bundespost (DBP), a highly transparent process. The deep historical roots of the DBP allow us to observe its slowly changing role with unique insight into both German society and the process of creative destruction.

Telecommunication as an example of the globalization of the world economy can be studied most effectively in the context of European telecommunication policy. The concept of globalization was evoked so frequently during the 1980s that it has become embarrassing to use the term. There is no question, however, that markets that were once primarily national, such as telecommunication, transportation, and steel, have become truly worldwide in both manufacturing and marketing. We shall discuss the forces turning telecommunication into a global industry, but shall emphasize the inherent contradiction that is created by applying national industrial policies to a highly competitive, technologically dynamic world market.

We shall emphasize throughout this volume the interaction of technological innovations, global market forces, and the existing historical, institutional, and political forces that have determined Europe's telecommunication policies on both the national and regional levels of the EC. It is our belief that the failure to understand the sociopolitical environment of European industrial policy has been responsible for failures of American corporate and government strategies, such as the recent GATT (General Agreement on Tariffs and Trade) fiasco in December 1990.

THE IMPACT OF TECHNOLOGICAL CHANGE ON EUROPEAN TELECOMMUNICATION POLICY

The global telecommunication industry has witnessed enormous changes during the past twenty years that have had and will have far-reaching technical, economic, and social consequences. The complex interaction between technological change and economic-political response makes the assessment of current conditions difficult and the prediction of future developments in the global telecommunication industry hazardous.

Only twenty years ago, telecommunication enjoyed a stable growth trajectory, in which the linear, incremental technological change of the postwar years coincided with a steady growth in the demand for and the market penetration of telecommunication devices and transmission systems. The regulated monopolistic Bell telephone companies delivered outstanding and reliable telephone service to the North American market, while the government-owned post, telegram, and telephone (PTT) administrations provided telecommunication facilities to its citizens worldwide; their local service varied from excellent in Japan and Germany, to adequate in the United Kingdom, to inferior in Mexico and Italy. Rapid, discontinuous technological change during the past twenty years, accompanied by partial deregulation in the United States, Great Britain, and Japan, as well as changes in popular attitude toward government ownership and control threatened to destroy the existing institutional structure of the global telecommunication industry.[5] The creative destruction of prevailing market equilibria enabled aggressive, entrepreneurial companies to challenge established monopoly positions and to threaten national and international institutional arrangements.

Observers of entrepreneurial behavior, such as Schumpeter and Peter Drucker, have recognized market and process incongruities as a major source of innovative opportunities; such incongruities could occur "within the logic or rhythm of a process between (management) assumptions and realities" and between "expectations and results."[6] The American and European telecommunication markets possess all of the above incongruities; American deregulation and rapid succession of discontinuous technological inventions have disrupted seventy-five years of stable, monopolistic processes that had been able to adapt themselves to continuous linear, incremental innovations. The assumptions of both European mercantilistic state monopolies and American deregulators are daily confronted with new technological realities that reward innovative undertakings and bypass regulatory restrictions. The dynamics of contemporary telecommunication markets lead to adaptive organizational behavior and strategies that neither Judge Harold Green, who presided over the Bell system's divestiture, nor the Justice Department, nor the PTT administrators could have anticipated. Judge Green has been administering the Modified Final Judgement (MFJ) of August 1982 that ended the eight-year federal antitrust suit against AT&T; his experience is a particularly good example of the inability to direct the thrust of technological change into politically desirable channels. The MFJ completely ignored the macroeconomic, trade, and defense implications of the AT&T divestiture and, in making Judge Green the guardian/administrator of the final judgment, assumed that technological change would also honor the AT&T–Justice Department agreement. Judge Green has been condemned, therefore, to maintain the Bell Operating Companies' (BOCs') regional monopoly against technological innovations in mobile telephone, personal network communications (PNC), and satellite transmission advances while preventing the BOCs from taking advantage of their competitive edge in economies of scale and scope to enter new fields. In this book, we shall discuss how these incongruities affected the European telecommunication industry and, in particular, the EC's and DBP's telecom strategies.

Deregulation in the United States responded to technological change, but created a new incongruity—the anomaly of an internationally accessible market. Japanese, Canadian, and European telecommunication equipment manufacturers, who retained their long-established relations with their state-owned, monopolistic provider of telecommunication services, promptly penetrated the open American market. (Deregulation in Japan had transformed Nippon Telephone and Telegraph from a state-owned monopoly into a quasi privately owned, dominant oligopolist.) Not surprisingly, the American government has attempted to convince the rest of the free world, especially Japan and Germany, to liberalize its telecommunication industry in accordance with the American model, and to open its market to international—and especially American—competitors. Most European PTTs and especially the DBP maintained during the early 1980s that they already possessed a free equipment market, and that the U.S. experience was a peculiarly American phenomenon that could not and should not serve as a model for European telecommunication policy. Although the European markets were not quite as restrictive as the Department of Commerce (DOC) trade negotiators claimed, no impartial observer could compare the openness of the American market with the institutional restrictions on foreign competition that prevailed in, say, France and Germany up until 1988 or 1989. We can appreciate, however, the enormous changes that have taken place since then in Europe, and especially in Germany, by recognizing that no serious European PTT manager today would refer to the prereform telecom markets of the mid–1980s as "free."

The American drive to deregulate the global telecommunication market has been supported by both the technological revolution that erupted in the once staid telecommunication industry and the recognition by European telecom companies that access to the enormous American market required liberalization of the home market. Some movement toward deregulation in Canada, and, more important, the privatization of the state telephone monopolies in Great Britain and Japan further strengthened the American position. Yet we must not overemphasize the American influence on the deregulation drive in the EC. European telecom liberalization was prompted primarily by the changing information technology and by new economic opportunities. The microchip and the microprocessor have merged the telecommunication and computer technologies to create a new information industry with estimated worldwide sales of over $1,000 bn by 1992, at least one-third of it in the United States.[7] The various estimates of worldwide information industry sales are rather soft, vary from source to source, and depend, among many other variables, on the definition of the "information industry." Estimates of specific telecommunication mar-

Table 1.1
Leading World Telecom Markets (in Millions of 1988 U.S. Dollars)

Country	$Sales
United States	24,009
USSR*	8,400
Japan	7,080
West Germany	5,800
France	4,482
Italy	3,916
United Kingdom	3,146
Canada	1,885
China	1,448
South Korea	1,422
Spain	1,403
Switzerland	1,380

Source: *Financial Times* (July 19, 1989): 23.

*The Soviet data are quite worthless since they are based on the official but wildly inaccurate official dollar: ruble exchange rate and on misleading numbers provided by the Soviet telecommunication ministry. These data should be ignored completely but are often taken seriously by American telcos.

kets are more accurate, particularly if they refer to past performance. Tables 1.1 and 1.2 show the magnitude of world telecommunication markets in 1989 on the basis of the most recent data available; they also provide an assessment of changes within that market. These estimates omit the overlapping of telecom and computer networks, such as Integrated Services Digital Network (ISDN) workstations and ISDN hookups that emerged in 1980.

The technological convergence of computer architecture and telecommunication systems did not, however, make it easy for computer manufacturers to enter the telecommunication market, nor did it enable telecommunication equipment manufacturers to flood the market with new mainframe or personal computers; IBM did not become a telecom power nor did AT&T succeed in the computer business. There has been, however,

Table 1.2
The Changing Nature of Global Telecom Markets (in Billions of U.S. Dollars)

Global Markets:	1988	1989	1993e	CAGR* 1989-83
Single Line	1.6	1.6	1.8	3.0%
Data Communic. Equipment	6.3	7.4	11.5	11.7
Switches	6.6	6.5	6.9	1.5
Call Processing Equipment	1.1	1.3	1.9	10.0
Fax Machines	2.3	3.4	6.7	18.5
Video Conferencing	-	0.1	0.2	25.7
Public Network Equipment	5.3	6.6	9.0	8.1
Public Value Added Services	124.8	127.9	144.6	3.1
Cellular Radio Phone	3.6	4.7	8.7**	16.6
TOTAL	152.6	159.5	191.3	4.6%

Source: Dataquest 1989; *Financial Times* (July 19, 1989): 23.

*CAGR = Compound annual growth rate

** More recent estimates put the mobile cellular market for 1993 at around $20 bn.

e = Estimated in 1989 on the basis of available 1980s data.

an increasing overlapping of computers and telecom systems, especially in the peripheral equipment and local area networks (LANs), to demonstrate the common scientific base of computers and telecommunication. The wildly competitive history of the computer industry, in which technological innovations determined the competitive advantage of an enterprise, differed greatly from the monopolistic or regulated telecommunication industry that experienced slow but steady incremental technological changes. The growing interdependence of the market-driven computer industry and the regulated telecommunication administrations with close ties to national equipment manufacturers led to worldwide changes.

Technological change not only made many aspects of government regulation irrelevant and unenforceable but also created enormous market opportunities for the leading telecommunication-computer enterprises in the major industrial countries. The disappearing barriers between the telecommunication and computer industries were epitomized by IBM's efforts to enter the telecommunication market and by AT&T's production and marketing of a full line of computers and sophisticated office equipment. Germany's Siemens A.G. and Japan's NEC, producers of both telecommunication equipment and computers for decades, have considered their rich experience in both converging markets as their major strategic asset in their attempt to gain a major foothold in the American market.[8]

The putative convergence of the computer and telecommunication industries has been accompanied by de facto disappearing national boundaries, either as the consequence of deregulation or as a result of technological innovations that undermine remaining monopolies. In addition to acquisitions and mergers, corporate alignments across industry lines (such as IBM-Rolm-Siemens and IBM-Fujitsu), or formation of transnational associations (such as AT&T-Telefonica Española, IBM-NTT, and Siemens-GEC), or the establishment of joint ventures (such as AT&T-Italtel, Compagnie Generale d'Electricté [CGE]-ITT, and Siemens-Corning Glass) have created a new global information-processing and transmission market. An ever-growing number of American, British, French, German, Italian, and Japanese enterprises have been, simultaneously, competing and cooperating in this enormous market in order to obtain the strongest possible global position and have, thereby, increased the supply of and demand for new, sophisticated information services.

The perceived market opportunities, the benefits of greater and quicker diffusion of knowledge and innovation in a deregulated telecommunication industry, and the hidden costs of administering regulations have prompted entrepreneurial PTT managers as well as farsighted politicians and government officials to advocate deregulation and a quicker response to the American liberalization campaign. It is important to note, however, that the broad masses of private telephone users in the United States and Germany (and France by 1980) had been quite happy with their existing telephone systems and did not clamor for deregulation. The liberalization of telecommunication was an issue for the elites—the multinational corporations, the computer manufacturers, the ideological supporters of the Reagan–Thatcher revolution. In Germany, for example, most senior civil servants in the Federal Ministry for Post and Telecommunication (BMPT), the powerful post employees union, managers of telecommunication companies that could not compete internationally, segments of the political establishment, and, above all, the public had been quite satisfied with the existing institutions and opposed any tampering with the status quo.[9] The same conflict between elites demanding deregulation and broad sections of the public supporting the status quo occurred in most European countries. In this volume we shall analyze how European but particularly German society and telecommunication industry responded to the revolutionary forces that threatened to undermine well-established institutions and crafts. The long, at times bitter struggle over the reorganization of the telecommunication system and telecommunication industry is a unique story.

NOTES

1. Joseph A. Schumpeter, *Business Cycles*, vol. 1 (New York: McGraw-Hill, 1939), chaps. 2, 4, 6, 8.

2. K. H. Narjes, vice president of the commission of EC, 1980. In Preface to Herbert Ungerer, *Telecommunications in Europe* (Brussels: Commission of the European Communities, 1988), 5.

3. We shall define "economies of scope" as the production by an enterprise of a range of related products, linked by technical and commercial ties such that the total cost of manufacturing and marketing is less than if each product were produced separately. See J. C. Panzar, and R. D. Willy, "Economies of Scope," *American Economic Review* 71, (1981): 268–72.

4. Joseph A. Schumpeter, *Capitalism, Socialism and Democracy*, 3d ed. (New York: Harper and Row, 1950), 83.

5. Herbert Ungerer, *Telecommunications in Europe*, (Brussels: Commission of the European Communities, 1988), 25–34.

6. Peter Drucker, "The Discipline of Innovation," *Harvard Business Review* (May–June 1981). See also Schumpeter, *Capitalism, Socialism and Democracy*, chaps. 7, 8.

7. Clifford Chance, *Information Technology 1992* (Brussels, 1990), 5–7; Peter Stern, *Annual Domestic and Global Forecast* (Montreal: Teleglobe, December 1991).

8. See "In die Höhle des Löwen," interview with Hans W. Decker, president, Siemens Corporation (U.S.), in *Wirtschaftswoche* (April 3, 1989): 52–55. Decker emphasizes the long-run, strategic goal of Siemens' North American policy, in particular the role of the United States as the "single biggest (electronics-telecom) market." Decker paraphrases Siemens CEO K-H. Kaske: "If one wants to be a world class player . . . one has to be represented in a market (i.e., the U.S.) that

constitutes more than one half of the global market" (p. 51). See also "Tanga für die Post," *Wirtschaftswoche* (April 3, 1987): 17–20, for a detailed discussion of the resistance to change in the DBP bureauracy.

9. The general popular satisfaction with the German PTT has been a major factor in establishing the broad consensus that dominates German telecommunication policies and dictates the choice of post-minister. The current incumbent, Christian Schwarz-Schilling, belongs to the liberal wing of his party, while his Social Democratic predecessor, Kurt Gscheidle, was a leading member of the promarket right wing of his party. There is little political-ideological difference between the two.

2

German Telecommunication Policy, 1970–89

Deregulation and divestiture in the United States were helped by the conviction shared by Bell System executives and Justice Department mandarins that AT&T access to the computer and data-processing industry would benefit both AT&T and the U.S. telecommunication industry. For very similar reasons, free market advocates in the German government and among German telecommunication executives, Bundestag members, and academicians were committed to liberalizing the German telecommunication system. Their position was strengthened by divestiture's successful stimulation of entrepreneurial activities in North America. Yet at the same time American deregulation, in European eyes, had chaotic consequences that supposedly led to a loss of network reliability and common standards and a fragmented communication infrastructure. Reform advocates, therefore, were emphatic that the liberalization of the German telecom system should not be a duplication of the American experience.

The proponents of German Bundespost liberalization included key Siemens managers who recognized that a rapid introduction of existing and expected information-processing technology into the Germany economy required prompt changes in the telecommunication infrastructure and in the prevailing DBP structure. Moreover, Siemen's strategy of full participation and further growth in the North American market made it a necessity that, in American eyes, the privileged Siemens-DBP relation be ended by removing apparent institutional barriers to the sale of American equipment in Germany. The obstacles to American equipment sales, however, have been exaggerated. Throughout the 1980s, Germany had a consistent deficit of about DM 250 with the United States in telecommunication equipment trade (see table 2.3). In 1986, during the height of the Market Access Fact Finding (MAFF) talks held by U.S. trade representatives in

Germany, exports from the Federal Republic accounted for 1 percent of all American telecommunication equipment imports, while the Japanese supplied 43 percent of all U.S. telecom imports. Regardless of American pressure, however, there also existed within the DBP strong voices that advocated quick liberalization, especially in the regulations pertaining to the "enhanced service area," in order to satisfy the desires of domestic customers and prevent the migration of multinational corporate headquarters to London.

In attempts to reach a popular consensus on important but potentially divisive political issues the German government has frequently established parliamentary commissions to study controversial issues and make policy recommendations. During the early 1970s German political and economic elites became dissatisfied with the state of the German telecommunication system. Excellent in the reliable though rather expensive transmission of local and intrastate telephone conversations, the DBP had been slow in adapting its system to the emerging new technologies. The slow introduction of digital networks and new services (electronic mail, facsimile transmission, videotex, etc.) threatened the technological competitiveness of the German infrastructure. During the same period the French government had undertaken a major investment program to build a digital telephone and data network, which succeeded in transforming France's telecom system from Europe's laughing stock into Europe's leading electronic communication system.

Yet in the mid–1970s most German voters were not eager to support technical or structural changes in the status quo. Moreover, there existed a vociferous group of influential leftist intellectuals that opposed any significant, "hard" technological investment as socially and technologically undesirable. Major DBP investments in digital networks, switches, and value-added services were opposed as a further step toward strengthening the power of the technocratic bureaucracy. Since the Federal Republic of Germany is a consensus-driven society that avoids alienating significant groups, the government, although supported by parliament and industry, had to rely on the commission approach to create the necessary consensus for political change.

In a telecommunication policy statement of January 18, 1973, Chancellor Willy Brandt set the guidelines for Germany's technical development program:

Innovations in the field of information processing and communications are having an increasing influence not only on technical and economic development *but also on the social life of the people*. In co-operation with the *Länder* and with scientists and economists, the Federal Government will work out its proposal for the further development of the telecommunication system. An important role in the development of communication technology will be played by the Deutsche Bundespost.[1]

In order to create the conditions for a national, long-run telecommunication policy that would gain the broadest possible support Post-Minister Horst Ehmke appointed in 1973 a "Commission for the Development of the Telecommunication System," generally referred to by its German acronym "KtK." Ably led by its chair, University of Munich professor Eberhard Witte, the seventeen-member commission examined the technological needs of the German economy. At the same time it provided ample opportunity for all strata of society to be heard. After two years of hearings it recommended prompt expansion of telecommunication services, and the development of a long-run program for providing a telecommunication structure "for the year 2000." The careful, consensus-building performance of the KtK diffused the short-run political issues; the broad acceptance of the KtK report enabled trade unions to justify to members their cooperation with a national policy that would give Germany the necessary telecommunication services for the twenty-first century. The antitechnology lobby muted its opposition.

The KtK was almost exclusively concerned with examining the emerging technological innovations and defining the telecommunication services that the German economy required in order to maintain or strengthen its international competitiveness. Once the need for a massive technological investment was no longer a political issue the question of how these services ought to be provided could be addressed.

It was essential for the establishment of a national consensus that the commission agree unanimously on fourteen out of seventeen recommendations and on all fifty-six "findings of facts" that had formed the basis of its discussions and recommendations. The KtK's seventeen specific recommendations included five noncontroversial ones that pertained to increased R&D spending and broadcasting issues; seven recommendations demanded the establishment of value-added services such as facsimile, videotex, and electronic mail transmissions; five recommendations urged the creation of pilot studies for introducing alternative broad-band telecommunication networks. The recommendations for value-added services did not specify whether the DBP or the private sector ought to provide the new technology; the broad-band network recommendations, on the other hand, specified that pilot projects be undertaken by the DBP, municipal agencies, and private enterprises.[2] The first step toward liberalization had emerged!

The KtK report, submitted in 1976 to Post-Minister Kurt Gscheidle, a former leader of the post employees union and a right-wing Social Democrat, played an important role in laying the basis for the slowly evolving consensus that ultimately led to the liberalization of the German telecommunication system.

Anglo-American observers and telecom managers completely misunderstood the political process that transformed, slowly but surely, the German telecommunication system. The Anglo-American view during the mid–1970s and 1980s—as represented by *The Economist* (November 23, 1985), *Business Week* (March 31, 1986), the *International Herald Tribune* (May 29, 1986), and the U.S. Department of Commerce—considered the DBP as the bulwark of mercantilism. *The Economist* called it the "Fortress on the Rhine" because the KtK report did not lead immediately to a U.S.-style deregulation.[3] The crucial function of the KtK commission, however, was to obtain a consensus to support aggressive investment programs to modernize the German telecom system in order to maintain Germany's position as a leading industrial society. Once this step had been accomplished, the organizational and economic restructuring of the DBP could be considered.

The prompt acceptance of the KtK's enhanced service recommendations and their quick implementation represented a considerable DBP accommodation to the new information age. DBP employees and unions had viewed services like electronic mail and facsimile transmission with a good deal of suspicion. Letter carriers and telegraphers, of course, understood fully the new technology's impact on employment. It is quite understandable, therefore, that any responsible union leadership and any competent DBP minister would welcome the KtK enhanced service recommendations as a much needed outside pressure to introduce necessary—but not necessarily welcome—innovations. The DBP's acceptance of the KtK recommendations to institute broad-band pilot projects in competition with similar municipal or private sector undertakings demonstrated a much greater DBP flexibility than Anglo-American critics recognized. Although a quick reading of the KtK discussion of broad-band networks might give the impression that this technology pertains mainly to television transmission, the report actually refers briefly, but explicitly, to the various telecommunication services, such as interactive videotex or telemetering, that could be provided by broad-band technology.[4]

The DBP's willingness to accept, or be pushed to accept, further liberalization was also evidenced by the decision of conservative (Christian Democratic Union of CDU) Post-Minister Schwarz-Schilling to designate once more the chair of the previous commission of inquiry, Witte, to head a new parliamentary commission that was charged with examining the structure of the DBP and the German telecommunication industry. The report of that committee was scheduled to be submitted after the 1987 parliamentary election.[5]

The KtK report and its acceptance by parliament and prompt implementation by the DBP provided a strong indication that there was no longer a mercantilistic "Fortress on the Rhine" (neither was there a "liberalizing" French PTT, as *The Economist* claimed). German telecommunication policy evolved slowly from a corporative network of public and private enterprises, political and institutional forces, trade union and technocratic organizations that managed to preserve a broad consensus while preparing for the gradual adoption of a long-run strategy.[6]

THE BUNDESPOST AND GERMAN TELECOMMUNICATION: HIGH-TECH IN A CORPORATIVE ENVIRONMENT

The development and operation of telecommunication systems in continental Europe have been managed by state-owned enterprises, the PTTs. Under regulations slightly differing from country to country, they have administered a legal monopoly in telecommunication transmission and, to a varying degree, in the provision, use, and service of terminal or customer premises equipment (CPE). In response to rapid technological change, business demand, deregulation in the United States, Japan, and the United Kingdom, and, most important, efforts by the EC to build a European telecom system, the PTTs have over the past fifteen years chosen different paths by which to adapt to deregulation pressures. The fact that the PTTs have chosen different strategies, although faced with identical technical and economic issues, emphasizes the importance of political, institutional, and cultural forces in the decision-making processes of the PTTs. Ultimately it was left to the EC, serving as a deus ex machina, to impose deregulation guidelines on the PTTs.

An important study by Godefron Dang-Nguyen from the mid–1980s identifies the crucial variables in the response pattern of the four major European PTTs. In West Germany, the search for consensus explained DBP behavior, while in France "technocratic dialectics," that is, rational cost-benefits analysis by the technocratic management determined telecommunication developments. In Italy, the all-important political struggle between the governing coalition and the opposition and within the coalition determined PTT decision making, while in the United Kingdom the inadequacy of a public enterprise in the current political climate led to deregulation.[7] We find ourselves in complete agreement with Dang-Nguyen's thesis and shall closely examine the importance of consensus in the policy determination of the DBP and the German telecommunication industry and reflect on the other PTT strategies.

A Brief History of the DBP

In order to understand the political and institutional issues that constrain German telecommunication policy, one must become acquainted with the DBP's history. The German postal system traces its beginning to 1482; it has been an imperial government monopoly since 1595. Administered efficiently by the legendary v. Thurn and Taxis family, the imperial Reichspost transported mail, goods, and persons reliably, efficiently, and profitably over a dense network throughout Central Europe.[8] Its yellow coaches and liveried employees became symbols of high-quality service. (The now money-losing postal components of the German and Austrian PTTs are still called the "yellow post," to distinguish them from the posts' telecommunication services.) Early forms of deregulation and technological innovation—Napoleon's destruction of the Roman-German Empire and, subsequently, the invention of the railroad—ended the first German communication monopoly. (The v. Thurn and Taxis, incidentally, quickly transferred their money into breweries, shipping, and railroads and are, until this day, one of the wealthiest families in Central Europe.)

The v. Thurn and Taxis family operated the postal service as a profit-seeking business and therefore neglected thinly populated areas such as the Mark Brandenburg (later Prussia) in northeastern Germany. Prussia had to develop its own postal system, a money-losing service that the state provided for its citizens. Academics who have dealt with the contemporary DBP have stated that the spirit of the Prussian postal system has had a greater impact on the Deutsche Reichspost (1871–1945) and its successor the DBP than the more entrepreneurial v. Thurn and Taxis post of Hapsburg Germany.

In 1880, shortly after the formation of the second German Empire in 1871, a government office for post and telegraph was established to be administered by a junior minister (*Staatssekretär*). In 1919 the Post and Telegraph Office became the Federal Ministry for Post and Telecommunication, and was charged with the management of the German postal service and the state-owned telephone and telegraph network. There were few changes in the German system until 1989. The DBP also managed a bus system and a savings bank service that was closely integrated with its postal and telecommunication components. The Weimar Republic's organization of the DBP was taken over, intact, by the post-World War II Federal Republic. Article 87 of the German constitution (*Grundgesetz*) of 1949 defined the sovereignty of the federal government over the telecommunication and postal services area. The Postal Law of 1953 provided the ground rules for DBP administration and duties until the postal reform legislation of April 1989.[9]

The DBP Management Structure before 1989

Prior to 1984 the telecommunication services of all continental European countries were provided by fairly independently administered state monopolies, the PTTs. Only in Germany was the DBP simultaneously a public enterprise and a ministry. From 1924 the Reichspost (now Bundespost) minister headed the administration of the PTT system. In accordance with the German constitution (art. 65) federal ministers managed their ministries independently, but in accordance with the overall guidelines determined by the federal chancellor. The post-minister, as a member of the federal government, participated in determining general policy and had the special assignment of furthering the development of the telecommunication system. At the same time the post-minister was also the CEO of the DBP, the largest government-owned enterprise with over 550,000 employees. The position of post-minister, then, combined the duties of a government minister with the tasks of an enterprise manager.[10]

The new post reform legislation of 1989 changed the organizational structure of the DBP, but did not alter the minister's authority. This dual role of the post-minister has been frequently criticized, although the growing importance of telecommunication for the entire economy may, belatedly, justify the presence of the chief DBP officer in the government.[11] The responsibilities of a post and telecommunication minster require policy coordination and jurisdictional arrangement with the economics and research ministries, as well as adapting the telecommunication policies to the political objectives of the chancellor and the governing parties. These important responsibilities, however, require full-time attention and are not easily made compatible with managing one of the largest and most important German enterprises. Under the new structure the minister may delegate managerial tasks but is not required to do so.

In recent years Germany has been quite fortunate in its choice of DBP ministers. The current CDU minister Schwarz-Schilling and his two immediate Social Democratic predecessors, Kurt Gscheidle and Horst Ehmke, were good managers and farsighted, effective politicians who made the most of a difficult political assignment. This was not always so. Particularly during the Weimar Republic, the DBP minister was frequently a political hack with fewer qualifications for that job than the party stalwarts appointed as postmasters general in the United States during the same period.[12] The organization of the DBP as a ministry rather than a public corporation created operational and policy problems. While, for instance, the Austrian and Swiss PTTs had a management board to develop strategy and to supervise operations, the DBP minister was assisted only by two junior ministers who divided managerial and political tasks. Since at the next level, the managers (*Ministerialdirektoren*) had specific operational assignments, and since precedence—or the fear of setting a precedent—has been particularly important in a bureaucracy with a long cameralistic tradition, the three-member top management was continuously overloaded with relatively minor but politically treacherous decisions.

The political pressures on the decision-making process were further augmented by the administrative council (*Verwaltungsrat*) that was supposed to participate with the post-minister in policy determination.[13] The twenty-four-member administrative council consisted of five MPs (members of parliament), five members of the Federal Council (Germany's less important "upper house"), seven DBP employee representatives, five representatives of private industry, and two telecommunication and finance experts. Quite clearly, by composition and design, the administrative council imposed a broad consensus requirement on the formulation and implementation of policy objectives and strategy. The strong representation of the highly unionized employees gave the postal union, de facto, a "codetermination" voice, in violation of existing legislation.[14] The de facto codetermination of postal employees and unions in DBP decision making—and especially the postal union's monopoly position in selecting the seven employee representatives for the administrative council—played an enormous role in delaying DBP introduction of technological innovations and in slowing efforts to liberalize German telecommunication laws. This fact has never been appreciated in the United States.

The Role of Union and Workforce

The postal union, representing 80 percent of employees and civil servants, held less than one-third of the seats in the administrative council, but could, if necessary, count on sufficient support of prounion MPs and MdBRs (members of the Bundesrat) to block any decision that conflicted with its interests, especially in the areas of personnel policy and employment security. For practical purposes, however, the pressure to reach a consensus was sufficient to prevent any major issue opposed by the union, or by industry for that matter, to even come to a vote.

Divisive votes, carried by small majorities that override the views of an important minority (*Kampfabstimmung*, "fighting vote"), are extremely rare in German society, and especially in the supervisory councils (board of directors) of corporations and public service organizations. The fact that the DBP employees union was a rather conservative organization whose officers and members belonged mainly to the right wing of the SDP or to the CDU-CSU strengthened its position further, both within the DBP's administrative council and with the public at large. The "statesmanlike" posture of the postal union during the mid–1980s did not interfere, however, with its vigorous presentation of the economic interests of its members. On certain issues of long-run macroeconomic importance, the leadership was torn between adopting an enlightened position and aggressively defending the short-run interests of the postal employees. In view of its structure and composition, it was not surprising, therefore, that the consensus-oriented administrative council showed little interest in developing or even discussing openly long-run strategies. The policies developed by the DBP (i.e., by the minister and his associates), on the other hand, were already formulated in a way that minimized controversy in the council. A minister convinced that substantial deregulation had to be introduced for the sake of the long-run interests of the German information industry would have been secretly pleased, therefore, if liberal economists and vociferous Americans demanded significant liberalization measures.

If the postal union imposed restraints on the German government and the DBP to formulate long-run telecommunication policies, its own ability to play a farsighted role was limited by German civil service legislation. In government enterprises the entire workforce—union and nonunion, letter carriers and senior civil servants—elects a "personnel representative council" (*Personalvertretung*), the government service's equivalent of the private sector works council. The *Personalvertreter* participate in all decisions pertaining to workplace design, introduction of new work methods and practices, productivity measures, and training, but are excluded from strategic decision making.

German social and labor legislation emphasize's cooperation. In private industry works councils and management are therefore able to make numerous quiet ad hoc arrangements on local levels that accommodate employees and management goals. In the DBP, however, all telecommunication services are performed according to uniform guidelines throughout the country. Very few modifications of existing procedures are arranged at the local level. Adaptation of existing guidelines to new technologies or changing employee needs requires, therefore, the attention of the DBP top personnel council (*Hauptpersonalrat*) and the equivalent DBP managers.

It must be noted that the economic interests of a senior DBP personnel manager who deals with the personnel council are also represented by that very council. The manager may participate in the election process. Since, however, the senior civil servants are, ordinarily, not active union members, and since virtually every *Hauptpersonalrat* member is a union member, the actual relations between DBP personnel managers and personnel councils are quite professional.

The postal union's traditional concern with workplace quality and employment security is undoubtedly reinforced by the existence of the DBP personnel councils and the council members' recognition that the DBP employees are concerned about the technological future. The council, therefore, has paid increasing attention to short-run job security issues and probably forced the union bureaucracy into a more aggressive defense of the status quo than their more farsighted leaders might have wished.

The chair of the postal employees union, Kurt van Haaren, unlike his predecessor former Post-Minister Kurt Gscheidle, vigorously opposed all proposals to liberalize the current system, and, for good trade union reasons, rejected all suggestions to separate the post and telecommunication services of the DBP into two independent, market-oriented public service corporations.[15]

Van Haaren's obstructionist position was not shared by all other union leaders or DBP employees. The former senior post official and active union member Franz Arnold, for instance, was one of the more outspoken critics of perceived union and DBP immobility, and other former union members and DBP executives can be found today in the most liberal European global telecommunication associations.

The postal union's excellent relations with the leadership of both political parties—especially with the parliamentary telecommunication committee—have given the union leadership the opportunity, however, to discuss informally long-run issues, and convey, off the record, a greater willingness to adapt itself to national needs than may be apparent. Union representation on the parliamentary telecommunication commissions provided another avenue for the union leadership to participate in the informal consensus-shaping process. At the same time, however, the union has not hesitated to use its political muscle to the fullest to protect the short-run interests of its members. As the discussion about the future of the DBP became increasingly heated during the late 1980s it became difficult to distinguish between leadership posturing and real beliefs.

The economy's growing interest in telecommunication policies, the importance of information technology and DBP revenues for the economics and research ministries, and the normal budget process assured, however, that substantial "countervailing" power existed to limit the role of the postal union. The importance of telecommunication for so many vital segments of the economy encouraged in German society all efforts to reach a policy consensus, even at the cost of delaying necessary changes in the status quo. Controversial subjects pertaining to technical change, employee policies, and deregulation were discussed in informal, quasi-academic settings, where senior bureaucrats, business executives, union leaders, politicians, and academics could consider the merits of specific issues.

The various government-appointed telecommunication commissions, as already mentioned, were a very effective force in setting the agenda for the telecommunication policy debate, while collegial get-togethers of managers, academicians, and union leaders, such as the Münchner Kreis, contributed immensely to the creation of a broad understanding of technical, economic, social, and geopolitical issues. We have already referred to the first government-sponsored commission, the Commission for the Development of the Telecommunication System (KtK). Appointed in 1973, it presented its widely read *Telecommunication Report* in 1975 in both German and English. In 1980 the German Monopoly Commission appointed a committee to study the impact of new technology on the DBP monopoly. The report by leading German economist Christian von Weizsäcker and his associates Günther Knieps and Jürgen Müller recommended far-reaching liberalization of the German telecommunication industry.[16] In 1985 a third committee was appointed by the post-minister with approval of parliament and the government to study the structure of the DBP in view of changing technological conditions. In order to build explicitly on the findings of the KtK commission, Witte was asked to chair this commission, which was instructed to submit its reports in September 1987.

This slow but effective process of formulating a consensus-based strategy—called *Willensbildung* in German, an untranslatable term—has been widely misunderstood in the United States and Great Britain and even in those circles in Germany that have not been part of the process.[17] Accustomed to the adversarial nature of Anglo-American policy discussions, English-speaking observers have taken ritualistic Bundespost pronouncements too seriously. For the sophisticated observer, it had been clear for a decade that the liberalization of the DBP would occur, especially in the areas of terminal equipment sales and value-added services although, of course, there was going to be no American-style deregulation. Most executives in the German, Swiss, and Austrian telecommunication industries expected that the parliamentary commission on the structure of German telecommunication (the Witte commission) would recommend a liberalization policy that could and would be implemented effectively.[18] Quite typical for the German decision process was the fact that the commission was charged to submit its recommendations only after the 1987 parliamentary election.[19]

The DBP Monopoly Position before 1989

We have already mentioned that the provision of telephone and telegraph services was a government monopoly from 1892, when the first telephone legislation was enacted by the imperial Reichstag. Exclusive government jurisdiction over telecommunication transmission was reconfirmed in the 1949 constitution of the Federal Republic.[20] The fact that the DBP monopoly position was anchored in the German constitution restricted deregulation possibilities; significant changes in the current system can and have been made, however, without encroaching on the constitution.

In order to emphasize the significant changes that have occurred in the German telecom system, we shall take a look at the conditions prevailing, de facto or de jure, during the mid–1980s, *before* the German parliament passed the post reform law of April 1988. The DBP was then (and still is today) the sole provider of public switching and transmission systems, including television transmission networks. Private establishment or ownership of all possible forms of telecommunication transmission systems, including satellite communication codes, was and still is "strictly forbidden," although, de facto, this latter provision is not enforced in reunited Germany for pragmatic reasons. The DBP's monopoly-monopsony position involved the following activities:

• the construction, maintenance, extension, utilization, and improvement of all telecommunication transmission and switching systems

- the specification, purchase, and service of network cables and network equipment
- the specification, purchase, service, and installation of terminal equipment (terminal equipment was deregulated in 1989; the first two provisions still prevail)

The DBP does not manufacture its own equipment, and, unlike AT&T, has never been a vertically integrated enterprise. It purchases equipment designed to meet very precise DBP standards. The DBP regulates the use of leased telecommunication networks but does not permit the lessee to share the equipment with customers or vendors. During the mid–1980s DBP officials—as well as their colleagues in the Austrian and Swiss PTTs— still emphasized that Central Europe had had a free equipment market for over eighty years. Foreign as well as domestic observers, however, often questioned the feasibility of penetrating that highly monopsonistic market; both new German and established foreign companies, however, had been able to sell various types of terminal equipment during the fifteen years that preceded the 1989 deregulation.

A crucial role in the DBP's purchase of telecommunication equipment was played by its "technical division," the FTZ (Fernmelde technisches Zentralamt), which supervised the licensing of terminal equipment in accordance with FTZ standards. The licensing process has followed the CCITT (Comité Consultatif International Télégraphique et Télephonique) and CEPT (European Post and Telecommunication Conference) standards, emphasized "maintenance and reliability," and insisted until 1988 on a uniform technology (*Einheitstechnik*).[21] The requirement that equipment manufacturers abide by an existing "uniform technology" was common to all PTTs (including AT&T) and had been used effectively to protest existing operator-vendor relationships. At the same time there is little doubt that the PTT managements in Bonn, Paris, and New York truly believed that the "uniform technology requirement" was designed to assure network and user security, compatibility, easy maintenance, and equipment adaptability to long-term policy objectives. During the late 1980s the DBP dropped its insistence on uniform technology to encourage competition among its suppliers, especially between Siemens and S. E. Lorenz (SEL/Alcatel).

The FTZ licensing policy made the penetration of the German market especially difficult for newcomers regardless of their nationality, although the German computer firm Nixdorf, Canada's Northern Telecom, and the various Japanese suppliers of telefax equipment had been able to gain access to the terminal equipment market. The DBP defended the FTZ licensing policy in terms that were reminiscent of preregulation AT&T and NTT arguments in defense of their monopoly position.

The emphasis on maintenance, compatibility, and reliability was also applied to the standardization of switching systems and PBX's private branch exchanges. Technically innovative equipment could be offered successfully only when the FTZ, in cooperation with the DBP's major suppliers, agreed on new standards and specifications. The joint "DBP-approved supplier" determination of new specifications delayed, for instance, the introduction of innovative newcomer Nixdorf's new digital PBX by years, until the established supplier Siemens could offer a competitive exchange; in that instance Nixdorf, at least, did finally obtain the opportunity to sell its PBX in the West German market. In neighboring Austria or France even large multinationals like Philips had given up attempts to crack the PTTs' bureaucratic licensing procedures, which surpassed Japanese ingenuity in maintaining established supplier relationships.

The DBP was the sole supplier of telephone sets, purchased from equipment manufacturers in accordance with published guidelines, and, during the fall of 1985, became the sole supplier of modems;[22] in extending its monopoly from low-speed modems to the entire digital analog converter market, the DBP followed initially general continental PTT policy that hoped to check the use of "illegal" enhanced services through control of modem use. In August 1986, however, the EC's monopoly commission ruled that the DBP's modem regulation constituted illegal restraint of trade. The German government promptly agreed to permit domestic and foreign vendors to sell modems directly to their customers. The government's rapid response to the EC's modem ruling stood in sharp contrast to its foot dragging and noncompliance with a previous EC commission's finding during March 1986 that had declared the existing European airline pricing agreements illegal. The ready, even eager, acceptance of the EC's modem ruling was another indication that the government had already made the decision to liberalize; outside pressures, whether from the EC or parliamentary commissions, provided welcome justification for taking necessary but politically hazardous steps.[23]

Although the DBP was legally the sole supplier of all terminal equipment, it permitted its suppliers to sell certain devices directly to its customers and stopped enforcing its equipment sales monopoly years before it was revoked. It was not always clear to what extent, if any, an overall strategy regulated the DBP's various policy decisions during the 1980s. Thus the DBP was only one of many suppliers in the important PBX market; it sold no telexes but licensed two domestic suppliers. After sharing the facsimile market with domestic and foreign enterprises, the DBP attempted to reassert its monopolistic claims in that market in 1985. The opposition of telefax manufacturers prompted the German antitrust agencies to intervene, and in a subsequent compromise the DBP was restricted to a 20 percent share of the expanding facsimile market; the 1989 reform removed the restraints on competition in the entire terminal market.

In summary, we can conclude that the German telecommunication equipment market never experienced the full, vertical integration of the pre-deregulation Bell System. In the switching and network market free access for all manufacturers was always theoretically possible, although in practice well-established relationships, reinforced by complex standardization and licensing procedures, created privileged positions for traditional, native suppliers. In the terminal equipment market, the DBP exploited fully its legal monopoly position only in the telephone apparatus, and, previously, the modem area, while licensing German and sometimes foreign companies to supply BPXs, telex, telefax, and facsimile equipment directly to the customer.

Close relationships between a handful of German firms (including S. E. Lorenz, the former ITT and now Alcatel subsidiary) and the DBP had developed in the key telecommunication markets that made it difficult but not impossible for outsiders to compete. During the mid–1980s the equipment market was less free than claimed by the DBP, but much more competitive than Anglo-American observers described it.[24]

THE GERMAN TELECOMMUNICATION INDUSTRY

The Telecommunication System

Modern telecommunication systems consist of three segments: (1) a transmission network that links one terminal unit with all others throughout the world; (2) accessible basic services and terminal equipment that can be located at a factory (robot), home (telephone), or office (multipurpose workstation); and (3) the value-added services (VAS) that have become available over the past two decades and put the use of databanks, data processing, and computer analyses at the disposal of the individual telephone owner. A country's telecommunication industry, therefore, consists of the network provider(s), the manufacturers of terminal and network equipment, and the sellers of enhanced or value-added services.

The convergence of the computer and the telephone into a revolutionary, global information-processing and -transmitting industry has prompted computer and telephone terminal equipment manufacturers as well as network owners and suppliers to invade each other's territory in order to increase their market share in all three segments of the telecommunication system.

The entry of famous computer makers into the telecommunication market, and the provision of glamorous value-added services to telephone owners by new providers may have distracted from the strategic importance the telephone network still holds in the telecommunication system. In the cases of the European PTTs, whose existing networks are still protected by strong legal monopolies, the establishment of a sophisticated, digital telecommunication infrastructure will strengthen for another decade the network owners' commanding position to determine telecommunication policy.

The Telecommunication System's Network Component

The crucial importance of the network rests on one economic and two technical factors. First, the revenues generated by payments for network use and (basic) network services comprised about 85 percent of total telecommunication income in Europe, Japan, and North America during the 1980s but are expected to decline to 80 percent before 2000.[25] We can assume that the latter percentage will remain stable only as long as the PTTs and other major network owners can prevent "bypass" competition. Second, the network connects all terminal equipment units with each other and with computers, databanks, and data-processing equipment. The need to merge voice and data transmission increases the importance of integrated networks and will assure network users standardized, compatible terminal equipment and services. Third, the providers of value-added services must either provide their own more or less specialized systems or use existing telecommunication networks. Even if they do use and market their own systems, in most cases final access to the terminal equipment must be made through the public telephone network. In Europe, the PTTs have required that all external value-added services be transmitted only through the public telecommunication net. Moreover the dominant role of existing networks enabled the major network providers—the PTTs (including the Bundespost), AT&T, NTT, and British Telecom—to introduce their own value-added services, and to extend their activities into the emerging growth market, primarily telecom-supported data processing.

It seems quite clear that the DBP has recognized the strategic significance of the telephone network and the policy leverage a sophisticated voice-data network, such as the Integrated Services Digital Net (ISDN), could provide. We shall discuss later both ISDN and the DBP's strategic objectives.[26]

The Telecommunication System's Equipment Manufacturers Component

The dominating enterprise in the terminal and network equipment market is Germany's second largest enterprise, Siemens A. G. Besides NEC it is the only company worldwide that has been active in both telecommunication and computers since the end of World War II.[27] Through a joint venture with Corning Glass, Siemens has also played a major role in the development of glass-fiber cables, as part of its strategy to lead in the development and installation of narrow-band and broad-band ISDN. The Alcatel (formerly ITT) subsidiary S. E. Lorenz and the Bosch subsidiary Telenorma are the next two most important German telecom firms; both have excellent although specialized R&D programs. SEL (S. E. Lorenz) developed together with another former ITT subsidiary BTM (originally, but long ago, Bell Telephone in Belgium) the System 12, a sophisticated network-switching device that had been marketed successfully in Europe, but could not be adapted to U.S. standards in its 1985 American debut.[28] Telenorma has developed cost-effective internal telephone systems, PBXs, and multipurpose extensions, and holds 20 percent of the German PBX in-house telephone system market.

ANT, DeTeWe, Tekade, and Hagenuk make up the final group of important German telecom equipment manufacturers that are commonly referred to as DBP *Hoflieferanten* (court purveyors), the group of manufacturers that had, or has, developed a close relationship with the DBP and has generally received most of its network equipment orders.

The electronic firm Nixdorf Computer (acquired by Siemens in 1990) and AEG/Telefunken were successful in entering that part of the telecom equipment market where computers were playing an increasing role. Nixdorf, Germany's version of the Apple success story, was a rapidly growing entrepreneurial firm that was led by its charismatic founder until his sudden death in the spring of 1986. Nixdorf was one of the first German computer manufacturers that produced specialized computers for the coming telecommunication market. It introduced, for instance, a sophisticated digital PBX system into the market several years before Siemens. AEG/Telefunken, a computer-electronic company whose management-marketing skills have not equaled its engineering competence in the past, has also entered the telecommunication market with specialized equipment; having become profitable again, since Daimler-Benz became its majority stockholder, it may emerge as a serious competitor in the global information market. The staid office equipment firm Triumph-Adler, acquired by Olivetti in 1986 and briefly associated with AT&T, was another enterprise that was expected to become an aggressive competitor in the terminal equipment market under new management and owners. So far this expectation has not come true.

In the past, the German telecom equipment market has not always been open to all international suppliers, as DBP officials have stated repeatedly; until 1980, at least, the DBP relied heavily on the top ten German equipment manufacturers (including the ITT/Alcatel subsidiary SEL, however) to supply network and terminal equipment. During the mid–1980s, however, foreign multinationals were able to both penetrate special terminal equipment markets that required DBP licensing and provide value-added service to German industry. Japanese companies (especially Toshiba and NEC subsidiaries) dominated the telefax (facsimile) market; Philips, Ericsson, and Northern Tel were making headway selling PBXs; IBM managed to sell the DBP, in late 1985, its obsolete 8100 computer and SNA (Systems Network Architecture) system.

IBM Germany's success in penetrating the DBP procurement market had several noteworthy aspects. The DBP's purchasing department chose the IBM computer and network over the offers of fourteen German and North American competitors, including DEC and Siemens. Four months after the sale, the IBM America headquarters announced that the 8100 computer would no longer be manufactured.[29] It had been questioned to what extent, if any, IBM Germany had advance knowledge of this decision, nor is it clear that IBM America was fully aware of IBM Germany's sale to the DBP. In order to assure the DBP objective to develop *quickly* an on-line net that would connect each post office workstation with all others and with the DBP mainframes, the DBP purchasing executives had wanted to purchase a "mature system." The purchase of overage equipment and an ISDN-noncompatible SNA network gives some indication that the Germany DBP may not be as protectionist as American observers claim.[30] For comparison, one may think of the reaction of the U.S. Congress if the U.S. Post Office decided to modernize its post office operations with German or Japanese computers and networks.

In summary, the German telecommunication equipment market during the mid–1980s became slowly more open and competitive, although Siemens and the other major suppliers still benefited from past "special relationships" that, in the Siemens case, had existed for nearly one hundred years.

Providers of Value-Added Services

Virtually every major German and international telecommunication computer firm, as well as a host of smaller German software and office equipment enterprises, offer various forms of information services to German industries. The convergence of telecommunication and computer technology has turned virtually all major enterprises in these two fields into actual or potential providers of value-added services—from inventory and production control systems, to electronic mailboxes, financial services, and access to diverse databanks, to displays of current theater programs and video information systems. All major multinational computer and telecommunication companies as well as the DBP offer these VAS and VANs (value-added networks) to German business and individual telephone subscribers. The advent of European broad-band glass-fiber ISDN systems by the year 2000 (Europe 2000 network) will integrate television and telecommunication, convert the television set into a two-way communication device, and increase both the competition and the offerings in the enhanced value-added service area.

The chief competitors in Germany's value-added market are the German subsidiaries of DEC, IBM, Ericsson, Northern Tel, Olivetti, Philips, Rank-Xerox, and Alcatel/ITT, as well as the major German computer-telecom firms Siemens, Nixdorf, Bosch, and AEG, plus a large number of smaller foreign and domestic firms. Although the lack of common standards and a proper fully integrated voice-data network has kept the providers of value-added services from realizing the full potential of the emerging information economy, the growth rate in this field is expected to range around 20 percent per annum during the remainder of this century.

Total value-added services represented but a small fraction of the $500 bn worldwide information-telecommunication market in the mid–1980s (in Europe, probably less than $200 m). Their potential was immense, however, especially since the demand for both office automation equipment and value-added services was highly interdependent and mutually reinforcing. A fair number of different estimates for past and future sales of computer-telecom equipment and services appeared during the mid–1980s. Thus, the U.S. Commerce Department's National Telecommunication Information Administration (NTIA) estimated $450 bn in sales for the global information industry in 1984, while ZVEI, the German Electronics Industry Association, as well as Siemens, estimated a 1985 DM 2250 bn market (about U.S. $1 bn at June 1986 exchange rates) for a similar but not identical market that included electronic components that had been omitted in the NITA statistics. There was no universal agreement on what was considered value-added services, enhanced network services, or standard services. Europeans believed that a major share of VAS and VANs in the United States served principally to overcome the chaotic lack of standardization that was a by-product of American deregulation.

The EC viewed the new telecommunication services as strategically important for the competitiveness of the European economy. The absence of reliable empirical studies prompted the EC in 1988 to order Scicon Networks to determine the market for value-added services (including value-added or enhanced networks) in Europe. In 1989, Scicon submitted its completed survey, *The Market for Value Added Services in Europe*, to the EC. We shall discuss this report below but will present the key 1989 findings now, in order to provide some benchmarks for the numbers bandied about in the mid–1980s (see table 2.1 for an overview).

No matter how imposing the estimates of information technology sales were, the market had not yet reached its potential. There was common agreement between sellers and potential buyers of office automation equipment and services, that only the absence of standardized products prevented an even greater exponential sales growth.[31] The arrival of a vendor-neutral integrated, standardized, digital voice-data network accompanied by standardized equipment and services will, according to industry spokespersons, generate the broad business acceptance of office automation the suppliers have been dreaming about. The value-added services market in Germany has been and will continue to be completely open to all domestic and foreign providers and hence highly competitive.

Table 2.1
The EC Market for Value-Added Services* (in ECU Millions**)

Online Databank Services (OLDB)	1275 Million
Electronic Mail (EM)	339
Electronic Funds Transfer (EFT)	247
Network Management (NWM)	73
Electronic Data Interchange (EDI)	51
Video Conferences	27
Temex and other services	14
Total VAS	2025***

Source: Scicon Networks, *Analysis of the European Market of Value Added Services*, vols. 1–6. Report to the Commission of the European Communities (London, 1989).

  *In order to adapt to the fluctuating dollar/mark and dollar/ECU exchange rate, we have throughout this book assumed a 2:1 DM:U.S. \$1 and hence a 1:1 ECU:U.S. \$ exchange rate. This is below the DM 2.30:U.S. \$1 purchasing power exchange rate that prevailed approximately for the 1988–90 period (2.50 DM:U.S. \$1 for the mid–1980s) but above the market rate for much of 1990 and 1991.

  **Scicon included only VAS that were offered to the business community against payments. Services to nonbusiness telephone users and intracompany services were not included. No distinction between VAS and VANs was made.

***The actual total of VAS reported was ECU 2024. The difference is due to rounding errors.

THE ROAD TO COMPETITION: DBP STRATEGY, 1976–87

The Sociopolitical Environment of German Telecommunication Policy

The broad acceptance of the first Witte commission's *Telecommunications Report* (1976) provided the DBP leadership with the political support needed to embark on an aggressive investment program to modernize the German telecommunication system. The immediate goal was to challenge France for technological leadership in European telecommunication systems; the long-run objective was to develop an infrastructure that would be as good or better than North America's. The emerging investment strategy was influenced, on the one hand, by efforts at the top government level to liberalize the German telecommunication system and, on the other hand, by the reluctance of senior DBP executives to accept significant changes in the status quo. There was, however, general agreement among both senior DBP managers and government officials that organizational changes were necessary to both cultivate an entrepreneurial spirit in the DBP's telecom bureaucracy and accommodate industry's demand for access to VAS.

The technical modernization strategy of the DBP was associated with a strong government program to strengthen the entire German microelectronic and information technology industries. A 1983 government study exposed the weakened competitive positions of West German and European industry in these two strategic sectors. Although Europe represented about one-third of the global market in microelectronic and information-technology products, its world market share had shrunk to 10 percent. Germany's telecommunication exports in the 1970s had attained second place in the world markets behind the United States but had fallen to third place by 1980, while Japan's market share had increased constantly.

Closer analysis of tables 2.2 and 2.3 shows that Germany had been able to maintain its leading position in medical technology and measuring instruments but lost market share in the microelectronic-information technology sector.

The German government believed that both Japanese and U.S. success was due to industrial policies that included strong governmental R&D support of civilian and defense projects (see figures 2.1 and 2.2). In accordance with its corporative history, the German government was determined to develop its own industrial policy to strengthen its microelectronic and information-technology industries, the strategic industries of the twentieth century. (Note that similar industrial policy efforts were already in progress in France and subsequently, in the mid–1980s, in the EC. The EC programs will be discussed below.)

The federal government's efforts to strengthen its computer and telecommunication sector obviously affected the DBP's investment strategy. Still, there were significant ideological differences in the underlying assumptions held by key DBP managers below the ministerial level. The center-right government that had come to power in 1982 as a part of the global Reagan–Thatcher revolution consisted of the Christian Democratic Union (CDU), its Bavarian "sister-party" the Christian Social Union (CSU), and the liberal Free Democratic party (FDP). The new government fervently expressed its faith in a social market economy and promised a *Wende* (change) from the previous government's guided economy toward a free market policy of deregulation, privatization of state-owned enterprises, elimination of subsidies, and lower taxes.

We should note at this point that Germany's de facto devotion to a market economy has not changed significantly since the Social Democratic-liberal coalition was replaced in 1982 by a Christian Democratic-liberal coalition. Helmut Schmidt, chancellor from 1974 to 1982, was probably a more dedicated and theoretically sophisticated supporter of market eco-

Table 2.2
West German Trade in High-Technology Products (in DM bn)

Changes in Trade Balance:

	1978	1980	1981	1982	1983
Data Processing	-0.4	-0.5	-0.6	-0.5	-0.5
Telecom. equipment	1.8	1.8	2.0	2.3	2.0
Electronic components	-0.6	-1.1	-1.1	-0.9	-1.0
Total information technology	.8	.2	.3	.9	.5
Measuring Instrument	1.6	1.9	2.3	2.7	3.0
Medical Technology	1.0	1.1	1.4	1.6	1.9
Total High Tech	3.4	3.2	4.0	5.2	5.4

Source: Adapted from Deutsche Bundesbank and K. H. Neumann, *Economic Policy Toward Telecommunications Information and the Media in West Germany,* WIK Monograph 8 (Bad Honnef, 1984), 21.

Table 2.3
Export of High-Technology Products in Select Countries

Export Shares is % of Selected Countries' Total

	1972	1976	1978	1980	1982	1983
West Germany	26.3	21.7	21.6	20.0	17.0	17.0
France	11.1	10.9	10.4	10.3	8.1	8.0
United Kingdom	13.8	11.5	11.7	12.6	11.1	10.0
Switzerland	3.5	3.6	4.1	3.6	3.2	3.0
Japan	13.0	18.2	18.5	18.2	20.3	25.0
United States	32.2	34.1	33.7	35.3	40.2	37.7

Export in U.S. $ Billion

	1972	1976	1978	1980	1982	1983
Selected Countries Total	8.4	20.6	29.8	44.2	49.7	54.0
West Germany	2.2	4.5	6.5	8.8	8.5	9.0

Source: Deutsche Bundesbank and K. H. Neumann, *Economic Policy Toward Telecommunications Information and the Media in West Germany,* WIK Monograph 8 (Bad Honnef, 1984), 20.

Figure 2.1
German Trade Balance with the United States in the
Telecommunication Equipment Industry, 1981–86 (in DM m)

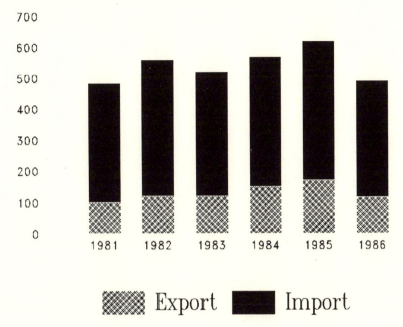

Source: Thomas Schnöring, *Changes in Telecommunication Equipment Trade: The Case of Germany*, WIK Monograph 12 (Bad Honnef, 1987), 19.

nomics that his conservative successor Helmut Kohl. Moreover, the liberal FDP, the permanent coalition partner in all German center-left and center-right governments since the 1960s, has always provided strong opposition to the corporative-interventionist tendencies that emerge in the German (and European) political spectrum as one moves from the liberal center to the left or the right. American observers of European politics are frequently misled in perceiving socialist tendencies in any effort to support or increase the government's role in the economy; they forget that European conservatives historically have had great faith in government intervention in the economy, provided, of course, the government was in the proper hands. The *dirigiste* core of most European governments, from Louis XIV to Mitterand, and from Bismarck to Kohl, is captured by a bumper sticker that proclaims: "Colbert is alive and well and still living in Paris."

In the case of the pre–1982 "social-liberal" coalition, it should be added that the very popular Chancellor Helmut Schmidt, a German Harry Truman, came under increasingly heavy attacks from the Social Democratic

Figure 2.2
German Trade Balance with Japan in the Telecommunication Equipment Industry (in DM m)

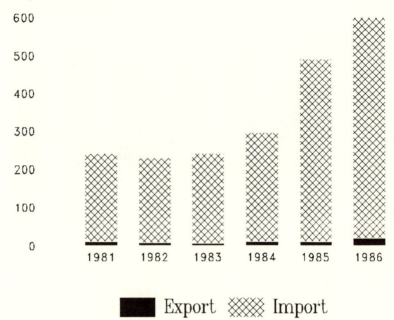

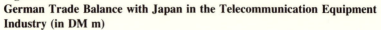

Source: Thomas Schnöring, *Changes in Telecommunication Equipment Trade: The Case of Germany*, WIK Monograph 12 (Bad Honnef, 1987), 20.

party's Marxist left wing. His promarket, pro-NATO, anti-Soviet stand constantly led to conflicts with important left-wing sections of the party and with the Union Federation (Deutscher Gewerkschaftsbund or DGB) establishment. The German Social Democrats (SDP) resemble the American Democratic party of the last decade: candidates that received the support of the party activists could not win an election, and candidates that could win would not be nominated.[32]

Given the ambivalent attitude toward deregulation among broad sections of the CDU-CSU and the traditional popular support for industrial policies to strengthen German key industries, we must not be surprised that Chancellor Kohl's *Wende*—the government's heralded withdrawal from intervention in the economy—had only superficial support in his own party and in the bureaucracy. At the same time, it must be emphasized that the philosophical concept of "competition" as an effective form of economic management has dominated German society since the Adenauer–Erhardt "economic miracle" of the 1950s. In particular, Nobel Laureate F. A. von Hayek's concept of competition as a superior "discovery procedure" has been widely and strongly accepted by virtually all segments of society, with the exception of the Marxist left, whose strength has lain primarily in the universities.[33] It is important to note that von Hayek considered competition to include entrepreneurial efforts with respect to innovations, product management, and quality. Von Hayek's views resembled Schumpeter's concept of creative destruction, and rested on a far more dynamic model than the static emphasis of orthodox Anglo-American economists on price competition as the only legitimate manifestation of the invisible hand.

The reconciliation between a philosophical attachment to competition in theory and support for limited government intervention in practice—a phenomenon not entirely unknown in American politics—is provided by Ludwig Erhardt's model of a social market economy. A government devoted to a social market economy encourages competition and lets the market allocate resources, except in those instances where the market mechanism would create socially undesirable outcomes, such as, for instance, the elimination of the family farm. The concept of the social market economy, hence, permitted the establishment of farm subsidy programs, and also justified telecommunication policies that subsidized "universal and uniform" local telephone service through high rates for business and long-distance users.

The policy of providing "universal and uniform service" required, first of all, that basic telephone service of uniform quality be available to all users throughout Germany at affordable rates. It also meant, however, that all services offered by the DBP, from telex to videotex, had to be offered, at uniform rates, to all subscribers throughout Germany. Thus, telex service, for instance, had to be available at identical rates for peasants in the Alps and bankers in Frankfurt, or for the general store in a Friesian fishing village and an automobile factory in Stuttgart.

The provision of universal and uniform telephone service as a socially desirable achievement was completely accepted by the German public and by the DBP's telecommunication management. There can be no doubt that DBP managers such as Helmut Schön, chief of telecommunication (*Abteilungsleiter Fernmeldewesen*) in the post-ministry, believed completely in the social desirability of the uniform and universal service policy. At the same time, this policy justified cross-subsidization and, therefore, required the continued existence of the DBP telephone monopoly in order to avoid "cream skimming." Whenever the demand for private sector value-added telecom services emerged, either from potential business users or from liberal politicians, Schön would immediately point out that private sector competition would serve only the most profitable service segments and would thus undermine uniform and universal service by reducing DBP profits.[34]

The devotion to a social market economy provided, therefore, a setting that simultaneously valued and encouraged competition, while expecting the state to maintain and even develop a modern infrastructure that would serve both industry and the individual citizen. The German government, supported by industry and parliament, embarked, therefore, during the 1980s on a policy to strengthen the entrepreneurial innovative capability of the microelectronic and information technology industry. Government policy consisted of simultaneously encouraging competition, providing research support, and maintaining a market of last resort for the telecommunication industry. The support for research projects in the computer and telecommunication sector had been, more or less, coordinated with similar EC efforts. The provision of reliable markets through government procurement came under increasing EC criticism during the late 1980s and will be abandoned by 1992 or 1993. In general, however, neither the German public nor the government saw any conflict between emphasizing the need for more aggressive competitive behavior in the telecommunication and electronics industry and simultaneously strengthening the government's role in research and development activities in strategic industries.

The Quandary of DBP Strategy, 1980–89: Liberalize but Maintain the Monopoly

The DBP strategy before the 1989 reform legislation consisted of three components:

1. Development of an ambitious investment program that would result in immediate modernization of network operations through new digital networks and value-added services. In the long run, by the mid–1990s or, respectively, the year 2000, narrow- and broad-band integrated services digital networks (ISDN) would give Germany an advanced telecommunication infrastructure (see figure 2.3). The investment strategy was to be accompanied by an effort to attain Europe-wide uniform standards for enhanced network services (e.g., the German videotex BTX) and open, that is, nonproprietary, VAS and VANs.[35]
2. Liberalization of the terminal equipment market and introduction of usage-based tariffs for leased lines with subsequent removal of usage constraints.
3. Emphasis on already existing competitive aspects of DBP procurement and operating policies to defend the essential maintenance of the existing monopoly. The social obligation of the DBP as well as its significant role in providing long-run investment funds were also stressed to foreign and domestic critics of DBP performance (see tables 2.4 and 2.5).

The various aspects of this strategy were presented effectively by Helmut Schön, chief of DBP's telecommunication department, in a speech on July 11, 1985, before the newly appointed government commission on telecommunication (Witte II). Schön was, if not the architect, the able spokesperson and aggressive executor of this policy until the elimination of his position in the 1989 DBP restructuring and (partial) deregulation.[36] Schön's speech presents a clear picture of the DBP strategy devised by the per-

Figure 2.3
DBP Strategy for Long-Run Network Integration

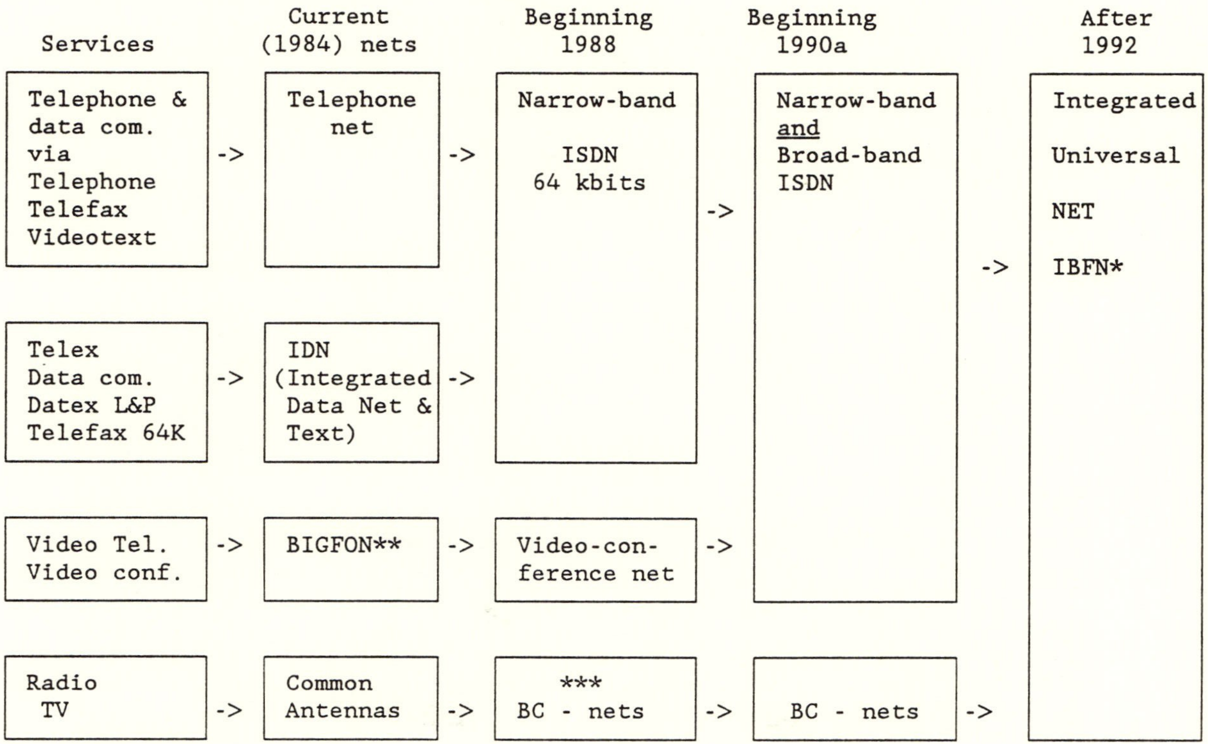

Services	Current (1984) nets	Beginning 1988	Beginning 1990a	After 1992
Telephone & data com. via Telephone Telefax Videotext	-> Telephone net	-> Narrow-band ISDN 64 kbits	-> Narrow-band and Broad-band ISDN	-> Integrated Universal NET IBFN*
Telex Data com. Datex L&P Telefax 64K	-> IDN (Integrated Data Net & Text) ->			
Video Tel. Video conf.	-> BIGFON**	-> Video-con-ference net ->		
Radio TV	-> Common Antennas	-> *** BC - nets	-> BC - nets ->	

Figure 2.3 (continued)

Siemens, *Leistungsstarke und Wirtschaftliche Telekommunikation für die Bundesrepublik Deutschland*; Unternehmens bereich Nachrichten und Sicherungstechnik, no author (München, May 1986), 10. Similar drawings also in *Konzept der deutschen Bundespost zur Weiterentwicklung der Fernmeldeinfrastuktur*, no author (Bonn, 1984), 22–26. The simple Siemens drawing reproduced here is based on a series of colorful drawings in Konzept.

*Integrated Broadband Fernmelde (Telecom) Net

**German acronym for Integrated Broad-Band Glass-Fiber Fernmeldeortsnetz (Local Telecomnet)

***Broad-band Coupling

[a]Broad-band ISDN nets were already introduced on a preliminary basis in 1989.

Table 2.4
Percent Share of DBP Telecom Investment, 1986–89, in Industry Sectors

Sector	1986	1987	1988	1989
Traffic and Communication	44.28%	45.86%	46.7%	*
Trade	30.17	30.04	28.61	*
Manufacturing	21.32	20.66	20.74	*
All enterprises	4.80	4.78	4.59	4.38

* No data available

Source: DBP/WIK *Newsletter* 1, December 1990, 23.

manent senior civil servants, and is a benchmark by which to evaluate the actual deregulation accomplished by the government's acceptance of the Witte II commission's recommendations.[37] The significance of Schön's speech extends beyond delineating DBP strategy. Virtually every regulatory and political telecommunication issue that affected the controversy between deregulators and traditional network operators in the United States and Europe is addressed. Rarely, if ever, can we find, however, a statement that discusses publicly, before a highly publicized commission, these controversial issues as clearly from the point of view of a beleaguered PTT. We shall present Schön's concepts, and try to put them in a European context.

By 1985 the DBP had already implemented virtually every recommendation of the Witte I commission and operated the following networks:

1. The analog telephone network with 24 million users. The telephone net could also transmit data, telefax, and videotex (BTX—the German acronym for video screen text). Digital nonvoice transmission could be managed through modems but became increasingly unimportant as the Integrated Data Network (DIN) developed.

2. The digital telex (teleprinter exchange service) net. First installed in Germany in 1933, it had always attained greater popularity in Europe and especially in Germany than in the United States. By 1990 the telex had been displaced by the telefax.

3. The digital switched datanet (DATEX-L). Through eighteen locations stored program control (SPC) switches operated an electronic data transmission system (EOS). During the mid 1980s 12,000 DATEX-L terminals were connected. The DATEX-L also transmitted the teletex service, a modernized version of telex that does not require specialized terminals.

4. The packet-switched datanet (DATEX-P). The DATEX-P was introduced in

Table 2.5
DBP Telekom (Sales, Employees, Investments in Comparison with the Five Largest German Enterprises)

Enterprise	Sales (DM million)			Employees (thousand)			Investment (DM Million)		
	1987	1988	1989	1987	1988	1989	1987	1988	1989
DBP Telekom	36,281	36,669	38,324	216.0	216.2	216.2	16,500*	17,000*	18,000*
Daimler-Benz	67,475	73,495	76,392	326.3	338.7	368.2	3,736	7,007	7,620
Siemens	51,431	59,374	61,128	359.0	353.0	365.0	5,313	5,210	7,872
VW	54,635	59,221	65,352	260.5	252.1	250.6	4,592	4,251	5,606
VEBA	40,475	44,391	49,208	74.6	84.7	94.5	3,989	4,366	7,075
BASF	40,238	43,868	47,617	133.8	134.8	137.0	2,758	3,495	3,950

Source: Annual reports, except for DBP investment estimates compiled by WIK.

*Estimated. Prior to June 1989 DBP investments in telecommunication had not been reported separately from those in postal service or postal banking.

1981 and switches packets of data. Several packets of data can be sent simultaneously over one physical connection. By 1984, six thousand customers were connected to DATEX-P.

5. The GENTEX net transmits the DBP's telegrams. Introduced in 1849 it was converted in 1985–86 into a digital, switched network.

6. Direct datanet (DIREKTRUFNETZ). It connects exchanges over fixed (not switched) lines that can transmit data at high speed (up to 48,000 bit/s) between two points. By 1985, 90,000 data terminals were connected.

7. The Integrated Text and Data Net (IDN). Starting in the mid–1970s the DBP developed the digital IDN to integrate all the nonvoice networks (i.e., services 2–6 presented above). The DBP claims that it was the first network administration worldwide to operate an integrated digital text and data network.

8. In addition to switched individual communication services the DBP also operates distributed communication nets, primarily broadcasting and television transmissions. These distributed services will become increasingly important as the broad-band digital networks emerge and become capable of sending voice, data, and moving images over the same network. Television sets will then become communication terminals and cable companies could become the next generation of mobile telephone service. By 1991 several aspects of this development were already used in the United States, the United Kingdom, and Germany.[38] (See table 2.6)

The DBP finally decided in 1979 to adopt the KtK commission's strong recommendation, and make the digitalization of the telephone network its number one strategic priority. The fact that it took the DBP planning staff four years to revise its previous investment policy is a testimony to the reluctance of technocratic bureaucracies to revise plans under political pressure and admit, even implicitly, that original decisions may have been flawed. Once the DBP committed itself, however, to a policy of rapid digitalization—the introduction of digital transmission systems and digital switches—it quickly decided to introduce an advanced digital system, the so-called Integrated Services Digital System (ISDN), which would simultaneously transmit voice data, text and, ultimately, moving images (television) over one network.

The strategy of creating a sophisticated digital network by introducing ISDN would enable Germany to leapfrog France, which had been leading in network digitalization. France had begun to replace its obsolete analog telephone system with digital transmission nets in the early 1970s. By the early 1980s it already had the most efficient telecommunication system in Europe. It had digitalized 50 percent of its central office (CO) switches and 60 percent of its long-distance circuits.[39] The introduction of an ISDN system, which for now we can consider as an advanced, multipurpose digital system, was considered to be the fourth and last step in the ambitious modernization of the French telecommunication system.[40]

To provide the additional ISDN capability for already existing digital

Table 2.6
The Telecommunication Services According to Their Economic Significance

Telecommunication service	Characteristic data (1984)	proceeds from sales 1984 (billion DM)	Work force 1984	Investments 1984 (billion DM)
a	b	c	d	e
Telephone service	25 m main stations 11 m extensions 26 billion calls subdivided into: 16.5b local calls 0.37b international calls	28	179,000	11.3
Telex service	160,000 telex stations 171 m national tx connections 78 m international tx connections	1	5,700	0.24
Broadcasting service	35 sound broadcasting transmitters 180 TV basic network transmitters 4,000 TV transposers 1 m broadband cable stations	0,66	10,300	1.7
Data communication service	71,000 telephone stations with modems 15,000 DxL main stations 7,000 DxP main stations 109,000 stations for switched connections	0,74	3,900	0.3
Telegram service	5,9 m national telegrams 3,6 m international telegrams	0.138	4,700	0.018

Service				
Radio paging service	92,000 radio paging stations	0.04	200	<0.01
Air raid warning and alarm service	64,500 siren stations 12,000 announcement stations 1 community announcement facility	0,022	360	<0.01
Radiocommucations service	11 senders 1,500 message receiving and recording stations	<0.01	110	<0.01
Teletex service	9,000 teletex stations	0.03	300	0.028
Phototelegraph service, Telefax service	266 phototelegraph stations 18,000 Telefax stations	<0.01	130	<0.01
Bidschirmtext service	30,000 Btx terminal stations (6.85) 3,700 Btx providers (6.85) 650,000 pages (6.85)	<0.01 (1985)	450	0.2 (1985)
Temex service	Teleindication (fire alarm, assistance for senior citizens, etc.) Telemetering (heating, gas, water, power supply, etc.) Telecontrol (illumination, sirens, etc.) Teleadjusting (traffic signs, machines, etc.)	service forthcoming	service forthcoming	service forthcoming

Source: Helmut Schön, *Telekommunikation in the Federal Republic of Germany, Today and Tomorrow* (Starnberg: J. Keller Verlag, 1985), 18.

network requires, however, the modification of the existing digital switches through additional software and perhaps even extra hardware components. The DBP strategy of installing the ISDN system as a means of converting the German telecom system into a digital network promised to provide an advanced, sophisticated system that could achieve, at least, the quality of the French system, at lower cost, over a shorter period of time. By the end of 1991 the French still had the world's most highly digitalized system, but the Germans had at least caught up by connecting 120 local exchanges and twelve key long-distance exchanges to the ISDN network (see figures 2.4 and 2.5) in former West Germany, and by connecting Berlin with the four largest cities in east Germany with an overlay ISDN net.[41]

The ambitious goal of providing ISDN service for all terminal equipment (CPEs) by 1993 seems certainly well within the reach of DBP capability from a 1991 viewpoint. Not all six thousand local exchanges will have been converted to digital technology by 1993; however, a rather ingenious technical procedure, the so-called *Fremdanschaltung* (nonlocal switching), will enable each ISDN participant connected to an analog local exchange to be attached to the nearest digital, ISDN-capable local or central office switch. We have been told by DBP telecommunication engineers that the rather expensive investment in the *Fremdanschaltung* technique is probably less costly than the French strategy to build a digital network first and then add on ISDN capability. European telecom engineers seem to be certain that either the German or the French procedures are more cost-effective than the American approach, in which numerous vendors supply often incompatible (only partially standardized) equipment to different network operators.[42] The DBP also emphasizes that they and the French have made greater efforts to develop adapters to convert existing CPEs to ISDN use than the Americans.

On the one hand, an ISDN network based upon common European or global standards can be an enormous incentive for entrepreneurs to sell new service and equipment, unfettered by proprietary standards, to any telephone user. On the other hand, the monopolistic—or, in the United States, oligopolistic—network operators (NOs) can provide many of these advanced communication services through the establishment of "intelligent networks." The question is whether the NO (in the German case the DBP), will provide many of these services to the customer within its own network or whether these services can be performed by equipment supplied to the user and attached to CPEs. The International Telecommunication Union (ITU), a UN-affiliated agency, has been the forum for technical discussion and through its advisory committee, the CCITT, has striven to maintain global standards. In particular, the CCITT and the ITU have been discussing how and where the customer terminals will be connected with the public ISDN network. There are three possible interfaces: S, T, and U (see figure 2.6). If the interface is

Figure 2.4
ISDN, 1988

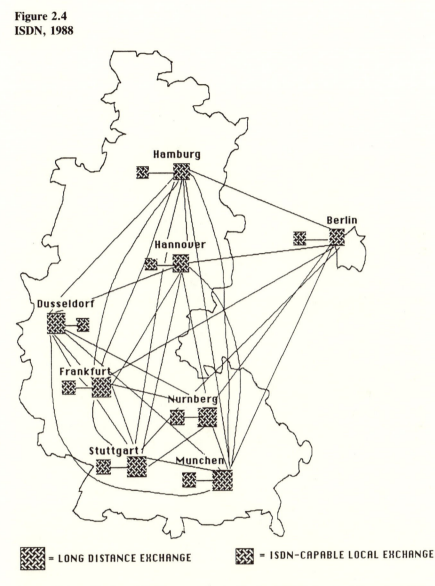

= LONG DISTANCE EXCHANGE   = ISDN-CAPABLE LOCAL EXCHANGE

Source: Reiner Kostka, "Einführungsstrategie für das ISDN" (paper delivered at ISDN Congress, International Council for Computer Communication, Dallas, Texas, Sept. 15–17, 1987), 37.

Note: The 1987 objectives had indeed been accomplished by 1988.

Figure 2.5
ISDN, 1990

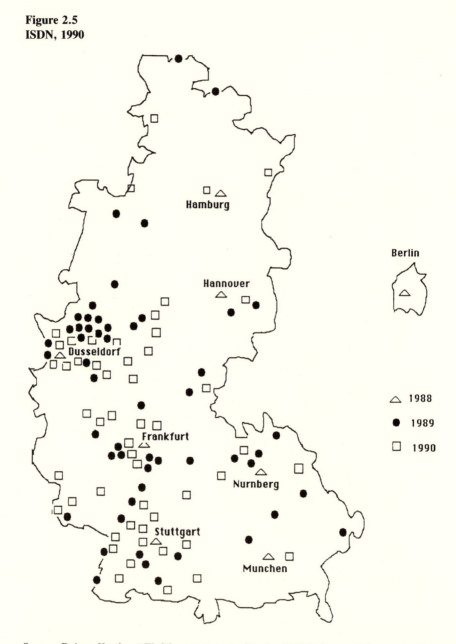

Hamburg

Berlin

Hannover

Dusseldorf

△ 1988

● 1989

□ 1990

Frankfurt

Nurnberg

Stuttgart

Munchen

Source: Reiner Kostka, "Einführungsstrategie für das ISDN" (paper delivered at ISDN Congress, International Council for Computer Communication, Dallas, Texas, Sept. 15–17, 1987), 39.

Figure 2.6
ITU Interface

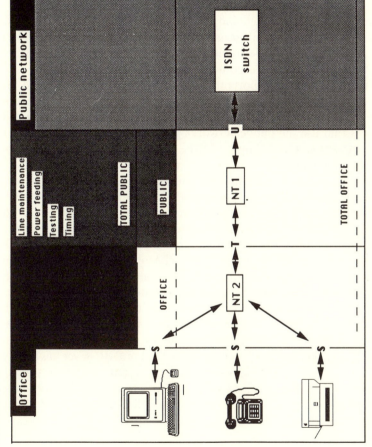

The International Telecommunications Union has defined two sets of tasks, NT1 and NT2, that need to be done to connect the office to an ISDN public network. If the network ends at point U, both NT1 and NT2 tasks will be done by office equipment; if at T, NT2 jobs will be done in the office but NT1 jobs by the public network; if at S, both sets of jobs will be done by the network.

Source: Ann Reid, "The World on the Line", *The Economist* (November 23, 1985).

placed deep within the network at point U, providers of equipment and value-added products (advanced data and message processing) can provide much of the necessary intelligence to deliver their services. If the interface is close to the customer's premises, the network operator can supply the intelligent network that could deliver most of the services provided by telecom enterprises with the exception of some terminal equipment. As a matter of fact the Centrex, a switching arrangement within the public networks that replaces a PBX, shows that an intelligent network can even replace customer terminal equipment.

Schön considered interface S as the proper interface location from the very beginning (see figure 8 in his paper cited above) and perceived the ISDN system as a means to protect the public telecommunication system from "cream-skimming" competition.

Providing ISDN service and, at the same time, charging customers on the basis of their system's usage rather than on a cost basis would make leased lines much less desirable but could enable the DBP to remove all constraints on resale of used line capacity to third persons.

This point is quite important, and can be easily misinterpreted. Schön, and the DBP, did distinguish between terminal equipment services provided by private telcos in a competitive environment and centrally switched services that use the public networks partially or fully; both these services could be accommodated by the DBP. Value-added services based on their own private networks, however, were inadmissible because they could resell their network capacity and undercut the DBP rate structure. "[A private network] offers ideal preconditions for undercutting the DBP tariff structure selectively and profitably since DBP activities are subject to conditions serving the public economic interest. . . . A fair competition between the DBP and private network operators is possible only when the DBP is exempted from the structural and social obligations to ensure uniform tariffs . . . and the equal treatment of customers."[43] There was no indication that the DBP management under Schön contemplated driving out the bulk of the value-added networks and services that depended on the public networks; DBP policy welcomed enhanced services provided they had to rely, at least partially, on the publicly switched system, and were therefore subject to supervision and regulation. While the DBP never has been wildly enthusiastic over leased lines since they represent a potential threat to its monopoly, it has encouraged value-added services and networks that deliver clearly defined products and do not threaten the DBP monopoly. Schön made this point clearly:

In 1973 the DBP, *without being pushed towards deregulation and many years before the USA, Great Britain or Japan*—initiated the liberal procedure of approval for data networks tailored to meet the needs of the customers. So e.g. the START network of the travel business, the DATEN network of the tax advisers and the

DIMDI network for medical purposes were approved without any difficulties. The ideological dispute over VANS which broke out in other countries is therefore almost nonexistent in our country. *This shows that a reasonable telecommunication policy does not require an artificial delineation between basic and enhanced or VAN services.* [Emphasis added.][44]

The DBP strategy attempted to respond simultaneously to industry demands for world-class information services and to government commitments to undertake some form of liberalization. In particular, liberalization decisions had to respond to both American criticism of the protectionist impact of existing access and procurement policies, and the conviction of the DBP leadership that it had to maintain its network monopoly in order to provide its social and economic contributions to society. In Schön's statement we see the type of liberalization the DBP leadership was willing to support. It contained the full liberalization of value-added services—an American term used reluctantly by Schön. These services could be connected to standardized "open systems," systems with clearly defined interfaces and fully compatible with the standard conforming products of many different vendors. Leased lines would be rented on the basis of usage, not cost-related, charges, released from all constraints. Schön realized that customers with an extraordinarily high volume of communication such as the large multinational enterprises would oppose usage-related rules, but claimed that this policy might help medium-sized enterprises to lease dedicated lines since the increased revenues from "volume tariffications" could lead to lower rates for all customers.[45]

The actual telecommunication reform did incorporate parts of Schön's strategy, but went considerably beyond it in many respects. The Schön reform vision provided, however, the basis for the liberalization controversy in both Germany and the EC. On one issue raised explicitly by Schön, however, he had the unqualified support of all parties, in the EC, in Germany, and throughout Europe: the issue of standardization.

Standardization and compatibility (i.e. open systems) are not an original goal of competition. On the contrary: for a system manufacturer incompatibility is an excellent way of establishing his own monopolistic submarket. . . .

Or frankly speaking: the EDP market is dominated by systems which are dependent on a specific manufacturer and the lack of standardization caused the whole industry to become somewhat dependent on the market leader.[46]

The threat of an IBM monopoly replacing a fully deregulated and divested DBP is raised here for the first time openly. It had considerable impact on the deregulation process in both Germany and the EC.

NOTES

1. See Komission für den Ausbau des technischen Kommunikationssystems, *Telecommunikationsbericht* (Bonn: Hans Heger Verlag, 1976), 17; emphasis added. Most citations will refer to the English version of the KtK report.

2. Ibid., chap. 6.

3. See "The World on the Line: The Fortress on the Rhine," *The Economist* (November 23, 1985).

4. See the English version of the report, *Telecommunication Report*, 178–79.

5. Still another commission under the auspices of the German Monopoly Commission studied the German telecommunication system in 1981. The commission members—the leading German economist Christian von Weizsäcker and his colleagues Günther Knieps and Jürgen Müller—also recommended broad deregulation and liberalization. A revised version of this report appeared in English under the title "Telecommunications Policy in West Germany and Challenges from Technical and Market Development," *Zeitschrift für Nationalökonomie*, suppl. 1 (1982): 205–22. We shall refer to this report below.

6. The apparent requirement to obtain a broad consensus for policy decisions in the German telecom industry has been compared to Japanese decision processes. In the telecom industry, however, we find far greater consensus in Germany than in Japan, where bitter antagonism prevailed for many years between the Japanese government and NTT management. See Timothy J. Curran, "Politics and High Technology: The NTT Case," in I.M. Destler, Hideo Sato, eds., *Coping with US-Japanese Economic Conflict* (Lexington Mass.: Lexington Books, 1982).

7. Godefron Dang-Nguyen, *État et entreprise publique: Les PTT européen* (Florenz, Italy: European University, 1985). Dang-Nguyen's thesis has been elaborated in T. Hafsi, "L'État en Affaires: Au Delà L'Idéologie," *Politique et Management Publique* 1/2 (1985), and T. Hafsi, *Entreprise publique et politique industrielle* (Paris: McGraw-Hill, 1984).

8. The first regular postconnection was established by Count v. Thurn and Taxis in 1490 between Innsbruck and Mechelen in the Austrian Netherlands (present-day Belgium). In 1595 the postal service was declared to be an imperial monopoly and assigned to the v. Thurn and Taxis family for administration. The Thurn and Taxis postal system reached its height during the reign of Maria Theresa and Joseph II. See H-C. Löhr, "500 Jahre Deutsche Post," *Zeitschrift für Post und Fernmeldewesen (ZPF)* (May 1989): 40–46; and G. Möller, "500 Jahre Post," *ZPF* (October 1989): 12–19. In 1990 Austria, Belgium, and Germany celebrated jointly the 500th anniversary.

9. Postverwaltungsgesetz (Post VWG) of 1889; (Post VWG) of 1953; and Poststrukturgesetz (1989).

10. See Ernst Herrmann, "Das Kräftespiel bei der Leitung der DBP," *Zeitschrift für Öffentliche U. Gemeinwirtschaftliche Unternehmen (ZÖGU)* 8/3 (1985): 285–300. After Germany's unification the DBP is the largest German "enterprise" in terms of number of employees, revenues, and investments.

11. See, for instance, Herrmann, ibid., 286–88 and *passim;* Günter Knieps, "Technological Revolution and Regulation," *Zeitschrift für die Gesamte Staatswissenschaft (ZgS)* 139/3 (1983): 390.

12. Hermann, "Das Kräftespiel," 286, relates the story that President Hindenburg refused in 1932 to designate Hitler as chancellor with the comment, "I wouldn't even appoint him post-minister."

13. Post VWG of 1924. The 1924 law established the post as a financially independent public corporation whose revenues and expenditures were no longer contained in the federal budget. The administrative council was designed to establish broad social oversight over the DBP, to counterbalance possible parochial policies. Employers and unions in the civil service sector do not participate in the codetermination process. Fearful that codetermination of employees might interfere with the parliament's policy-making responsibility, participation of civil servants in workplace-related decisions are regulated in the *Personalverwaltungsact* of 1954.

14. Employees of corporations with more than two hundred employees participate in decision making by selecting almost 50 percent of the supervisory board and by electing works councils. (See Alfred Thimm, *The False Promise of Codetermination* (Lexington: D. C. Heath, 1980), chap. 2.

15. Van Haaren wrote well-publicized letters to Chancellors Schmidt and Kohl demanding the dismissal of both Gscheidle and Schwarz-Schilling. The postal-union is held responsible for Gscheidle's resignation shortly before the SPD-liberal coalition was replaced by the current CDU-liberal government. Observers well acquainted with the SPD-union relations insist that the union's demand had little or nothing to do with Gscheidle's resignation (see his book). CDU Chancellor Kohl has ignored Van Haaren's letter.

16. Monopolkomission, *Die Rolle der Deutschen Bundespost im Fernmelde-Wesen* Sondergutachten 9, Monos (Baden-Baden, 1981). A revised version, "Telecommunication Policy in West Germany and Challenges from Technical and Market Development," has appeared in the bilingual *Journal of Economics* (*ZfN*), suppl. 2 (1982).

17. See, for instance, the previously quoted telecommunication survey in the November 23, 1985 issue of *The Economist* on "Can Europe Untangle Its Telecommunication Mess"; note also a similar article in the March 31, 1985 issue of *Business Week*. Generally, the *Business Week* articles on European telecom policy have not been enlightening.

18. The impact of German telecom liberalization on Swiss deregulation efforts is analyzed in Jürgen Plagemann, *Der Entwurf zum Neuen Fernmeldegesetz der Schweiz* (Bad Honnef: WIK, 1988).

19. For this section, the author has relied especially on the following sources: *Telekommunikationsbericht* of the KtK, as well as its English version *Telecommunication Report*; Knieps, Müller, and Weizsächer, "Telecommunications Policy in West Germany"; Günter Knieps, "Is Technological Revolution a Sufficient Reason for Changing the System?" *Zeitschrift für Gesamte Staatswissenschaft* (*ZgS*) 139/3 (1983); Herrmann, "Das Kräftespiel"; Dang Nguyen, *État et entreprise publique;* OECD, *Telecommunication, Pressure and Policy for Change* (Paris, 1985).

20. In 1892 the "law on telegraphy" established exclusive government jurisdiction over telephone and telegraph services. The DBP administers the telephone-telegraph service for the German government exclusively in accordance with article 87 of the *Grundgesetz* (constitution) of 1894. The postadministration law (Post VWG) of 1953 defines administrative procedures.

21. During the 1980s, the CEPT cooperated closely with the European community in its policy formulation. The CCITT, the standards committee of the International Telecommunication Union (ITU), also followed EC policy on standards.

22. Modems connect computer equipment to telephone outlets by transforming digital into analog data and vice versa.

23. See "Can Europe Untangle Its Telecommunication Mess," *Business Week* (March 31, 1986): 68; and "West German Modem Monopoly," *Network World* (August 4, 1986): 2.

24. In this context, we should mention the claim by G. Tenzer, a senior DBP manager and currently member of the DBP Telekom management board, that Germany has experienced free competition in telecommunication trade "for more than 80 years, and that other countries are just catching up." See G. Tenzer, "Aspekte der Endgeräte Politik," in *Jahrbuch der Deutschen Bundespost* (Bonn, 1985), 67. The DBP's role in establishing and maintaining television transmission networks has been ignored so far in this book. As discussed below, the DBP plans to establish broad-band television networks that will permit two-way communication that will make it impossible in the future to distinguish between telecommunication and television transmission systems. German studies of future telecommunication policy, especially the above-mentioned KtK report, include *Medien Politik*, that is, the issues of cable and commercial television in their considerations. An excellent analysis of German media issues and policy is provided by Eberhard Witte, *Ziele Deutscher Medienpolitik* (Munich: Oldenbourg, 1982). The possible impact of broad-band networks on German television is discussed in E. Witte, *Neue Fernsehnetze im Medienmarkt* (Heidelberg: Rv Decker-Schenck, 1984).

25. See the unsigned Siemens memorandum: *Leistungstarke und Wirtschaftliche Telecommunication für die Bundes-Republic Deutschland* (1986), appendix.

26. The DBP's ISDN strategy developed over a decade, under post-ministers Gscheidle and Schwarz-Schilling. The chief architect of the ISDN policy, however, was the senior Social Democratic civil servant J. Elias, who left the DBP in early 1986 to become a telecommunication consultant. ISDN will be discussed below.

27. Since its acquisition of AEG/Telefunken in 1986, Daimler-Benz has replaced Siemens as Germany's largest enterprise.

28. S. E. Lorenz, the well-known former ITT and now Alcatel subsidiary in Germany, is regarded as a German firm by the general public and the DBP. This is quite common among ITT subsidiaries, especially in Austria, Belgium, and France (before the nationalization of CGTE). The ability of its subsidiaries to pass as national companies reflects the hands-off policy with which ITT CEO Geneen ran the enterprise. The difficulties in installing SEL's S–12 switch in Europe may have been due, in part, however, to the lack of coordination among the various ITT units. See "The ITT-CGE Deal," *Financial Times* (July 28, 1986).

29. See "Ärger bei der Post," *Wirtschaftswoche* 21 (June 16, 1986): 60; and "Telekommunikation," *Wirtschaftswoche* 6 (January 31, 1986): 72.

30. In an interview with the author, a Philips executive referred to the IBM sale as a "victory of marketing over engineering"; Philips was *not* a potential supplier.

31. The World Center for Office Information and Communication Technique (CeBIT) held for the first time its own trade fair in Hamburg in March 1986. Hugely

successful, it brought together for the first time German (and other Central European) users and sellers of information equipment and provided a good understanding of customer needs and products. The *Süddeutsche Zeitung* covered the exhibition exceptionally well and its articles provided a good description of the optimistic atmosphere that prevailed (see "Elektronik Industrie auf dem Sprung" [March 15/16, 1986]; "In jedes Zweite Büro zieht Elektronik ein" [March 13, 1986]; "ITT drängt noch mehr nach Europa" [March 11, 1986]).

32. The SPD proved this point in 1990 by nominating the radical Oskar La Fontaine as the chancellor candidate. La Fontaine received only 35 percent of the vote; exit interviews indicated that about 20 percent of those voting for him did so only because polls showed that he would *not* win.

33. F. A. von Hayek, *Der Wettbewerb als Entdeckungsverfahren* (Neue Folge: Kieler Vorträge, 1968).

34. See Helmut Schön, "Gegenwart und Zukunft der Telekommunikation in der Bundesrepublik Deutschland," *Zeitschrift für das Post und Fernmeldewesen* (*ZPF*) 2 (August 10, 1985). An English reprint was subsequently published by the DBP: *Telecommunications in the Federal Republic of Germany, Today and Tomorrow* (Starnberg: J. Keller Verlag, 1985). We shall repeatedly refer to this important statement of DBP–Telecom positions during the mid–1980s. We shall generally refer to the English text, unless certain nuances emerge more clearly in the German original.

35. *Konzept der Deutschen Bundespost zur Weiterentwicklung der Fernmeldestruktur* (Bonn, 1984). See also *Mittelfristiges Programm für der Ausbau der Technischen Kommunikationssysteme* (Bonn, 1986).

36. See Helmut Schön, *Telecommunications in the Federal Republic of Germany, Today and Tomorrow*, reprint of Schön's article in *Zeitschrift für Post und Fernmeldewesen* (October 28, 1985) (Starnberg; Josef Keller, 1985). The reprint appeared in a combined German and English version, to emphasize that it was directed at least partially at the Anglo-American critics of DBP policy.

37. The senior civil servants below the ministerial level chosen to manage departments or governmental enterprises belong ordinarily to the political party(ies) of the government and are expected to resign or retire if the government changes hands. It must be remembered, therefore, that Schön and the next level of managers, the *Ministerialdirektoren*, were CDU members. Schön was born in 1931, received a degree in communication engineering from the University of Bonn in 1955, joined the DBP in 1955, and became head of telecommunication in the ministry of post and telecommunication in 1982.

38. See "Telecom Regulations: Talking Pictures," *The Economist* (January 12, 1991).

39. "Objectiv RNIS" (Objective RNIS: RNIS is the French acronym for ISDN) *France Telecom* 61 (February 1987): 28, fig. 3.

40. Ibid., "Une course en quatre étapes."

41. Thomas Schnöring, "Die Entwicklung des Telekommunikationssektors in den neuen Bundesländern," *WIK Newsletter* 3 (June 1991), and Thomas Schnöring and Uwe Szafran, "Telekommunikativer Aufschwung Ost," *Wik Newsletter* 5, (December 1991).

42. For a perceptive analysis of the American ISDN systems from a user's viewpoint, see Ham Mathews, "It's Not Love at First Sight Between Cautious Users

and ISDN," *Telephony* (December 17, 1990): 7.12. The issue of compatibility is raised continuously in advertisements in *Telephony*. See, for instance, the Pulescom ad, *Telephony* (January 14, 1991): 17.

43. Schön, *Telecommunikation*, 25.
44. Ibid., 22.
45. Ibid., 24, 25.
46. Ibid., 21.

3

The Final Phase of the German Telecommunication Reform, 1987–90

During recent years the German telecommunication system has experienced a significant de facto and de jure liberalization. The entire scope of the DBP restructuring and the concomitant establishment of a free market in services and terminal equipment has not yet fully penetrated the consciousness of the Anglo-American telecommunication community. Although Germany has today, after Great Britain, the second least regulated telecommunication system in Europe, the image of the DBP as the mighty (mercantilistic) fortress on the Rhine, so eagerly drawn by the Anglo-American press, still prevails among American telco managers and government officials; this misconception is depriving some American enterprises of existing market opportunities.

Part of the reason for the restrained reception of the German reform legislation has been the government's ambivalent motivation in drawing attention to the scope of its DBP restructuring. On the one hand the government has always insisted that the German telecom market was much less regulated than Americans believed; hence it was difficult to emphasize further deregulation. On the other hand the government was compelled to downplay the significance of the change in the telecommunication system in order to pacify the often virulent internal opposition to its reform legislation. It was, therefore, not completely surprising that the English-speaking world did not immediately and fully comprehend the scope of the reform. The battle over the liberalization of the German telecommunication system had been closely connected with the reform recommendations of the Witte commission and with the way the commission performed its assigned task. A close look at the internal struggle and pragmatic objectives of the commission's deliberations will explain many of the peculiarities of both the German and the European reform process.

THE WITTE COMMISSION

The appointment of the Witte commission in March 1985 to consider structural reforms in Germany's telecommunication system signaled the government's intention to deregulate and restructure the DBP. The appointment of the chairman, Witte, who was well known for his ability to find common ground among conflicting viewpoints, demonstrated the government's objective of obtaining the broadest possible consensus in support of DBP reform. Through the careful selection of the individual members of the twelve-member committee the government intended to provide a voice for the most important interest groups affected by a liberalized telecommunication policy but still assure that a majority for a pragmatic reform would emerge. The government, principally Post-Minister Schwarz-Schilling and Chancellor Kohl, succeeded in this difficult task of consensus management. We shall, therefore, take a closer look at the commission's composition.

Chairman:

Eberhard Witte, professor, University of Munich. Witte was well known for his (in European terms) liberal views and strong sympathies for the United States. He had at the same time excellent relations with the trade unions and with many leading Social Democrats.

Deputy Chairmen:

Albert Stegmüller, vice chairman of the German postal union, a union apparatchik who had the confidence of the union leadership, but was polite and businesslike in commission discussions.

Edmund Stoiber, chief of the Bavarian Chancellory, a close friend and ally of Franz Josef Strauss, the late dynamic, mercurial leader of the CSU.

Jürgen Terrahe, member of the management board (senior vice president in American terminology) of the Commerzbank, Germany's third largest bank.

Members:

Dieter Fertsch-Röver, a leading member of Germany's liberals, the Free Democratic party (FDP).

Peter Glotz, member of parliament and secretary (*Geschäftsführer*) of the Social Democratic party; an able and well-liked man who belonged to the party's right wing; he has been called the "conscience of the SPD."

Hans Heinz Hauser, parliamentary whip of the CDU-CSU, member of parliament.

Wernhard Möschel, law faculty, University of Tübingen. Möschel, an ardent libertarian, advocated vehemently complete privatization of the DBP, and became Witte's most aggressive antagonist on the commission.

Tyll Necker, economist and president of the German Industry Association (BDI), the German equivalent of the American Manufacturers Association.

Ingolf Ruge, engineering professor, Technical University Munich, and one of two telecommunication engineers on the commission.

Horst Schwabe, chairman of the association of German construction firms of telecommunication installations.

Gerd Wiegand, chairman of the information and communication sector of Germany's large and influential Electrotechnical Industry Association (ZVEI).

Clearly every important political, economic, and trade union interest was represented on the commission. The objective of shaping a consensus or obtaining, at least, a large majority in favor of effective reform recommendations was going to be a difficult task.

The Witte commission held numerous meetings throughout West Germany, giving all interested groups as well as professional experts ample opportunity to present their views. In addition, close, continued contact with the DBP, the finance, research, and economics ministries provided timely "feedback" between the evolving commission position and the political and economic realities.[1] The deregulation experiences of Great Britain and the United States had a striking impact on the commission's deliberations. The commission visited the United States several times; discussions with AT&T, Bell Atlantic, Motorola, the Departments of Commerce, Justice, and State, the FCC, and users' associations gave the commission, and especially Witte, an excellent survey of the strength and weaknesses of America's "telecom regulations through partial deregulation."[2]

To many observers, it quickly became apparent that the commission would recommend broad deregulation of the telecom system that would, however, leave the DBP's basic network monopoly intact. The existence of the constitutional provision of state ownership of the telecommunication network, articles 73 and 87 of the "Basic Law," makes any tampering with the monopoly status of the DBP's telecommunication system politically impossible.[3] The trade union opposition to deregulation made it certain that a two-thirds majority necessary to rewrite the constitution could not be obtained. Most other aspects of deregulation seemed to be negotiable, however, provided the discussion would retain an objective, nonideological tone. Witte's commitment to deliver, once more, a virtually unanimous recommendation, if possible, also made it likely that highly sensitive topics, such as private networks and DBP procurement policy, would be approached in a way that could create compromise solutions and would give the vested interests some time to revise their positions. Interestingly—and perhaps fortunately from the point of view of the reformers—the sharpest attacks on the emerging consensus and on Witte himself came from those, both within the commission and outside, who demanded the complete abandonment of all DBP monopoly positions. The spokesman for the "ultraliberals," in the European meaning of the term, was the law professor and commission member Wernhard Möschel, who not only argued force-fully for his views within the commission, but also leaked commission discussions to the press, a virtually unheard of violation of German "com-mission collegiality."[4] The politically unrealistic demand for full deregu-lation advanced by Möschel and three industry representatives on the commission made it easier, however, for representatives of groups that were, at best, lukewarm about DBP reform to support Witte's pragmatic telephone reform recommendations.

In the final sessions of the commission, devoted to drafting the final recommendations, Möschel moved that the government license one or more network operators to compete with the DBP. The motion obtained six votes in favor and six votes against and, therefore, failed. The fact that half the commission favored, at least in principle, the complete deregu-lation of the German telecommunication system helped in establishing subsequently a large majority in favor of a less radical reform that would not touch the DBP's network monopoly. In the end, the Witte commission's key recommendations were adopted by 10:2 or 9:2 majorities.[5]

THE REPORT OF THE WITTE COMMISSION

The commission's recommendations contained four key points:

1. Reorganization of the DBP
2. Maintenance, with some constraints, of the existing network monopoly
3. Liberalization of services
4. Deregulation of terminal equipment

We shall examine briefly the most significant components of these four points and comment on their political implications.

Reorganization of the DBP

The commission proposed two significant structural changes:

(1) Separation of the DBP into two independent, publicly owned, profes-sionally managed enterprises: telecommunication (Telekom) and postal services (Postdienst). Although the reorganization of the DBP has not generated much interest in the United States, it was by far the most con-troversial issue within Germany. The German postal union correctly per-ceived this reorganization as a threat to its political power and organized a vehement opposition to the entire reform concept. The postal union was able to gain the support of the German Trade Union Federation (DGB) and the majority of the Social Democratic parliamentary caucus.

The key issue in the DBP reorganization involved the large cross-subsidies that had been flowing from the DBP's extremely profitable te-lecom operation in the generously staffed, highly labor-intensive, money-losing postal services. The commission had proposed that the subsidies be phased out over a five-year period, and that the top management levels of the new telecom agency, Telekom, be exempted from civil service legis-lation and be paid according to market requirements.[6] The separation of postal and telecom services would invariably lead, in the postal union's opinion, to staff cuts in the postal services and a lowering of the quality of the *Bürgerpost* (a term that cannot be quite translated into its English equivalent, "citizen's post"). The exemption of top management from civil service pay standards would also weaken considerably the influence of the union on DBP personnel policy.

Telekom was encouraged to be entrepreneurial and to provide new ser-vices but was compelled to avoid possible predatory behavior. The new enterprise had to separate, therefore, its accounting systems for regulated activities from the new, entrepreneurial, nonregulated undertakings. (This provision was quite similar to Judge Green's "modified judgment" in the AT&T divestiture.)

(2) Separation of the post-ministry's regulatory and managerial func-tions. The post-ministry regulated the German telecommunication system through such departments as the network access-granting FTZ (Fernmelde Technisches Zentralamt) and simultaneously chose and supervised the DBP management. The Witte commission recommended that the ministry retain the regulatory responsibilities but urged that the DBP's telecom and postal components become independent, public enterprises, with the gov-ernment as the only stockholder. Both enterprises would still remain under the supervision of the post-minister. A similar organizational arrangement already had been made previously with the German Federal Railway with subsequent improvements in enterprise performance.[7]

The regulatory tasks that were to be carried out by the Post and Telecom Ministry (BMPT) included the following: representation of Germany in international telecom institutions (ITU, CCITT, CEPT, EC, etc.); regu-lation of rates for DBP monopoly services (telephone, leased lines); pre-vention of cross-subsidization of DBP competitive tasks through monopoly profits; approval of the DBP budget; appointment of top management; standardization policy; network access approval through an agency inde-pendent from the DBP but within the ministry.[8]

Network Monopoly

The commission recommended that the DBP retain the network mo-nopoly provided it leased telephone lines on "fair and competitive" con-ditions. The government, not merely the BMPT, was to monitor the development of competition in the telecom system every three years. In the case of unsatisfactory market developments the government would permit the installation of competitive networks.[9] Already existing private networks should remain but receive a more "liberal" treatment (existing private networks were operated by public enterprises such as the Federal Railways and the Autobahnen, but also by private pipeline operators and several large corporations, such as Siemens).[10]

The wording of the network provisions represented a compromise between those six members who favored network competition and those six who wanted to maintain the network monopoly. The phrasing is, therefore, quite vague. The charge that the DBP had to manage the network in a "fair and competitive" manner was clearly not operational. We shall see that the final government legislation submitted to the parliament omitted the provision that the government should monitor competition in the telecom industry every three years; the omission was meant to be interpreted as a compromise gesture that would garner SPD support.

Service Liberalization

Drawing on the U.S. and U.K. experience, the commission distinguished among the three types of possible telecommunication services:

- monopoly services
- regulated services
- unregulated services

The pure telephone voice service (POTS, plain old telephone service in American terminology) was to be the only monopoly service to be provided by the DBP. All other telecommunication services should be offered in competition with private service providers.[11] The commission used the term "pure telephone service" in lieu of "basic telephone service," since the DBP, and especially Helmut Schön, had repeatedly questioned the operational value of the American terms "basic" and "enhanced" services. Schön considered the term "basic service" an adjustable concept; as new services became familiar, each telephone user would consider them basic, and receive these services from the DBP.[12] The Witte commission tried to anticipate attempts to modify the POTS concept by defining it as "real-time voice"; hence every voice storage or voice transformation (e.g., voice mail) constituted a value-added provision that would be provided under competitive conditions.[13]

The rates for monopoly services had to be approved by the BMPT in cooperation with the Economics' Ministry (BMW) and would be a function of costs (not usage time, as proposed by Schön and other DBP executives). In addition to the monopoly service the DBP had to provide certain obligatory services (*Dienst Leistungen*) in competition with private firms. These types of services, such as telex, were to be defined by government directives. Implicit in the discussion of obligatory DBP services was the assumption that international standards and international competition would generate competitive world market prices for telecommunication services.

In cases where the obligatory services would require unprofitable DBP performances (e.g., telegram delivery to isolated areas) regulated rates could be imposed by the BMPT. These rates would, conceivably, apply to all service providers. The commission's statement on this issue was not clear.[14] The unregulated services were not defined since all services not expressly specified as monopoly or obligatory were free, and left to the market forces of supply and demand. It was also left to Telekom to decide which services it would offer in competition with private providers.[15] No unregulated service required any form of approval (unlike the Japanese reform, which distinguished among various types of "free" services).

The DBP's policy toward leased lines had been criticized severely in the past by both German and foreign-owned corporations operating in the Federal Republic. The Witte commission recognized the controversial role of leased-line and private networks and included in its service liberalization (*Freie Leistungen*) provisions the recommendation that every telephone user had a right to obtain a leased line, and that these leased lines could be integrated into a private network by connecting fixed and switched circuits.[16] This recommendation was interpreted as a threat to the very core of the DBP's structure since it would have weakened its network monopoly. The provision to liberalize the creation of private networks was, therefore, not included in the final government legislation. By 1990, however, the DBP had liberalized both its leased-line policy and its tariffs on an administrative basis to such an extent that one could speak of a "fundamental break with past policies" (freely translated quotation from WIK director K. H. Neumann's March 1, 1991 letter to the author). Throughout 1991 and early 1992 corporate leased lines—especially the private IBM network—have been put temporarily at the disposal of the DBP Telekom in order to augment the east German public network. This experience has led and will lead to further liberalization of the leased line regulations.

Terminal Equipment

The DBP had always followed a rather liberal equipment policy. By 1987 it had given up enforcing its legal right to be the sole supplier of terminal equipment. German department stores sold telephones and other CPEs routinely, and special stores had emerged, particularly in West Berlin, which sold sophisticated customer premises equipment of East Asian origin that had not obtained an access approval (license) from the DBP's FTZ, the access-granting agency.

The commission recommended that the terminal equipment be completely deregulated, and that each customer be permitted to buy any equipment desired. The commission proposed, furthermore, that the DBP compete in the terminal equipment market by selling, leasing, and maintaining equipment purchased from vendors of its choice. The DBP's participation in the terminal equipment market was considered a desirable learning experience that should help the DBP's research and innovation performance. (Implicitly, the commission suggested an enlarged R&D activity for the DBP, a recommendation that was already made by the KtK [Witte I] commission in 1975.)

Americans should note, however, that the term "free terminal equipment market" applied only to products that had received an access license. This restriction is very much in line with the German practice of requiring, de facto or de jure, the approval of most manufactured products by standards organizations such as the nonprofit TÜV (Technischer Überwachungs Verein), an agency similar to the American Underwriters Insurance Agency. The difference, however, between these two agencies consists of the far greater role TÜV plays in the German economy. One simply cannot buy any electrical or mechanical equipment in Germany that has not been approved by TÜV. Given the importance of the network access-granting agency, the commission, therefore, recommended that not only an organization independent from the DBP grant access but that even equipment sold by the DBP must undergo the access licensing process. The commission also recommended that only network integrity and compatibility be examined, and that access standard needs meet the lowest possible safety demands.[17] Equipment included in the DBP's obligatory service category, whether sold by the DBP or private vendors, had to meet existing international standards as set by the CCITT or the ISO (International Standards Organisation). By 1990 the European Technical Standards Institute (ETSI) had become the dominant standard agency and all telecommunication products had to meet existing ETSI standards.

Summary of the Commission's Recommendation

The Witte commission recommendation proposed a considerably liberalized telecommunication system that consisted of four segments:

- A continued monopoly regime in network and basic voice telephone service
- A quasi-regulated competition in the DBP's "obligatory service" market, where the DBP and private vendors would compete freely, but where the obligatory nature of the DBP services could turn the sales of some DBP products into unprofitable activities
- A free market open to all, including the DBP if interested
- A free market in equipment products open only to private manufacture

Segments 1 and 4 continued existing relationships, but segments 2 and 3 suggested significant liberalization and deregulation measures that were to have a strong impact not only on the German reform legislation, but also on the liberalization directives subsequently issued by the EC.

The Witte commission's report represented the maximum liberalization that could be obtained within the consensus nature of German politics. As a matter of fact, within the government coalition the conservative-populist CSU and its leader Franz Josef Strauss were opposed to several aspects of the Witte report. Strauss's representative on the commission, Edmund Stoiber, objected repeatedly to various deregulation recommendations, and abstained on the final commission vote that accepted the report 9:2. Once the report was submitted to the government, all vested interests became extremely active in efforts to persuade both the public and the parliament to accept or extend or reject the report. We shall take a closer look at the opposition to telecom reform, not only because it sheds considerable light on German society but also because the very same issues are still affecting the emerging telecom regimes in the EC.

THE LAST BATTLE OVER THE DBP REFORM: THE OPPOSITION TO TELECOM LIBERALIZATION, 1987–89

In the previous chapter we referred briefly to the institutional and ideological opposition to DBP deregulation and restructuring that prevailed among the public at large, the trade unions (especially the postal union), the DBP bureaucracy, and segments of the German telecommunication industry. The submission of the Witte commission recommendations intensified the efforts of the various opposition groups and brought key philosophical and ideological arguments into the open. It should be emphasized again that similar clashes of ideology and economic interests occurred in other countries, but were not discussed as openly and vigorously as in Germany. In France, for instance, an open public debate was delayed until 1988, when socialist Paul Quilés replaced the conservative post-minister Gérard Longuét, and refused to carry out the liberalization program of the previous government until a *débat public* could be held.[18] We shall, therefore, take a closer look at the vigorous debate about the respective role of the state and the free market in shaping Germany's telecommunication infrastructure.

Opposition to the liberalization of the European telecommunication systems has been based on economic self-interest, philosophical-ideological views, or both; moreover, self-serving arguments were often advanced in the guise of national objectives or social aspirations. The close and subtle relationship between the German telecommunication industry and the DBP provided a sharp focus on the economics of liberalization. As already mentioned, at least seventy medium-sized firms, so-called *Mittelstand* enterprises, supplied the DBP with equipment and services, frequently as subcontractors to the "Big Four" (Siemens, SEL/Alcatel, Bosch/Telanorma, and DeTeWe). Foreign suppliers such as Cable and Wireless, Ericsson, GPT, IBM, Mitel, Northern Telecom, Olivetti, Philips, and Toshiba did manage to gain a foothold as DBP vendors, but the German telecommunication enterprises enjoyed a special relationship—dubbed "court purveyors to the DBP" by the German press—that assured the Big Four high prices as a form of R&D subsidy, and the rest of the industry a reliable, profitable market share.

It was widely believed in Germany that implementation of the Witte II recommendations would force the DBP to dissolve its special relationships and require all its vendors to meet market prices. Under these conditions, Siemens/Nixdorf, SEL/Alcatel, and perhaps Telanorma and DeTeWe could cope successfully with international competition in the terminal equipment market, and only Siemens and Alcatel in the switches-network equipment segment. This prediction has turned out to be incorrect so far. For instance, in 1990 Siemens/Nixdorf/Rolm held about 40 percent of the PBX-CPE market, SEL/Alcatel about 12 percent, all foreign firms (excluding SEL and Rolm) about 5 percent, leaving 45 percent to the dozen medium-sized German enterprises. This was very much the same market share they had enjoyed in 1987. Very similar conditions prevailed in other CPE markets.

The DBP has played a major role in purchasing and distributing PBXs to its customers. Only Siemens, SEL, and the foreign firms distributed their own PBXs. Since the DBP makes a profit on distributing the products of firms that do not have their own marketing channels, and the smaller firms continued to supply high-quality products, it seems that the traditional DBP vendors—all GMBHs (limited liability companies) such as ANT, DeTeWe, Hagenuck, Krone, Loewe, Merk/Telenorma, Quanta, and TeKaDe—were in a better competitive position than had been anticipated. The future had seemed much darker, however, to these medium-sized enterprises in 1987, and through their manufacturers associations—especially the telecommunication division of ZVEI, the powerful electronics association—they put great pressure on the government coalition parties to modify the Witte commission's recommendations.[19] These efforts had some success with the CSU, whose conservative-populist agenda has strong support among small and medium-sized business and the skilled crafts, Germany's powerful, prestigious, and conservative guilds. Franz Josef Strauss, the flamboyant leader of the CSU and chief of the Bavarian government, opposed both the reorganization of the DBP and the liberalization of the telecommunication system. It is generally believed that if he had not died shortly before the final session of the Witte commission, his friend and representative Stoiber would have opposed the majority recommendations instead of abstaining. The CSU caucus (*Fraktion*) in the national parliament played a significant role in forcing the government to make several changes in the Witte commission's recommendations in the reform bill finally presented to the parliament a year later (May 1988).[20]

Except for Siemens, and to a lesser extent SEL/Alcatel/ITT (ITT still owned one-third of Alcatel), the German telecommunication enterprises sold their products almost exclusively in the German market in 1987, and therefore, did not worry about the international trade implications of maintaining their privileged position with the DBP. The very influential Federation of German Industries (BDI) and its very effective president Tyll Necker did not support the telecommunication equipment companies, and lobbied vigorously first for a much broader liberalization than the Witte commission had actually proposed, and subsequently for the implementation of the commission's recommendations "as a first step." Necker was one of the members of the commission most frequently quoted by the press and television; he effectively presented the viewpoint of the German industry, primarily from the points of view of the exporting industries and telecommunication users.

Necker, together with Möschel, FDP representative Dieter Fertsch-Röver, and banker Jürgen Teerahe added a minority statement (*Sondervotum*) to the commission recommendations.[21] Although supporting the preponderant part of the commission's recommendations, the four representatives of industry, banking, and German liberalism believed that the liberalization "did not go far enough to create the optimum, future oriented framework for the strategic area Telecommunication."[22] Only the introduction of full competition in all areas—including the network—would provide the free market in telecommunication the economy needed.[23]

Given the corporate tradition in Germany's intraindustry politics, clashing economic interests and aspirations are discussed in public in muted tones by industry and enterprise representatives. The opposing positions of the BDI and the telecom section of the ZVEI presented considerable public relation difficulties for both Siemens and the leadership of Germany's influential electronics industry, ZVEI. Siemens' top management, especially its impressive and widely respected CEO K-H. Kaske, had made it abundantly clear that Siemens' global aspirations required that its "special relationship" with the Bundespost be sacrificed. Although in the mid-1980s only the very top of Siemens' management recognized that access to the American market required ending even the perception of a privileged procurement position with the DBP, by 1988 senior Siemens management paid at least lip service to the liberalization of Germany's telecommunication system.[24] Although Siemens' enterprise strategy was fully compatible with the Witte commission's recommendations it clashed with the public position and perceived economic self-interest of the telecommunication industry. In the corporate German setting Siemens, the traditional spokesman for the industry, could not simply overlook the economic interests of the telecommunication equipment manufacturers. Hence Siemens' public announcement in the 1987–89 debate over the future of Germany's telecom system was generally subdued, and emphasized "reciprocity," that is, the opening of the North American and East Asian telecommunication markets in response to German liberalization.

We should interject at this point that, in European eyes, the American market was never as "open" as portrayed by the Departments of Commerce and State. The institutional barriers to American market access were hardly less daunting than similar nontariff obstacles in France, Germany, or Japan. As Karl-Heinz Kaske observed on several occasions during that period, it cost Siemens $1 million to have its switches tested in America for conformity to U.S. standards, while Germany's FTZ performed this service virtually for free. Similarly, even the American enterprise ITT could never adapt its European (German)-built S–12 switch to American network requirements in spite of lengthy and expensive efforts. The sale of ITT's European telecommunication empire to Alcatel in 1986 was a consequence of ITT's failure to penetrate the American market. The call for "reciprocity" in response to American heavy-handed MAFF efforts is very popular in Germany and Europe, and provides leading CEOs with the opportunity to maintain peer support while advocating unpopular policies.

The representative of ZVEI in the Witte commission, Gerd Wigand, belonged to the pragmatic core of the commission that attempted to formulate a realistic, feasible, but effective liberalization program. The role of Wigand and others close to the electronics-information industry, such as Horst Schwabe, chairman of the Telecommunication Installation Association, and electrical engineering professor Ingolf Ruge, does indicate that the telecommunication industry's opposition to reform may have been exaggerated in the media, especially by the *Wirschaftswoche*. Too much attention may have been paid to the comments of SEL's flamboyant CEO Helmut Lohr, who consistently attacked all reform proposals.[25]

Collectively German industry generally supported the telecom liberalization, but, at the same time, maintained sympathy for the "losers" in the restructuring fight. BDI's outspoken president Necker probably did not represent the bulk of German business owners in his campaign for complete dismantling of the DBP monopoly. The argument of telecom equipment representatives that full liberalization would help primarily "the foreign multis" (multinational enterprises like IBM, NEC, and AT&T) was widely recognized as a self-serving argument; it was also considered, however, to contain some truth. Given the pervasive ambivalence toward the restructuring of the telecommunication system, the Witte commission's recommendations and the subsequent government legislation probably presented the maximum liberalization that was feasible.

Any legislation that destroys a long-existing equilibrium will have winners and losers. The DBP vendors deprived of their hidden subsidies were only a small proportion of the potential losers. The real losers were believed to be the post employees—particularly in the post delivery component of the DBP—who, it was believed, could face reduced employment opportunities, and the postal union together with its ally the Association of Social Democratic Post Employees. Given the nature of German society and German civil service legislation, the notion that a restructured DBP would reduce employment in the overstaffed "yellow post" by the thousands was of course absurd. The possible loss of cross-subsidies from telecommunication, however, would make the postal service's money-losing operation transparent, and could have led to losses in union bargaining power in collective bargaining sessions. Losses in bargaining power would translate into real losses in political power for Kurt van Haaren, president of the German Postal Union (Deutsche Post Gewerkschaft), and Peter Paterna, senior SDP member of the parliamentary telecommunication committee and chair of the Social Democratic Federation of postal employees. (Paterna was also the German equivalent of a SDP shadow-minister of the DBP.)

From the point of view of the trade union-SDP opposition (actually, only the SDP left wing opposed the reform) the restructuring of the DBP into two separate, entrepreneurial profit-seeking government enterprises represented the greatest danger in the reform recommendations, and much of its opposition to the reform was directed to "maintain the German citizen-post" (*Bürgerpost*) and prevent "a liberalization that would benefit only IBM."[26] The concept of the *Bürgerpost* emphasized the unprofitable post and telephone services provided (below cost) for isolated villages and lower-income groups. There also prevailed in Germany the belief that the state monopoly DBP, if deregulated, would be replaced by a new, private monopoly created by IBM and perhaps other foreign multinationals. It is difficult to understand in the early 1990s the awe in which IBM was held in the mid–1980s. A proreform position paper of the BDI had noted that "lack of competition in (provision) of terminal equipment and services have failed to satisfy existing market demand, and has been responsible for delayed introduction of innovations and excessive rates."[27] Paterna and his associates in the DBP countered by affirming that "the chief objective of the DBP can not be the provision of tailor made services for specific groups of customers."[28]

The hardball and at times almost violent response of the postal union and its supporters in the SPD came, I believe, as a surprise to commission chairman Witte, and to the broad group of politicians and industry officials that had supported the commission recommendations. During the commission's deliberation Social Democrat Peter Glotz and postal union vice chairman Albert Stegüller had been cordial and cooperative, but were now forced into the apparent defense of the status quo. Their position was not made any easier by Marie Antoinette-like statements by van Haaren and

Paterna. For instance, faced with a McKinsey consulting report for the DBP that criticized the slow introduction of electronic value-added services such as electronic mail, Paterna countered that "at least we have in the Federal Republic, unlike Japan or the U.S., still a working postal special delivery system" (and therefore did not need new electronic services).[29]

The blatantly self-serving, naive, but demagogic attack on the Witte commission's reform package did help to forge a vigorous, populist alliance of some trade unions, the hard left, populist conservatives (CSU), and romantic economic nationalists who endowed the *Bürgerpost* with all kinds of Germanic virtues and created the strawmen IBM and the foreign multinational enterprises as the benefactors of liberalization. The sound and fury of the demagogic class warfare tirades, however, preached only to the choir and probably helped to persuade the "silent majority" to take some interest in the telecommunication reform issues, and to support finally a "reasonable" reform.

The final government reform legislation did contain some concessions to reform critics, but these modifications were primarily due to the strong hold the political-economy paradigm of the *Gemeinwirtschaftslehre* (school of cooperative economics) has had on broad sections of the German public.[30] The economic theory of the *Gemeinwirtschaftslehre* has its roots in the mid-nineteenth-century attack on the "destructive nature" of classical economics that seemed to unite European Marxists, nationalists, and conservatives in efforts to protect "the fabric of society."[31] The attack on classical liberalism in Germany, France, and, to a much lesser extent, England evoked a sophisticated reconsideration of classical economics that resulted during the last quarter of the nineteenth century in the simultaneous appearance of neoclassical economics in England (A. Marshall), Francophone Europe (L. Walras), and Germanic Central Europe (A. v. Menger, E. v. Böhm-Bawerk). In Central Europe the conflict between the neoclassical defenders of liberalism and the nationalist opponents of classical economics culminated in the bitter *Methodenstreit* (argument over methods of analysis) between the German historical school and the neoclassical "Austrians." Although much of the argument between the two schools dealt with the deductive, quasi-mathematical theorizing of neoclassical analyses versus the historical, empirical approach of the institutional school, the role of the state lay really at the heart of the matter. The institutional school in general, and its offspring, the *Gemeinwirtschaftslehre* (*Lehre* is translated by "school"), insisted during the last quarter of the nineteenth century that it is the responsibility of the state to maintain and protect the organic nature of society; hence the state should play a role in all those economic activities where the market results are undesirable.[32] Note that the contemporary German concept of "social market economy" is compatible with the nineteenth-century *Gemeinwirtschaft* concept. In many respects, most Germans—with the exception of a handful of liberal groups in the universities—have accepted the overall responsibility of the government to prevent market forces from upsetting the social equilibrium and to maintain the infrastructure of the economy. The German Railroad, DBP, Lufthansa, and Autobahn are the quintessential components of this infrastructure, and can draw on a large amount of goodwill when attacked.

The modern *Gemeinwirtschaftslehre* (GWL) has established the responsibility of the government to protect society if, and only if, the market cannot perform a socially desirable task. A leading contemporary exponent of GWL observed:

Modern *Gemeinwirtschaftslehre* is not concerned with economic systems, e.g. "the planned economy." At the center of its research are such enterprises as, *within an economic system which is in principle a market economy*, . . . are oriented primarily and directly towards the fulfillment of public tasks. . . . [T]he state should become active only when and to the extent that private enterprises . . . do not produce results which are acceptable to the prevailing political opinion. Public enterprises are instruments of economic policy, and that alone.[33]

Americans may perceive a common objective in the GWL and U.S. regulatory policy. The GWL has also noted that American regulations pursue a public interest but GWL proponents fail to find any American regulatory application to the German issues because of the "ponderousness, the bureaucratic nature, and the enormous costs of such commissions."[34] If we compare the concept of the *Gemeinwirtschaftslehre* with, for instance, the statement on the DBP future by Helmut Schön or with the actual management behavior of the DBP and the federal railway, we must recognize that the *Gemeinwirtschaftslehre* provides a strong ideology for state-owned enterprises that also seems to be accepted by broad segments of the public including the CSU and the right wing of the Social Democrats. (The left wing, influenced by the antitechnology attitude of the "Institute for Information and Communication Ecology," adopted an absurd position that opposed technical modernization and urged maintenance of the analog networks.)[35]

The view of those who recognized that modernization and some sort of liberalization were necessary but still accepted enough of the *Gemeinwirtschaftlehre* to mistrust a complete market-solution of telecommunication policy was best represented by Social Democrat Peter Glotz. Glotz was a hard-working, influential, and cooperative member of the Witte commission. Until the very last months of the commission's deliberations, when trade unions and the Social Democratic party expressed increasing hostility to the emerging DBP reform, Glotz was expected by many observers to support the recommendations. In the end, he cast one of the two dissenting votes. His dissenting vote is of considerable interest because it indicates the changes in German and even European telecommunication policy that might be introduced if the SPD won the next election in 1994. (Although there was more interest in Glotz's position before the SPD lost the December 1990 election, the current German telecom legislation leaves enough discretionary authority in the hands of the post-minister to enable a minister to change the nature of the system even without legislation.)

Peter Glotz's Disagreement with the Witte Commission Majority

Glotz emphasized in his dissent that the commission's report contained many recommendations with which he agreed. He finally voted against the report for three reasons:

1. The limitations and reductions of the DBP network monopoly
2. The subsequent weakening of the German telecommunication industry that would be exposed to foreign competition without having the same access to foreign markets
3. The creation of the independent enterprises Telekom, and the elimination of the cross-subsidization of the postal (post office) system

Glotz emphasized his support for a reorganization of the telecommunication system and for more competition in the value-added services and terminal equipment sector; he considered the establishment of a public (i.e., government-owned) enterprise freed from both bureaucratic civil service limitations and interference from other ministries as absolutely necessary but he believed that the three shortcomings of the report noted above would:

1. destroy the existing synergies between telecommunication and postal service and lead to higher postal rates and massive lay-offs (all arguments advanced by the postal union)
2. introduce "free trade" in telecommunication at a time when the German telecom industry did not have free market access in the "deregulated" foreign countries (meaning the United States and Japan)
3. lead to a sharp reduction in the DBP investment funds necessary for the development of the ISDN and broad-band-ISDN infrastructure
4. cause economic hardship for the individual customers, as well as for small and medium-sized businesses, while benefiting primarily big business enterprises

In Glotz's minority report we do find the sympathy for the putative "losers" in the reform—the postal union, the small business community, and the telecommunication industry. The German media, in particular the *Wirtschaftswoche*, have claimed that Glotz was under great pressure from his constituency (SDP and trade unions) to raise these points. Although there is no evidence, it is quite possible that Glotz might have supported the majority report if he had not been under pressure from his constituency to express his misgivings. The important point, however, is that his stated reasons for opposing the recommendations have been widely shared by the general public, including groups that either failed to oppose or even supported the reform legislation. The spirit of the *Gemeinwirtschaftslehre* still plays an important role in Germany.

Glotz's reservations about telecommunication reform were and are not restricted to center-left Germans. The Frenchman Hubert Prévot, in his remarkable *Le Débat Public: Rapport de synthese*, confirms the strategic role of telecommunication and the duty of the state to provide the proper infrastructure to support an industrial policy.[36] It is not difficult to reconcile the views of Glotz and Prévot.

Prévot's position in the French political spectrum is not unlike Glotz's. A socialist senior civil servant rather than a member of parliament, he shares Glotz's view that a reform of the system is necessary but, much more than Glotz, he is not willing to reduce the role of the state but speaks of a consensus that "the great network, the infrastructure and basic services must be built and exploited under a (state) monopolistic regime."[37] There are few unqualified endorsements of market forces in Prévot's report, except for an appeal to consider the wishes of customers and users.[38] De facto there is probably little difference between Prévot's recommendations (implemented in December 1990) and Glotz's view of a German telecom reform; the formulation, however, is different. For Glotz it is necessary to defend state intervention in the market; for Prévot, president of the Public Service Association, it must be demonstrated that there are sufficient reasons for the state to withdraw and permit the market forces to allocate resources. This significant difference between a leading German Social Democrat and a prominent French socialist sheds a good deal of light on the different views on European telecommunication and on the post–1992 EC that are battling for supremacy within Europe. The future of European telecommunication and European society will be shaped by this conflict.

The Libertarian Attack on the Witte Commission's Recommendations

We have so far emphasized the views of those who for philosophical or economic reasons opposed the restructuring of the DBP proposed by the government commission. As noted, there existed on the commission and in public life an important group of economists and business leaders who believed that the reforms were insufficient. Since plain old telephone service (POTS) produced 90 percent of DBP revenues in 1987, and was still expected to provide 80 percent by 2000, a reform that did not destroy the DBP network monopoly was simply not sufficient. We have already briefly referred to the minority report (*Sondervotum*) of J. Terrahe, D. Fertsch-Röver, W. Möschel, and T. Necker. Subsequently, in March 1988, an important manifest was published by a group of well-known liberal German economists that provided an academic justification for the demand to deregulate the German telecommunication system along the lines of the British reform.[39] The main impact of the liberal-libertarian demand for full deregulation was to offset the postal union demand for complete maintenance of the status quo.[40] The unrealistic demands of the academics and the self-serving perseverance of the trade unions made both the Witte commission recommendations and the subsequent government legislation appear as a moderate, middle-of-the-road consensus. Although the liberal manifest *More Competition in Telecommunication* had comparatively little influence on the emerging reform legislation it is of some interest to North America because it expresses the view of the senior British-German liberal civil servants and commissioners in the EC, such as current British trade commissioner Leon Brittan and German economics commissioner Martin Bangemann, German telecommunication policy chief Herbert Ungerer, and former British commissioner Lord (Arthur) Cockfield (author of the "Europe 1992" strategy). The liberal manifest *More Competition in Telecommunication* supported the Reagan–Thatcher deregulation philosophy and had more influence in Brussels than in Germany. *More Competition in Telecommunication* "is a conviction that what is needed on the national and international scale is as little state and collective regulation as absolutely necessary, and as much competition and individual freedom as possible. A market economy reconciles conflict interests better than state intervention, fosters more growth and greater prosperity and thereby indirectly serves the human need for self-determination and freedom."[41]

In line with the sentiments expressed in the introduction, the manifest demanded competition at the network level, reduction of political control, rate setting through competition, no restrictions on establishment of private networks, open competition in the DBP equipment procurement market, expansion of competition in terminal equipment to network-user interfaces in order to provide alternatives for establishing intelligence within networks, and the end of cross-subsidization of postal services. The recommendations contained in *More Competition in Telecommunication* were far-reaching, and, if implemented, would have gone beyond any existing telecom liberalization in the United Kingdom or the United States. At the same time we can conceive of this manifest as a goal that may very well be reached on a continental level in a post 1992-Europe if the free market forces in the EC prevail over the mercantilistic traditions.

The Restructuring of German Telecommunication: From Government Concept to Legislation, 1987–89

Once the Government Commission on Telecommunication submitted its report in September 1987 it became obvious very quickly that the Kohl government was pleased with the scope of the reforms suggested and would move swiftly to have the recommendations accepted by parliament. The impression that the Witte commission recommendations would almost certainly be implemented may account for the vigorous attacks—vicious by German standards—on the reform legislation launched above all by the postal union and its allies in the Social Democratic party. Both the government and perhaps also the commission were surprised and taken aback by the passion of the attack.

It is not clear whether van Haaren, Paterna, and the other advocates of the status quo actually felt as strongly about the issues they raised, or whether they accurately assumed that under fire the government would make some "face-saving" concessions to the postal union leadership. The consensus nature of German politics did force the government to make some, mostly procedural, concessions. To reduce tension the government, furthermore, emphasized that several key reforms were demanded by the EC and could be considered imposed on Germany by outside forces. Lastly, the government reaffirmed that the DBP's long-run investment and infrastructure strategy, formulated under SDP and CDU-CSU postministers, would not change, and that there was no disagreement between SPD and CDU, Glotz and Schwarz-Schilling on the DBP's responsibility to build a strong infrastructure.

Much of the credit to embark upon a policy that made only minor de facto changes but did pacify the opposition belongs to the post-minister, Christian Schwarz-Schilling, who showed great political skill not only in steering the reform package through the political labyrinth, but also in providing the setting for the Witte commission's investigations and recommendations. It was Schwarz-Schilling who took on the responsibility of submitting the outline of the government reform package, about eight months after the submission of the Witte commission's report and about a year before the reform legislation was passed by parliament.

The concept of the federal government for the restructuring of the telecommunication system was adopted by the cabinet on May 11, 1988, and published shortly thereafter under the title *Reform of the Telecommunication System.*[42] The Witte commission's final recommendations seemed very much in line with the government's overall expectations; predictably, the liberal (FDP) economics minister Martin Bangemann (now EC economics commissioner in Brussels) asked the government to consider also the *Sondervotum* submitted by the four liberals on the commission. The ambivalence of the CSU (the Bavarian branch of the Christian Democratic Union) toward telecommunication reform, on the other hand, provided good reasons for introducing at least cosmetic changes in the reform bill in order to maintain the full parliamentary coalition support. Post-Minister Schwarz-Schilling had shown great skill in emphasizing the economic and foreign policy reasons for DBP liberalization without antagonizing completely the bureaucracy in his own ministry. With the full support of Chancellor Kohl Schwarz-Schilling endeavored to minimize the opposition to telecom reform in both parliament and the country, but at the same time, preserve the important features of the commission's recommendations.[43]

Schwarz-Schilling is one of the very few conservative ministers in any Western government since the end of World War II who was not coopted by his own bureaucracy and, as a matter of fact, even achieved the amazing feat of changing the ideological disposition of his senior civil servants. The selection of the Witte commission and the establishment of the think-tank WIK (Scientific Institute of Communication Services) helped enormously to change slowly the attitude of the DBP. Schwarz-Schilling's constant emphasis on long-run *European* deregulation, while emphasizing the already existing, or perceived to be existing, liberal aspects of DBP policy, kept him always one step ahead of his senior bureaucrats in striving for DBP restructuring but maintained his position as a defender of DBP interests and accomplishments. Schwarz-Schilling's skillful performance has not been acknowledged sufficiently by the German press, and has been completely misjudged by Anglo-American journalists and telecommunication managers, who have insisted on viewing him as the personification of the "Fortress on the Rhine."

In spite of political and economic pressures, Schwarz-Schilling managed to have the government abide by its deregulation policy and submit its *Concept for the Reform of the Postal Telecommunication System* in May 1988, with the intention that the final passage of the necessary legislation should occur in early 1989.[44] Between May 1988, the submittal of the "Reform Concepts" for pubic debate, and May 1989, the final acceptance of the legislation by both houses of parliament, further minor changes were made in the government bill in order to obtain the necessary majority in both houses.[45]

THE GOVERNMENT'S TELECOMMUNICATION REFORM

Since the government's legislation followed the Witte commission's recommendations in most important aspects we shall summarize merely the main points and note the few discrepancies between the original recommendations and the final bill.

DBP Restructuring

The reorganization of the DBP was of relatively little interest to the Anglo-American telecommunication community but generated the most intense internal opposition. It was, therefore, in this area that the final government bill made the most concessions to provide face-saving "successes" for the union leaders, to mute SPD opposition, and to obtain the support of the *Länder*. None of these changes in the Witte commission's organizational recommendations have had, so far at least, any operational significance. The two significant commission recommendations—separation of the DBP's regulatory and administrative-managerial functions and the division of the DBP into three separate and distinct telecommunication, postal, and bank service enterprises—were fully implemented (actually the original Witte commission proposal contained merely the separation of telecommunication from all other post-ministry services). The separation into three rather than two units accommodated the interest of the banking industry that expected an entrepreneurial, profit-seeking post bank to operate more like a profit-seeking German bank and less like an exponent of *Gemeinwirtschaft* concepts.

The three separate units—DBP Telekom, DBP post service (Postdienst), and DBP post bank—were to be managed by executives drawn from private industry as entrepreneurial public enterprises, removed from day-to-day political control. The original Witte commission's recommendation to exempt the three new enterprises from the civil service legislation had to be sacrificed in view of the public service union and postal union opposition. The post-ministry (BMPF) was permitted, however, to pay almost market salaries to top management in all three enterprises. (Schwarz-Schilling had little difficulties in finding able managers for the top positions: Helmut Ricke, previously CEO of the telecom equipment enterprise Loewe Opta GMBH, for Telekom; Klaus Zumwinkel, ex-CEO of the giant mail order firm Quelle, for the Postdienst; Günter Schneider, former CEO of the KKB Savings Bank, for the post bank. Each sacrificed some income for higher prestige and possible political advancement.)

In order to satisfy postal union opposition to the "destruction of the citizen-post" a coordinating body, *Direktorium der Deutschen Bundespost*, was established to maintain "synergies" among the three enterprises. The *Direktorium* consists of the three DBP enterprise CEOs and is located on the organizational chart between the ministry and the three public corporations (see figure 3.1). In spite of the coordinating body, each enterprise was supposed to be market-driven and its management was to be judged by its financial performance. Cross-subsidization of the postal service was to be retained until 1993 and then to be eliminated gradually.

Networks

"Pure transmission" through the public network will remain a monopoly, although a possible relaxation of the transmission monopoly in the future is not completely ruled out. The switching of value-added information in network nodes is permitted and the old Telecommunication Installations Act (FAG 1928) has been modified accordingly.[46] "[In order to provide value-added services] it has become necessary to make specific [switching] functions of the telephone network available to other services."[47]

Figure 3.1
DBP Organization Chart, 1989 Post Restructuring Law

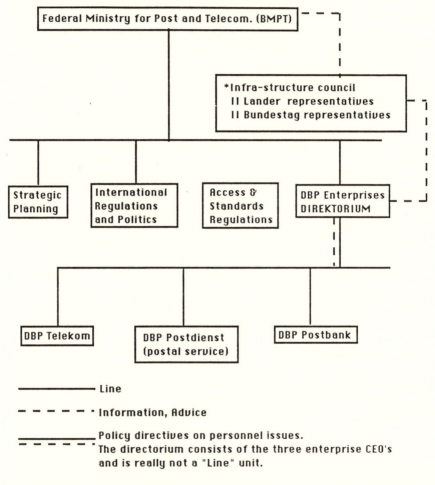

Source: Adapted from *ZPT* (February 22, 1990).

*The infrastructure council is supposed to give the Länder and parliament an opportunity to affect tariff and investment decisions. Nobody knows how the council will work out.

The government bill did not accept the Witte commission's recommendation to permit operations of private multilocation networks, but encouraged a more liberal policy toward establishing leased-line communication systems:

[In addition] private suppliers of telecom services are free to engage in business activities in fringe areas of the network if

(1) this does not undermine the monopoly for the telephone service which is to be maintained to safeguard the DBP's financial viability and

(2) innovation becomes possible which could otherwise not be put into practice

From the present day point of view these conditions are met in satellite and mobile radio communication.[48]

Leased lines, a major area of concern for multinational companies operating in Germany, remained subject to Telekom monopoly, but the government required that "leased lines must be offered to all service providers at reasonable conditions."[49] To avoid any Telekom foot dragging on the controversial leased-line issue the government authorized the federal minister of post and telecommunication to "ensure within the framework of his regulatory authority that competition [in services] is not impaired by the inadequate provision of leased lines."[50] The government "concept" encouraged application of a cost-based rather than usage-based tariff policy to both the public network and leased lines, but defended the increase in leased-line rates that had been introduced by the Telekommunication Regulation of January 1, 1988.

The Telekommunication Regulation had applied Schön's strategy of "liberalizing leased lines" by applying usage-dependent rates to leased-line users in lieu of the previously prevailing cost-based tariffs.[51] (The installation and maintenance cost of networks make up a huge proportion of transmissions costs. Usage tariffs, based on volume used, are virtually independent of actual transmission costs.) The 1989 Telecommunication Regulation was imposed by Schön and colleagues as a defiant gesture at a time when the commission recommendations and Schwarz-Schilling's comments had made it quite clear that telecommunication deregulation, including liberalization of leased-line traffic, would be implemented.[52] Considered by many as "Schön's last hurrah," proponents of a pragmatic DBP liberalization at WIK and in the universities played down the significance of the Telecommunication Regulation, an apparent decision to tighten regulations, by declaring that "of course, if the Parliament passes the government bill, the Telecommunication regulation will become mute!"

Apparently, Schön and his associates represented the end of an era, and nobody was going to make the change more painful than necessary for the upper-level DBP bureaucracy.

The "leased-line" provisions in both the government publication and the actual final legislation had been considered vague by many foreign observers. G. Pfeiffer and B. Wieland, two leading young experts on European telecommunication policies, were pessimistic about any actual liberalization. In fact, the experience as of spring 1992 has been quite reassuring, especially as far as leased-line tariffs and network access are concerned. There has been continued competitive pressure on the rates, which led to significant revisions. By September 1990, for instance, the DBP's New York City office provided potential customers and telecom consultants with a new, sharply reduced list of leased-line tariffs and indicated that further reductions might occur in the not so distant future. Ad hoc reductions have been introduced, as a matter of fact, especially in eastern Germany, but a revised leased-line tariff schedule has not yet emerged. The significant financial contribution the DBP Telekom will have to make to help finance German unification and the immense costs (estimated at DM 60 bn by 2000) of bringing the eastern German network up to western German standards have squelched attempts to lower DBP Telekom tariffs during 1991–92.

The reduction in leased-line tariffs was only one step in the Telekom strategy to reduce the scope of its network monopoly administratively. The September 1990 DBP publication *Basic Points for the Definition of the Federal Government Network Monopoly* provides the transparent, narrow definition of the DBP's monopoly regime the European commission had been recommending as part of its open network policy (ONP). The DBP effectively deregulated administratively part of its network and voice transmission monopoly, and liberalized its leased-line policies beyond the original Witte commission's recommendation. We must note here a very important phenomenon that has been completely overlooked by Anglo-American telecommunication analysts and executives. Significant deregulation measures that, for political reasons, could not have been legislated have been introduced administratively by the post-ministry (BMPT) and DBP Telekom. Rather than exploiting to the fullest extent the remaining network monopoly regime, the "new" German telecommunication management has limited the application of its monopoly powers. It is also noteworthy that the liberal interpretation of its monopoly jurisdiction is explicitly tied to the EC's open network policy directives.[53]

The commission of the EC has played a significant role in "harmonizing" and liberalizing leased-line policies among its member states as part of its "open network" strategy. The EC governments adopted in 1990 the "open network provision" (ONP) drafted by the EC commission. ONP obliges member states to publish leased-line tariffs and operating conditions. In February 1991 the EC commission proposed a further directive to the council of ministers to simplify the access of private companies to lines leased from public networks in a "nondiscriminatory transparent way" and to eliminate "predatory pricing conditions" imposed by public authorities.

The Germans have frequently opposed the EC commission in the drafting stage of legislation, but—like the British—have been very fast in adopting EC directives once they have been approved by the council of ministers. We can expect, therefore, further liberalization of leased-line operating conditions and tariffs. Liberalization of the use and installation of leased lines accompanied by lower tariffs will accommodate most of the requirements of middle-sized firms and meet most of the need of international enterprises. The deregulation of switching equipment and services, combined with the existing and anticipated changes in German (and European) leased-line policy, will enable multinational enterprises (MNEs) operating in Germany to construct their own networks by integrating leased lines with their own transmission facilities and in-house networks.[54] (Currently private lines may connect different units in a private network only if the different properties are within twenty-five kilometers of each other.) The establishment of uniform standards throughout Europe should make the interconnection of private networks easier and will probably undermine completely the network monopoly of the DBP by the year 2000.

Basic, Mandatory, and Value-Added Services

Pure voice transmission remains, as already noted, a government monopoly although a precise definition of "pure voice" transmission has not been made. "Mixed services," voice transmission with some "enhancement" (e.g., video telephone), will be considered to be a part of the "pure voice" monopoly, provided "voice" is the dominant communication component. The regulatory agency within the Federal Ministry for Post and Telecommunication (BMPT), not the DBP, will decide, however, which mixed services fall within the monopoly provision of the new telecommunication law. There seem to be some indications already that the BMPT, under a Schwarz-Schilling at least, may not be inclined to provide a generous definition of monopoly services.[55] Under a different government and a different post-minister, the network monopoly might be extended, as many critics of the reform predicted. The entire technological development, however, will continue to undermine network monopolies. The DBP will face more rather than less network competition during the next decade.

All telecommunication services except for voice (POTS) transmission will be offered in a free competitive market. The government fears, however, that profit-seeking enterprises might neglect marginal groups that, either for reasons of location, income, or narrow, though vital, needs, constitute an unpromising market. The reform legislation, therefore, created the category of "mandatory services" (*Pflichtleistungen*) that requires the DBP to maintain the infrastructure concept of "uniform and universal" service by providing vital infrastructure services, regardless of profitability, to all German telephone users. "Unlike all other [telecommunication systems] throughout the world we [the German government] have placed the maintenance and further development of the infrastructure next to the principles of competition into our legislative concept. I believe this is one of the essential points of the German solution in this question."[56] Private enterprises are free to compete with the DBP in supplying "mandatory services," but are not required to do so. Telekom may compete or fail to compete with private suppliers in all nonmandatory VAS and VAN.

The government has been slow to define mandatory service but has, in the meantime, committed Telekom to continue all services that had been offered in 1989. The upgrading of eastern Germany's telecommunication network after the October 1990 reunification led to further ad hoc liberalization of the telecom system. In order to overcome quickly the most striking shortcomings of the east German system, the DBP suspended regulation of satellite transmission, permitted use of leased lines by third parties, and installed temporary satellite–mobile phone links that included Danish networks. The proposed licensing of a third mobile phone operator also indicated a flexible response to the existing emergency. In my opinion, moreover, postminister Schwarz-Schilling and his new advisory committee (incidentally, again presided over by Professor Witte) exploited the challenge of rebuilding the East German telecom system by deregulating further the DBP Telekom to reduce its basic service monopoly.[57] The conversion of the DBP Telekom to a profit-motivated enterprise has already had the consequence that Telekom managers have begun to question the application of the "uniform and universal" service to anything beyond POTS. Is it really necessary, some Telekom managers and economists ask, that ISDN service be offered in all Bavarian Alpine hamlets and North Sea fishing villages? Is broad-band ISDN (B-ISDN) still "plain old telephone service" that must be offered throughout Germany regardless of the opportunity cost? We can expect that these questions will be raised more vigorously in the years to come, as Germany struggles with the immensely costly task of rebuilding the telecommunication infrastructure of eastern Germany. Regardless of the scope of the mandatory services, however, the vital innovation and rapidly growing telecommunication service sector (VAS and VAN) has been fully deregulated; American telcos should note, however, that access permission is still required for any product offered in the service market.

Terminal Equipment

By the time the German parliament passed the post reform bill, the terminal or customer premises equipment (CPE) market had been, de facto, already fully liberalized. The new bill merely acknowledged the fact that telephone users could attach any customer premises equipment to the network without DBP permission. All equipment sold on the market still had to meet the access approval standards although cheap telephones from Southeast Asia that have not been approved can be bought today in most German department stores. The DBP may and does purchase terminal equipment and distributes it to its customers in competition with private suppliers. The DBP continues to maintain the terminal equipment it has sold to its customers, but does not repair CPEs bought on the free market. The DBP's provisions of prompt maintenance service should assure it a continued, large slice of the terminal equipment market.

THE GERMAN POSTAL REFORM IN THE CONTEXT OF EUROPEAN TELECOMMUNICATION DEREGULATION

German telecommunication reform, in particular the Witte commission report, had considerable impact on the EC 1987 Telecommunication Green Paper[58] and on the efforts of the Chamoux commission[59] to propose a deregulation concept for the French government in the fall of 1987.[60] Witte, Chamoux, and H. Ungerer, the chief architects of telecommunication reform in Germany, France, and the EC, have communicated with each other and have actually helped out each other's endeavor. The EC Green Paper appeared propitiously just as the opponents of DBP reform attacked the Witte commission recommendations vociferously; the similarities in the EC and Witte commission recommendations gave the German government the opportunity to emphasize that its legislation was in step with European attempts to create a competitive information infrastructure. Similarly, Chamoux could and did refer to the German reform to gain support for his proposal.[61] (Chamoux's reference to German and EC examples was in vain since the 1988 elected socialist government withdrew the PTT reform bill.)

Liberal German telecommunication experts, such as Witte and the head of WIK Karl-Heinz Neumann, initially had great reservations about the EC's role in telecommunication reform.[62] They viewed the Brussels EC bureaucracy originally as a stronghold of European mercantilism but changed their mind with the emergence of the Green Paper. By 1989 there was general agreement among German reform advocates that at least in the area of telecommunication the EC was a liberalizing force.

The EC commission is under severe pressure from countries and industries that favor a protectionist industrial policy. France and Italy have lobbied strongly in Brussels against specific interpretations of EC directives that would open markets to international competition. In general the German government, Post Minister Schwarz-Schilling in the European council of (post) ministers, and German EC economics commissioner Bangemann have been strong proponents of maintaining a liberal EC telecommunication policy.

German telecommunication reform has resulted in a liberal regime that is surpassed in Europe only by Great Britain in permitting market forces to promote innovation and to allocate resources. The DBP's remaining monopoly services will be undermined further by technological innovations but, in the meantime, do provide a focus for social policy and a source for infrastructure innovation that is admirable and very much in line with the values of German society. This industrial regime, widely admired by Anglo-American intellectuals, would be a disaster if transplanted to America, but does work reasonably well in Germany.[63] The same can be said of American-type ad hoc deregulation and reregulation that did provide more competition in telecommunication. This regime probably has worked quite well, so far, in the United States but would undermine the social equilibrium in Germany. In the United States telecommunication is viewed as a vital market for an information society; in Germany it is the "foundation of social intercourse."[64]

NOTES

1. Bericht der Regierungskommision Fernmeldewesen, *Neuordnung der Telekommunikation* (Heidelberg, 1987), 11–12, 158–61.

2. This phrase has emerged frequently in European (especially German) discussions of American deregulation, and implies that the extent of U.S. deregulation has been exaggerated since the typical Bell regional holding company monopoly extends over an area larger than France or Germany. The term was originally coined by G. Knieps and P. T. Spoiller, "Regulations by Partial Deregulation," *Administrative Law Review* 35 (1983): 391–421.

3. In the government mandate to the commission, it was noted that the members had to recognize that articles 73 and 87 of the "Basic Law" made the government responsible for post and telecom.

4. Möschel had especially good connections with the *Wirtschaftswoche (WW)*, Germany's equivalent to *Business Week*, which is closely allied with the liberal FDP. One of the *WW* editors, economist Wolfram Engels, belonged to a liberal group, the Kronberger Kreis, that published an influential statement, discussed below, on telecom reform in 1988. This group advocated full deregulation of the DBP.

5. See *Neuordnung der Telekommunikation*, 3. The commission's report consisted of forty-seven separate recommendations, of which at least eight were adopted unanimously.

6. Ibid., 114, rec. 37.

7. Ibid., 116, rec. 38.

8. Ibid., 108–9.

9. Ibid., 82.

10. Ibid., 83.

11. Ibid., 90–91.

12. See H. Schön, "Telecommunications in the Federal Republic of Germany,

Today and Tomorrow," *Zeitschrift für Post und Fernmeldewesen* (October 28, 1985): 21–25.

13. *Neuordnung der Telekommunikation*, 90–91.

14. Ibid., 94.

15. Ibid., 95.

16. Ibid., 95–97, recs. 17, 18, 19.

17. Ibid., 100–3.

18. See Hubert Prévot, *Le Débat Public: Rapport de synthèse, ministere des postes, des telecommunications et de l'espace* (aout 1989), 7–9. Also note J. P. Chamoux, *The State of the Reform Process in France* (Bonn, WIK Conference: 1988).

19. Since the CSU was a member of the government coalition, the business opposition to the DBP reorganization preferred to use the party close to small and medium-size businesses, the CSU, in attacking the government proposal. In July 1988, CSU-governed Bavaria made a motion in the upper house (the Bundestag, representing the government of the *Länder*) that private PBXs in offices and factories should in the future be operated only by the DBP. The CSU motion had almost full support of the SDP-governed states and lost by only a small margin. Since the PBX market had been Germany's completely deregulated market since the days of the Weimar Republic, a regulated PBX market would have meant a major step backward. See "Postreform: Verkehrte Fronten," *Wirtschaftswoche* (July 15, 1988): 28.

20. See *Reform of the Postal and Telecommunication Systems in the Federal Republic of Germany: Concept of the Federal Government for the Restructuring of the telecommunication Market* (Heidelberg: R. V. Decker Verlag; G. Schenck, 1988). The differences between the government bill and the original Witte commission recommendations will be discussed below.

21. *Neuordnung der Telekommunikation*, 134–39.

22. Ibid., 134; author's translation.

23. Ibid., 135–36.

24. See *Leistungstarke und Wirtschaftlice Telekommunikation für die Bundesrepublik Deutschland*, internal strategic memorandum produced by the Siemens communication division Nachrichten und Sicherungstechnik, Munich, May 1966. This important Siemens document suggests liberalization policies that are fully compatible with the Witte recommendations; several proposals, such as leased lines and private network deregulation, go beyond the Witte II commission recommendations (p. 12). In its infrastructure recommendation the Siemens document, on the other hand, is compatible with the DBP infrastructure strategy (pp. 9–11).

25. In January 1991 Lohr's flamboyancy got him into trouble with the income tax authorities and the press over excessive contributions to the CDU leader and first minister of Baden-Würtenberg, Lothar Späth. Lohr, no longer CEO at that time, had to resign all his positions with both SEL and the parent company Alcatel. One of his major misdeeds was paying for the horseback riding lessons of Späth's daughter—hardly in the same league with the "Keating five."

26. Paraphrased translation from a Paterna quote in "Tanga für die Post," *Wirtschaftswoche* 15, (April 3, 1987): 17.

27. Ibid., author's translation.

28. Ibid., author's translation.

29. Ibid., author's translation.

30. The German word *Wirtschaft* can be translated "economics and business administration." In the universities the discipline is subdivided into *Volkswirtschaft* (economics) and *Betriebswirtschaft* (business administration). The literal translation of *Betriebswirtschaft* as "business economics" conveys the wrong meaning. The word *Gemeinwirtschaft* is difficult to translate. Günter Pfeiffer and Bernhard Wieland (*Telecommunication in Germany* [Berlin: Springer-Verlag, 1990], 40) have suggested the term "social economy." I prefer the term "cooperative economics," to distinguish it clearly from Anglo-American "welfare economics." I shall use the German term throughout.

31. The German conservative economist Adam Müller (1779–1834), one of the prime examples of Keynes' observation on the durable influence of long-forgotten philosophers, provided the model for the conservative anticapitalistic attitudes that have permeated much of German and subsequently European Catholicism. The two encyclicals *Rerum Novarum* (Pope Leo, 1890) and *Quadragesimo Anno* (Pope Pius XI, 1931) reflect Müller's views, which are also compatible with Franz Josef Strauss's and the CSU's opposition to weaken the DBP. For a discussion of Müller, see J. Finkelstein and A. Thimm, *Economists and Society* (New York: Harper and Row, 1973), 112.

32. The best known representatives of the *Gemeinwirtschaftslehre* were Albert Schäpfle, Emil Sax, and Adolf Wagner. Their most important contributions appeared in 1867, 1878, and 1887, respectively. All three of them were clearly influenced by the German-American economist Frederick List (1789–1849).

33. T. Thiemeyer, "Deregulation in the Perspective of the German Gemeinwirtschaftslehre," *Journal of Institutional and Theoretical Economics* 139 (1983): 406; emphasis added. Thiemeyer's influence on DBP policy is discussed in *Werner Titterhoffer, die Deutsche Bundespost als Teil der Gemeinwirtschaft* (Frankfurt, 1978).

34. Thiemeyer, "Deregulation," 407. It should be noted that Thiemeyer was one of the many expert witnesses who testified before the commission.

35. A prime example of the "infantile left" is Barbara Mettler-Maibon's *Breitbandtechnologie* (Opladen: Westdeutscher Verlag, 1986).

36. Note especially recommendations on pp. 144–95 under the heading "Confirm the role and authority of the state" (Confirmer le rôle et l'autorité de l'État), and pp. 145–48, under the heading "Give the two branches of the PTT (Telekom and Post) the means corresponding to their mission" (author's translation).

37. Ibid., 37, 38; author's translation.

38. Ibid., 84.

39. W. Engels, et al., *More Competition in Telecommunication*, Frankfurt Institute, March 1988.

40. Commission member A. Stegmuller, vice president of the German postal union, presented the undiluted trade union opposition to the reform proposal in his minority report (*Neuordnung der Telekommunikation*, 142). Although the core of his reform is not very different from Glotz's, his rhetoric is aggressive and uses the class warfare idioms of the trade union disputes.

41. Gert Dahlmann, director, Frankfurt Institute, in the introduction to the English version of *More Competition in Telecommunication*, 1.

42. *Reform of the Postal and Telecommunication System in the Federal Republic of Germany* (Heidelberg: R v Decker-Schenck, 1988).

43. See "Die Post soll 1989 umgestaltet werden," *Frankfurter Allgemeine Zeitung* (*FAZ*) (September 16, 1987), for a perceptive discussion of the political issues constraining reform.

44. *Reform of the Postal and Telecommunication System.*

45. May 1989 was the date when the Bundesrat finally gave its approval to the reform legislation, which had already passed the Bundestag, Germany's equivalent to the British parliament. The Bundesrat consists of delegations from the governments of the *Länder* (states). By 1989 the governing center-right coalition had lost its majority in the Bundesrat, as a result of several defeats in *Länder* elections. It required the support of two Social Democratic *Länder* to gain the necessary majority in the Bundesrat.

46. *Reform of the Postal and Telecommunication System*, 90.

47. Ibid., 42.

48. Ibid., 45.

49. Ibid., 83.

50. Ibid., 52.

51. Ibid., 84.

52. Note, for instance, Schwarz-Schilling's speech of December 3, 1987 describing government deregulation policy. The speech was subsequently published as "1988: Ein Wichtiges Jahr für die Deutsche Bundespost," *ZPF* (January 26, 1988): 4–6.

53. "The basic points also take into account relevant EC provisions set up by the EC council directive of June 28, 1990, realizing the internal market for telecom services and the open network provisions (ONP–90–387-EC)" (*Basic Points for the Definition of the Federal Government's Network Monopoly*, Federal Minister of Posts and Telecommunication, Bonn, September 26, 1990, 4). See also "EC Plans for Telecom Leasing," *Financial Times* (February 21, 1991): 4.

54. Pfeiffer and Wieland came to a different conclusion in their *Telecommunications in Germany* (1989). The difference in our views is entirely due to the fact that we have the benefit of the 1990 and 1991 experience that was shaped by strong liberalizing efforts by DBP-Telekom management and EC telecom policy.

55. The unification of Germany required ingenious, free-market approaches to create the necessary telecommunication infrastructure. Schwarz-Schilling and the BMPT were perfectly willing to permit, albeit on a temporary basis, the establishment of private networks with the aid of radio and satellite transmission. Interestingly, the new free market Telekom CEO Helmut Rickes objected strenuously, but in vain.

56. Christian Schwarz-Schilling's speech before the German parliament (Bundestag) on April 20, 1987, opening the final debate on the "Postreform." Reprinted in the DBP journal *ZPF* (*Zeitschrift für Post und Fernmeldewesen*) (June 22, 1989): 6; author's translation.

57. See Thomas Schnöring. "Die Entwicklung des telekommunikations Sektors in den neuen Bundesländern," *WIK Newsletter* 3 (June 1991): 24–27; Thomas Schnöring and Uwe Szafran, "Telekommunikativer Aufschwung Ost," *WIK Newsletter* 5 (December 1991): 5–8.

58. *Toward a Dynamic European Economy*, Green Paper on the Development

of the Common Market for Telecommunication Services and Equipment, COM (87) 290, Brussels, June 30, 1987. EC Green Papers represent proposals subsequently submitted to the council of ministers. Subsequent approval results in EC directives to member-states. The EC Green Paper had been implemented to a considerable extent by early 1991. Virtually full implementation can be anticipated by 1992. For further discussion, see chapter 5. The senior EC civil servants H. Ungerer and Tjakko Schuringa (now managing director of Sony Europe) have been considered the architects of the EC Green Paper.

59. Mission à la Réglementation Générale called after its chair the "Chamoux commission."

60. "L'avant-projet de loi sur les télécommunications," first draft of a telecommunication law, fall 1987.

61. J. P. Chamoux, "The State of the Reform Process in France," speech given at the WIK conference "Die Zukunft der Telekommunikation in Europa" (The Future of Telecommunication in Europe), Bonn, November 14–15, 1988, 7.

62. See, for instance, K-H. Neumann's "Die Deutsche Bundespost vor der Herausforderung der Europaischen Telekommunikationspolitik" (The DBP faces the Challenge of European Telecommunication Policy), November 1986. This is a very skeptical evaluation of EC policy.

63. See Alfred L. Thimm, *The False Promise of Codetermination* (Boston: Lexington, 1981).

64. Richard Wohlfahrt, "Kommunikation—Grundlage des Gesellschaftlichen Wandels" (Communication—Foundation of Social Intercourse), *ZPT* (October 22, 1990): 4.

4

The Reform of the French Telecommunication System: A Case Study in Industrial Policy

During the last two decades, technological and economic forces undermined existing telecommunication state monopolies throughout Europe. The actual adaptation to the forces of creative destruction was determined, however, by the institutional structures and political history of each country. While the winners and losers in the struggle to shape a new telecommunication system were quite similar in Great Britain, France, and Germany, their political strategies and effectiveness in determining the changes in the system were different. In France it was the history of mercantilistic centralism, of an industrial policy managed by a technocratic elite from Louis XIV to de Gaulle to Mitterrand, that has shaped the administrative rationale for its telecommunication strategy. Colbertism, the centralized industrial strategy guiding the economic development of the French state, has remained the one policy common to the various metamorphoses of the French government: the Bourbon's ancient regime, the revolutionary Jacobins, the Napoleonic empires, and the five versions of the French Republic, from Clemenceau to de Gaulle to Mitterrand.[1]

For our purposes, it is important to note briefly the strategies underlying de Gaulle's and Mitterrand's industrial policies. During the 1950s and 1960s the French developed a government-dominated economic development strategy, called *Le Plan* on both sides of the Atlantic, that guided massive investment in strategic industries through close cooperation of government-planning technocrats, key financial institutions, and the private and state-owned sectors of industry. In particular the rapid and, at least originally, successful development of world-class petrochemical and nuclear industries caught the imagination of those sectors of the North American political community that had favored a national industrial policy as a remedy for the perceived ills of the American and Canadian economies. For a short time, France and *Le Plan* became the wave of the future, and futurologist

Alfred Kahn even predicted that France would surpass Germany and become Europe's dominant economic power during the last third of the twentieth century. Colbert was alive and well and living in Washington's National Press Club as well as in Paris.

The enormous environmental costs of building a polluting petrochemical industry along the once beautiful Mediterranean coast, along with chronic inflation and overcapacity in the global chemical industry, deprived *Le Plan* of much of its glamor, and forced North American advocates of industrial policy to look for a new paradigm, such as MITI (Ministry of International Trade and Industry), the putative architect of Japanese economic success, or codetermination, supposedly the root of Germany's economic miracle.[2] During the 1970s and 1980s, the mechanics of French *dirigism* were no longer front-page news, and *Le Plan* lost its international attraction. The concept of supporting the development of "leading industries," however, remained a fundamental goal of the French government.

During the 1970s and 1980s and into the 1990s the information-technology industry became the government's prime industrial target, under both the conservative Giscard d'Estaing and the socialist Mitterrand. The apparent and actual changes that have taken place in France's telecommunication system during the past twenty-odd years can be understood only within the context of both France's industrial policy to create a world-class information technologies (IT) industry and the history of France's centralism. Moreover an understanding of the institutional framework of France's telecommunication reform will also help to explain France's often opaque attempts to restrain the EC's policy to liberalize Europe's telecommunication infrastructure.

French telecommunication reform has been an integral component of its industrial strategy. The modernization of France's archaic telecommunication system during the 1970s was to be accompanied by a reform of the administrative structure that would improve management efficiency but would maintain the government's role in setting national goals. The elusive goal of French reform policy was to create a telecommunication system that would be sufficiently autonomous to adapt itself to customer demands and innovative opportunities, yet remain an effective tool of the government policy to develop a world-class telecommunication infrastructure for a globally competitive information-technology industry.

In the German telecommunication debate, the *Gemeinwirtschaftslehre* concept played a major role in reserving a decisive role for the state in order to assure a socially acceptable system performance. The notion of *service public* has played a similar role in France. Only the state through an institution representing the public can assure telecommunication users a uniform, universal service that will protect equally the rights and aspirations of all users; moreover, only a public service institution can achieve both the necessary infrastructure investment to modernize the network system and an "autonomous" administration that can respond to consumer needs and market opportunities.[3]

The policy decision in the 1970s to modernize France's telecommunication system by replacing an aging, inefficient analog transmission system with a digital network was an enormous success—one of the few examples of a well-planned, effectively executed, massive investment in the construction of a modern communication infrastructure. The 150-year-old traditional PTT structure (Postes, Telegraph et Telephone until the 1950s; Posts, Telecommunications et Telediffusion until the late 1960s; Direction Generale des Telecommunication [DGT] until 1987) with its tight, centralist organization was perfectly able to manage, during the 1970s, the investment program that transformed a legendary inefficient telephone system into Europe's, if not the world's, most advanced digital network.[4]

Once France had achieved its objective of having a modern, dense telecommunication network, the government-planning authorities advanced the goal of designing a system that could cope with the new challenges: a perceived convergence of telecommunication and computer science (*informatique*), a strong demand for new telecommunication services for large and medium-sized enterprises, and the emerging international competitors in an increasingly global communication system. There was general agreement among the socialist and conservative governments of the 1980s that the DGT France Télécom would have to be reorganized in order to acquire greater entrepreneurial and adaptive capabilities to meet the changing requirements of the new telecommunication system. There was, however, and still is, a disagreement between the left and the right about the nature of the changes that should be introduced. In order to understand the telecom reorganization debate of the last decade we shall briefly define the three types of public service organizations possible. It may have been the inability to understand the French administrative system that encouraged sophisticated observers, such as *The Economist* or OECD's Ann Reid, to overestimate the liberalization plans of the DGT.

THE STRUCTURE AND OBJECTIVE OF *SERVICE PUBLIC*

The highly centralized nature of French public administration is reflected in the past and present organization of the telecommunication system. A very essential characteristic of the administrative centralism is the focus it provides for the chief executive officer, that is, the French president of the Fifth Republic. (During the pre-de Gaulle Third and Fourth Republics, the permanent civil service bureaucrats in the prime minister's office provided the continuity for the centralized administrative process.)

The role of the president of the Republic as the powerful chief executive officer of a highly centralized administration is defined by the constitution of the Fifth Republic. The full powers of a presidential government have been used as effectively by the socialist Mitterrand as by the Fifth Republic founder, the nationalist de Gaulle. The president and his government have a very strong position in respect to the parliament, since the president has broad powers (*pouvoir réglementaire*) under article 37 to govern by decree in those areas in which no existing legislation exists. Ordinarily the president will act through his prime minister, but if the latter, who must win a vote of confidence in parliament, does not represent the president's position, he can bypass both parliament and prime minister, as happened in the 1986–88 "cohabitation" period of a joint rule by a conservative prime minister and a socialist president. The president also can effect the implementation of parliamentary legislation by decreeing the manner of its execution.

The considerable constitutional powers of the French president— equaled perhaps only by the British prime minister among leaders of Western democracies—were further increased by the massive nationalization introduced by Mitterrand's victorious socialist-communist alliance in 1981. It is precisely the nationalized industries or the *service public* institutions administering railroads, telecommunication, and electric utilities that can be guided by presidential suasion to implement industrial policies that may have bypassed parliamentary approval. Thus, for example, a simple directive to route all Japanese electronic consumer products through Tours, a small town in central France, for customs processing provided virtually 100 percent protection to the French electronics industry without any potentially embarrassing parliamentary discussion.

A centralized, unitary, hierarchical organization has been the predominant administrative organization in the French civil service, the *service public* organization, and in both the nationalized and the private industry. During the last decade efforts to increase decentralization have been noticeable, especially in the telecommunication sector. At least since the 1986 conservative-liberal Chirac administration, attempts have been made to find an organizational structure that will decentralize authority, create quasi-profit center administrations, and will permit both greater managerial flexibility and entrepreneurial response to market forces.

For an assessment of French telecommunication reform we must distinguish among the three types of organizations that are at the disposal of the French government in assigning *service public* tasks. In searching for a new format for France Télécom, the various governments during the 1980s could choose among public (i.e., government-owned) corporations, *regie enterprises*, or *établissements publics à caractére industrie et commercial* (EPIC).[5]

A public government corporation operates under regular French corporate law, but has the state as the sole or at least majority stockholder. The enterprises nationalized by the socialists in 1981 after Mitterrand's first presidential election were managed as incorporated public enterprises.

Public corporate enterprises, fully owned by the state, are the most common structures of nationalized industries throughout Europe. During the 1980s, the British Steel Corporation and the German Saltzgitter A. G. were two examples of well-managed enterprises, where the state, as shareholder, set the same standards as regular private owners. The same cannot always be said for public corporations owned by the French or Italian governments, but at least annual income statements provide a relatively transparent record of the economic performance of the state-owned enterprise.

The *regie enterprise* is today a primarily French phenomenon, although the roots of this structure go back to the *imperium regal*, the imperial monopoly of the Middle Ages. The German emperor Maximilian II conferred in 1491 on the v. Thurn and Taxis family the post monopoly as an *imperium regal*. In general, imperial state monopolies could either be administered by the ruling house or bestowed upon an individual or group of individuals (e.g., the royal corporate charter that established the East Indian Company). In contemporary France a *regie enterprise* is, essentially, a component of the state administration, in which the annual budget becomes a special part of government income and expenditures. The best-known French *regie enterprise* is the Renault Corporation, whose frequent annual losses have been absorbed by the government. The Chirac administration had planned to transform Renault into a public corporation, against the violent opposition of the unions, but lost the 1988 election before it could carry out the reorganization. Attempts to transform a *regie enterprise* or EPIC enterprise into a public corporation are often called "privatization" by opposing trade unions since public corporations must conform to regular corporate law. We shall see that attempts to turn France Télécom into a public corporation have been called "privatization" by socialist and trade union opposition even though the French government would have owned 100 percent of the outstanding shares.

The *établissement public à caractére industrie et commercial* (EPIC) falls somewhere between a public corporation and a *regie enterprise*. EPIC is a legal entity under public law and is managed by a *conseil d'administration*, an executive structure similar to a German supervisory board. The *conseil d'administration* is appointed by the minister responsible for its supervision, and the members of the *conseil* essentially serve at the minister's pleasure. The French railroad (SNCF) and electric utility (EDF) are the two best known examples of long-established EPICs. While the (public) corporation is regulated by the French corporation law the EPIC is not constrained by French administrative law. The statutes of an EPIC are defined on an ad hoc basis by the government and responsible ministry in accordance with its purpose. Various EPICs differ in organization, effectiveness, and independence from ministerial supervision. The 1990 restructuring of France Télécom chose the EPIC structure for the "new" France Télécom.

The last decade provided anecdotal evidence for both successful execution of ambitious industrial policy objectives and bureaucratic failure to reconstruct money-losing operations. If the telecommunication infrastructure and certain sectors in the IT industry are examples of successes, the state-owned computer manufacturer Bull and the automobile company Renault are examples of unmitigated, expensive industrial policy failures.[6]

We shall not attempt to evaluate the success or failure of the French planning structure. The novelty and putative successes of *Le Plan* during the de Gaulle–Pompidou era have waned, but "planification" (the coordination of public enterprise objectives with government strategy) still determines the efforts of nationalized enterprises and public institutions. There is sufficient evidence to assume that the industrial policy to create a strong modern telecommunication infrastructure and the framework for a globally competitive IT industry has been successful. To the extent planification has been successful, however, it has been due to the existence of a small, highly trained elite of professional technocrats—the graduates of the highly selective *haute écoles*—that hold the key positions in the government ministries, the *service public* institutions, and the top management positions in the private and public sectors. Moreover, moving from public to private to *service public* management positions has been well established as a proper career path for promising technocrats; hence the coordination of private and public corporate strategies, of *service public* and government ministries is carried out successfully in an informal manner that cannot be understood by examining French legislation.[7]

CONTINUITY AND CHANGE IN THE ORGANIZATION OF THE FRENCH TELECOMMUNICATION SYSTEM, 1970–90

From the days of the French revolution until 1878, the early telecommunication system l'Administration des Télégraphes had been attached to the ministry of the interior and used primarily for government communication. France Télécom traces its origins to 1854, when a *direction général* was created within the ministry to administer the telegraph network. In 1878–79 the PT ministry (ministère des postes et Télégraph) was established but failed to provide entrepreneurial or innovative impulses to the network. Paraphrasing French historian Patrice Carré, we can say that from 1878 to 1970 the telecommunication service was a stepchild of the French government.[8] Underfunded and frequently squeezed into awkward organizational structures, the Third and Fourth Republics—which roughly corresponded to the 1878–1960 time period—never considered telecommunication to be a key industry, worthy to be included in government planning activity.

The postal service dominated the PTT ministry, and seemed to consider telecommunication as a mere supplement to the postal delivery system.

As recent as the 1960s most Parisians considered the *post pneumatique* a more reliable means of communication than the telephone.

The low financial commitment to telecommunication, particularly in the interwar period, and the absence of a sense of organizational mission affected the morale of the PTT bureaucracy. Moreover, while all employees of the DBP were represented by one postal employees union, several different unions with disparate ideological and political commitments represented various groups of employees in the French PTT.[9] In 1941, the Vichy government reorganized the PTT and created a separate structure for telecommunication, the direction genéralé des telecommunications (DGT), organized on a regional basis, with regional chiefs. A few years later, in 1944, the postgraduate technical institution Centre National d'Études des Télécommunication was established, and subsequently validated by a de Gaulle directive in 1946. The Centre National and l'École Superieure des Postes et Télégraphie made a career in telecommunication academically and professionally legitimate.[10]

In spite of the slow recognition that telecommunication was a promising and important discipline, the position of the DGT in the government's investment priorities did not change until the early 1970s. At that time the technological changes that suddenly undermined the global equilibrium of monopolistic PTTs threatened to make the French system completely obsolete. In the PTT ministry and throughout the government a recognition emerged that France needed a modern telecommunication network, and that only an autonomous decentralized telecommunication administration could carry out the necessary investment and reorganization to achieve this goal.

It is important to recognize that the issue of reorganization of the PTT emerged as a reform strategy in the government and the top administrative levels of the PTT. There was no demand for competition as a discovery path as had been the case in Germany; there was no assumption that exposure to the market mechanism would improve the telecommunication system, as in Great Britain or in Germany. What was wanted was some organizational format that would make the DGT more responsive to technological change and customer wishes, and would give the DGT the autonomous management structure needed to permit quick implementation of the new top-priority strategy to transform France's creaking telecom system into Europe's, or the world's, most advanced network.

A change in any equilibrium position creates winners and losers. Quite clearly, the decision to reorganize the DGT created conflicts within the hierarchy, among government ministries, between the unions and the government, and between the government and the opposition. During the 1970s the dominant issue was to find the proper organization to manage the massive investment to modernize the network. During the 1980s conservative/liberal and socialist administrations tried various ways of providing an autonomous, entrepreneurial environment for France Télécom that would, in line with EC directives, deregulate services and terminal equipment but maintain the government's role in shaping the important telecommunication infrastructure.

The DGT France Télécom has had a long history of internal conflict between its engineers, for the most part graduates of the famous l'École Polytechnique, and its nontechnical management, which received its training from the l'École Nationale Superieur des PTT (ENSPTT).[11]

During the 1940s, 1950s, and 1960s the nontechnical administrator from ENSPTT dominated the DGT and emphasized essentially the maintenance and service of the existing network. During the same period the French government did not include telecommunication in its five-year plans, and provided fewer investment funds for telecommunication than any of France's neighbors. Only during the fifth five-year plan (1966–70) did modernization of the telecommunication network appear for the first time among the industrial policy priorities, to emerge during the sixth and seventh five-year plans (1970–80) as the top policy priority.[12]

The government's sudden emphasis on telecommunication modernization and the high rate of technological change that had begun to affect the nature of global networks strengthened the role of the engineer/scientist in the DGT, but also prompted a search for a new organizational structure that would confer greater managerial autonomy for the DGTs. Note that the reorganizations of the "télécoms" have been political and organizational issues, discussed by and within the technocratic echelons of the government and the DGT, with little participation of industry, customers, or American trade representatives. Even the EC and the trade unions began to influence the restructuring of France Télécom only during the mid–1980s.

During the 1970s the DGT managed to administer the changes in strategic objectives, investment funds, and technological sophistication largely in its existing organization. The increasing separation between postal services and telecommunication provided the DGT and its regional directors with greater authority, and flexibility and technical competence and training became the basis for advancement. In turn the DGT top management participated significantly in determining industrial, commercial, and tariff policy.[13] Although there were complaints in the press and among the emerging French version of the German "Greens" that a new high-tech communication system was imposed upon the French public, the success of creating within ten years a modern telephone network, with the highest percentage of digital transmission systems in Europe (and the world) mobilized broad popular support for the DGT effort.

From 1975 to 1985, during the sixth and seventh five-year plans the DGT's managerial competence and investment funds were consistently enlarged. The creation of Europe's densest (95 percent penetration rate in 1989) and most sophisticated telephone network was a victory for the French technocrats and planning bureaucracy. France Télécom was especially proud of extending and replacing its archaic analog system with a digital network that comprised 60 percent of its total transmission system by the mid–1960s and 80 percent by 1990, probably the highest percentage in the world. While Germany and the United Kingdom relied on copper wire overlay nets to establish digital ISDN-capable networks, France Télécom pioneered in the establishment of a massive optical fiber network. (Taking the technological lead in the early to mid–1980s may have made it more difficult for France Télécom to introduce state-of-the-art ISDN switching technology in the late 1980s and early 1990s. Certainly Alcatel's digital switch E10, Télécom's mainstay, no longer ranks among the world's top five.) In addition to its technological competence, France Télécom displayed considerable entrepreneurial skills; its packet-switching data network Transpac expanded globally, and it became a world leader with its videotex Minitel.

The physical networks built under DGT director general Gerard Thery during 1975–85 were, however, only the most noticeable aspect of the new engineering-driven DGT. In order to build a modern state-of-the-art telecommunication system the DGT had been charged with expanding its research and development operation, arranging for technology transfer between DGT and industry, and strengthening the ties between telecommunication and computer science. (The convergence of computer and telecommunication technology has been called *télématique*, a term that has also been adopted by the EC.) The relatively narrow base of the French telecommunication industry had already produced close ties among France Télécom and the two large electronic conglomerates (CGE-Alcatel and Thompson S. A.), the nationalized ITT company CGCE (now Matra/Ericsson Telecommunication or MET), and France's largest computer manufacturer, the nationalized Cie. Machine Bull (losses for 1990 U.S. $1 billion).

Equally significant for establishing a profile of the "new" France Télécom were its efforts to establish various joint international ventures with both European PTTs and international telcos. From Argentina (a France Télécom-led consortium, combining the political influence of Latin American communications and finance enterprises with French technology, acquired the northern half of Argentina's public telecommunication network) to Mexico (France Télécom–Southwestern Bell consortium strove to acquire Mexico's PTT Telmex), to Japan (joint marketing product developing venture with Japan's ITJ), to Canada (France Télécom joint venture with Canada's international carrier Téléglobe), to Germany (France Télécom–DBP Telecom joint venture to sell network management skills and VAS), France Télécom has acquired international telcos.

By the mid–1980s the globalization of the world economy, the concomitant conflict between corporate demand for international private networks and national telecom monopolies, the emergence of a supranational EC driven by a liberal European commission, and the impact of the Reagan–Thatcher revolution created strong pressures in France to liberalize the French telecommunication system.

The March 1986 parliamentary election produced a conservative-liberal victory that aligned France with Great Britain and Germany in an effort to push back the power of the state, privatize nationalized industries, and liberalize state monopolies. The Chirac administration pledged itself to return to the private sector the large number of enterprises nationalized from 1981 to 1985, and in particular to liberalize the telecommunication system in accordance with the EC Green Paper and with current developments in Germany and the Netherlands. A complete destruction of the state telecommunication monopoly along the lines of British or American experience, however, was never under consideration.

Although the Chirac administration made a liberalized telecommunication system one of its main priorities, it continued the industrial policy established by Giscard d'Estaing in 1975 to develop a world-class information technology (*télématique*) industry that could compete with Japanese and American enterprises. The Chirac administration, moreover, was a strong supporter of the "Europe 1992" project, and also was very influential in encouraging the EC policy of promoting a European telecommunication infrastructure as a part of a European information-technology industry. The EC research projects RACE and ESPRIT and the EC-sponsored unsuccessful cooperation among Europe's large computer firms Bull, Philips, and Siemens, all had strong French support.

Although there seemed to have been a contradiction between the Chirac administration's simultaneous devotion to a liberal telecommunication regime and to a strong industrial policy commitment, this view is not necessarily correct.[14] Even the public corporation France Télécom would have been still under the supervision of the post and telecommunication ministry, and private industry would continue to cooperate with the government's planning process. It is important to note that liberalization, even under a French center-right administration, is quite different from similar events in Great Britain or Germany. To the opponents of the Chirac reform program, the putative conflict between telecommunication liberalization and an industrial policy designed to protect France from American-Japanese domination was sufficiently obvious to attack the Chirac administration for selling out to the "multinationals." As in Germany, IBM became the specter that would dominate France's information technology if the government monopoly were weakened. It was precisely this type of opposition, including massive strike threats by the trade unions, that prompted the Chirac administration to delay the restructuring of France Télécom until after the May 1988 election.

Although the Chirac administration was not able to implement its telecom reform, we shall take a brief look at its agenda to compare the reforms of a liberal administration with the 1990 Télécom legislation passed by a socialist government.

The French Telecommunication System, 1986–88

By 1986, the distribution of television and radio programs had already been separated from France Télécom's jurisdiction (law of July 1982) and placed under a new administration, the TDF (Télédiffusion de France). Similarly the separation of the postal and telecommunication component of the PTT (Postes Télécommunications et Télédiffusion) also was completed, leaving France Télécom's administration in charge of the management of the telecommunication system. The Chirac administration established a new administrative unit within the PTT, the Mission à la Régelementation Générale (MRG). In line with the EC Green Paper, the MRG would administer regulatory functions of the PTT, leaving to France Télécom the managerial tasks. This separation (actually no full separation took place; France Télécom retained some regulatory authority) of regulatory and managerial assignments was very much in line with the Green Paper provisions and was very similar to the Witte commission recommendations in Germany. The establishment of the MRG with its dynamic chief J. P. Chamoux was an important first step in the liberalization process.

In the view of the international business community, the deregulation of the value-added networks (decree of September 24, 1987; note that an administrative decree bypasses parliamentary approval) was the most important aspect of the Chirac deregulation. Value-added networks (VANs) had been previously deregulated on a pragmatic ad hoc basis, but had been limited essentially to provide "enhanced services" through publicly switched networks. Under the September 1987 decree VANs could now be sold to third parties on leased telecommunication lines.[15] The 1987 deregulation of value-added networks had several additional provisions, buried in rather obscure language, which should be noted briefly. Leased line-based value-added networks had been divided into two categories, according to size and level of enhanced services. Category I VANs merely had to be announced to the PTT ministry, and thereafter could be sold freely to all telephone subscribers. Category II VANs required the access permission of the PTT minister, who consulted with the CNCL (Commission Nationale de la Communication et de Libertés), the commission established to supervise the deregulation of radio and television, in the above-mentioned 1982 regulation. As part of the liberalization of the mass media the CNCL was also allotted several regulatory functions. Needless to say the liberalization of VANs was complicated enough to give, de facto, the

PTE ministry ample opportunity to screen the introduction of large, sophisticated VANs.

By the end of 1986 the French PTT organization looked as pictured in figure 4.1. France Télécom maintained its twenty-two regional districts and a central administration. In addition, it set up a holding company (COGECOM, Compagnie Générale des Communications) to supervise and coordinate the numerous subsidiaries France Télécom had acquired by the mid–1980s. The COGECOM subsidiaries are administered, on an ad hoc basis, as private corporations, with private sector salary structures and discretionary transfer pricing procedures. Although the private sector structure of the subsidiaries freed France Télécom management from the rigid civil service reward and recruiting structure, it also reduced its control since the government and not France Télécom appointed the subsidiaries' top management and defined their strategic objectives (see table 4.1).

The vitality and autonomy of the France Télécom subsidiaries, especially Transpac and Minitel, may have given observers the impression in the mid–1980s that France Télécom was abandoning the monopolistic PTT position more readily than the DBP. Another interpretation might have been that France's industrial telecommunication policy was ready to rely on entrepreneurial organizations as long as state control was not threatened. A closer look at the reform process during 1986–90 will illuminate this question further.

Telecom Liberalization, 1986–88: Success and Failure

The Chirac administration strove to privatize the enterprises nationalized by the socialist-communist administration during 1981–83, the relatively brief period during which Mitterrand attempted to lay the foundations for a socialist France. The rapid drop in the value of the franc, accompanied by unemployment and capital flight, brought the attempt to actually implement the socialist election platform to a sudden end. All nationalized companies remained, however, in the ownership of the state, until 1986–88, when the Chirac administration succeeded in denationalizing the more promising enterprises. (There seems to exist a broad consensus among French parties that important but money-losing enterprises, such as France's largest steel company Usinor-Sacilor, the electronics firm Thompson S. A., or the computer manufacturer Machines Bull should remain the property of the state. Thus France's vaunted industrial policy does not merely pick winners but also protects losers!)

In the telecommunication and information technology area, Gérard Longuét, the minister for post, telecommunication, and space (PTE, Ministre des Postes, Télécommunications et de L'Espace), believed strongly that competition had become the driving force, as had been established already in the United States. Longuét and Chamoux, his chef de la mission à la

Figure 4.1
Organization Chart, French PTT, 1986

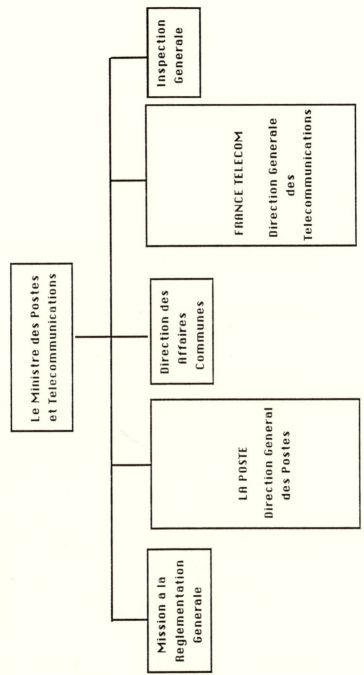

Source: Décret n° 86–1083 du 7 octobre 1986; décret n° 86–129 du 28 janvier 1986.

Table 4.1
Important France Télécom Subsidiaries, 1986–87

1.   France-Cables et Radio (FCR)

      Founded (as a Private company in 1913 owned
      100% by France Télécom
      Sales of 0,7 by FFR
      700 employees
      FCR operated primarily abroad
      Operates Underwater telecommunication cables, provides
      consulting services for office communications
      such as teleconferences, digital VAS transmission

2.   France Télésystems
      Founded 1969
      Owned 9.9% by France Télécom
      Sales of 0.6 bn FFR
      1800 employees
      Télésystems operates computer centers, provides
      network management and databanks, produces software

3.   Transpac
      Founded 1978
      owned 98.6% by France Télécom
      Sales of 1.6 bn FFR in 1986
      650 employees
      Operates and sells worldwide France Télécom packet-
      switched data transmission system, as well as the
      message transmission system 400

      The establishment of Transpac, one of the technical
      achievements of the 1970's investment policies as an
      entrepreneurial, profit-seeking subsidiary emphasizes
      the pragmatic nature of France Télécom management. (A
      similar venture by the DBP, say the administration
      of its IDN data service as an independent subsidiary
      would have been politically and institutionally
      impossible.)

4.   Entreprise générale de Télécommunication (EGT)
      Founded 1965
      Owned 100% by France Télécom
      Sales .5 bn FFR in 1986
      450 employees
      Responsible for the sale of terminal equipment
      Teletex services
      Radio telephones
      Telecopier
      Eurosignal
      Answering services

Source: DGT, *Rapport d'activité 1986.*

réglementation, became known throughout Europe for praising competition as a dynamic factor in the information-technology sector and announcing the imminent liberalization of France Télécom.[16] The proposed Longuét reforms had three objectives:

1. Transform France Télécom into a public corporation, with the government as the only stockholder. (This proposal, as mentioned, had been termed "privatization of France Télécom" by the trade unions, an appellation that seems to have baffled and misled foreign observers.)

2. Separate completely regulatory and managerial tasks. (The 1986 establishment of the Mission à la Réglementation within the PTE ministry had been merely a first step, that still left additional regulatory authority with France Télécom and CNEC, the television authority.)

3. Open the telecommunication system to competition within certain constraints, but give France Télécom the administrative structure to enable it to compete effectively in the value-added service sector and in the sale of terminal equipment. To provide equality of opportunity among private and public telcos, France Télécom would become subject to the value-added tax, but in turn should be protected from political interference.

Strong opposition from the trade unions, especially the communist-dominated Confédération Générale du Travail (CGT), the last bastion of French Stalinism, and the social democratic FO (Force Ouvriére PTT), ordinarily the enemy of the CGT, prompted the Chirac administration to delay introducing its proposed "Legislation for Competition in Telecommunication" until after the 1988 presidential election. Instead the Chirac administration in the fall of 1986 presented a reform legislation draft "L'avant-project de loi sur les telecommunications" to the public. A victory in 1988 would have provided the conservatives with the public approval to push through the telecommunication law against trade union opposition.[17]

The December 1988 authorization of the Societé Française de Radiotéléphone (SFR) had already added a privately owned, competitive mobile telephone network to the existing France Télécom mobile network. Unlike its staid government competitor, private mobile telephone flourished in the mid–1980s.[18] Thwarted in carrying out its reorganization plans for France Télécom, the Chirac administration was successful in supporting the deregulated mobile telecommunication and radio message sector through various decrees.

The SFR, a joint venture of the privately owned and financially strong water utility Compagnie Générales des Eaux, the Finnish mobile telephone specialist Nokia, and Alcatel, had been chosen by the ministry to provide telephone service with the hope that competition would stimulate France's lagging mobile cellular sector. The ministry explained that France Télécom's emphasis on establishing a digital telephone network had led to the neglect of the mobile cellular telephone system. Moreover, what interest in mobile networks France Télécom management displayed was directed toward the establishment of a digital cellular network that would conform to the proposed European /ETSI-approved GSM digital standard. The GSM Standard—a tightly written book of technical specifications the size of a medium city's telephone book—was, however, not fully approved by ETSI before the summer of 1991 and will not be operational before the fall of 1992 at the earliest. The explosion of personal mobile communication, supported by personal communication networks (PCN) in the United Kingdom, Sweden, and more recently Germany, has made the allocation of appropriate frequencies a controversial European issue that has delayed further the full acceptance of GSM.

France Télécom's digital strategy led, therefore, to the neglect of analog mobile services, that grew almost explosively in France's neighbors, especially the United Kingdom, Sweden, Finland, and Germany. France's backwardness in regard to a mobile telephone system enabled the Chirac administration to strengthen competition in the French system, without encountering strong opposition. The Générale des Eaux–Nokia–Alcatel consortium committed itself to a significant investment in the growing analog network that covered 85 percent of France by the end of 1991. A second consortium consisting of Nokia, Alcatel, and AEG (a German electronic-computer company owned by Daimler-Benz) had promised to provide the equipment for the digital net by the summer of 1992. Altogether the network brings competition, investment, and a technology transfer from Nokia and AEG to Alcatel.

THE REFORM OF THE FRENCH POST AND TELECOMMUNICATION SYSTEM, 1988–91

The socialists won the presidential election of May 1980, and the re-elected President Mitterrand chose Michel Rocard as his prime minister. The choice of Rocard, the leader of the Social Democratic right wing of of the Socialist party and an old Mitterrand adversary, signaled that no second wave of nationalization or renationalization of recently denationalized enterprises would occur. The Rocard administration was neither going to extend nor push back the role of state ownership and state economic policy. There was a strong commitment to the Europe 1992 project and a more or less public commitment to the harmonization of European standards and policies.[19]

Although the Rocard administration seemed satisfied with maintaining the existing private-public sector demarcations, Rocard's minister of post and telecommunication, Paul Quilés, made it clear, under union pressure, that he wanted to revise the liberalization steps that had been introduced by his predecessor Longuét.[20] Shortly after taking over the PTT ministry,

Quilés announced that he was going to reform the post and telecommunication administrations, and establish a structure along the line of the *service public*.[21]

Quilés rejected the reform design of the previous administration, and also announced his intention to revise the September 1986 Freedom of Communication Law (which deregulated television and privatized one government television channel, FTI) and its regulatory agency CNCL (Commission Nationale de la Communication et des Libertés; the CNCL resembled the FCC). The CNCL had been intended to be independent of the French government, and particularly the PTT ministry, and had regulatory authority that extended beyond the mass media into the telecommunication field (approval of leased-line networks) and thus limited the regulatory scope of the PTT ministry.[22] Quilés was able to revise the 1986 communication law in 1989, and replace the independent CNCL agency with a government-appointed regulatory commission, the CSA (Conseil Supérieur de l'Audiovisuel), whose jurisdiction was confined to supervision of public and private television and radio programming.[23] The 1989 revision of the so-called media legislation extends the CSA's ability to suspend television stations if the provisions of the legislation are violated.

The revision of the 1986 TV Deregulation Act was a rather minor rollback of the Chirac administration's liberalization efforts. There still remained the task of bringing the French telecommunication system into conformance with the EC Green Paper that was rapidly implemented during the late 1980s. France also had to respond to the ongoing reform efforts in Germany, and the virtually complete liberalization of services and private networks in the United Kingdom. After some initial dithering, a September 1988 manifest of all the unions represented at France Télécom that threatened a strike in case any form of privatization was carried out, prompted Quilés to search for a politically acceptable strategy that would reform the entire post and telecommunication system.[24]

Reopening a public debate about the future of France Télécom, Quilés chose one supposedly independent expert, Hubert Prévot, to explore the sentiment of interested groups and the public at large. No other European government would have dared to instruct *one* expert to carry on a public debate. The fact that Prévot was a senior socialist civil servant, commissaire général du plan (1981–84) in the finance ministry among other assignments, would have challenged even further the government's pretensions to have chosen an independent expert to illuminate all aspects of a complex issue in a public debate.

Quite surprisingly, from the point of view of foreign observers, Prévot was able to open a broad discussion in which the trade unions, employer and industry associations, user groups, government and opposition parties, and even the public at large participated vigorously. Perhaps not so surprisingly, in view of France's history and the general approval of the role of the *service public* institutions, Prévot was able to demonstrate that there did exist a broad consensus that under avoidance of ideologically loaded terms such as privatization, could permit a reform of the PTT that would accommodate the EC telecommunication policy, be comparable to the structural changes in the German PTT, and still maintain a strong role for the government in shaping its infrastructure policy.[25]

Prévot came to the conclusion that a reform of the post and telecommunication system was necessary. Acknowledging that the "realisation of the common European market (will) modify profoundly the conditions and developments of the postal service and France Télécom," Prévot proposed a restructuring of the system in order to attain four objectives:[26]

- A clear definition of the public service mission according to the needs of the user and the coming of "1992"
- A regulatory structure in accordance with the rapid development of the telecommunication sector
- A system of motivating PTT personnel
- A management structure that would provide an "autonomous administration" for the executives of France Télécom and the postal service[27]

Prévot provided a detailed list of recommendations.[28] Since the government accepted fully Prévot's recommendations submitted August 1989, we shall omit further discussion and present the various decrees and laws of 1990 that have changed the structure of French telecommunication and have made the demarcations between monopoly and competition more transparent.

The Reorganization of Post and Telecommunication

The first step in the PTT reform was the reorganization of the postal and telecommunication system into two autonomous *service public* institutions, accompanied by a reorganization of the ministry. As in Germany, the organizational restructuring was the politically most controversial step, but Quilés' skillful management of this issue brought him broad support in and out of parliament.[29] The CGT and the Force Ouvrière PTT opposed Quilés' reorganization bill, claiming, probably correctly, that it was not very different from the Longuét proposal. A *service public* organization and a public corporation can operate under very similar guidelines. Since, however, the reorganization proposal was advanced by a socialist government and seemed to be acceptable to the PTT employees, the trade union position was much less vehement. Quilés' assurance that the new France Télécom would maintain the *fonctionnaire* (tenured civil service) status of its middle- and upper-level employees undermined union-PTT employee opposition. There is no American equivalent to the French *fonctionnaire* or the German-Austrian *Beamte*, who hold a prestigious if not privileged position in society. The French and German civil service distinguishes between mere employees—low-skilled workers—and the *fonctionnaire* or *Beamte*, who has at the very least a lycée (gymnasium) baccalaureate or a technical or university degree. A *fonctionnaire* not only holds a life-time job, but also is assured of reasonable career advances. Both Witte in Germany and Longuét and Chamoux in France had tried to remove the civil service stigma from the new telecommunication enterprise and both failed.

If the trade unions and the hard left opposed Quilés' reorganization for undermining employee achievements and state control, the conservative-liberal opposition objected that the Télécom deregulation and autonomy were not far-reaching enough; in particular the opposition complained that the ministry did not really relinquish control, and hence there was no real separation of regulatory and entrepreneurial tasks.[30] Recent events (March–April 1991) seem to have confirmed the misgivings of the conservative/liberals that the government had not really relinquished its control over France Télécom.

During April 1991 the French government continued to use France Télécom as a tool of its industrial policy by channeling a substantial part of its F 8.5 bn (U.S. $1.15 bn) bailout of Thompson S. A. and Cie des Machines Bull through the supposedly autonomous telecommunication enterprise. The profitable France Télécom is already a reluctant minority stockholder in Thompson and Bull, and would have preferred to use its capital in promising international ventures.[31] French restructuring legislation, very much like the German, leaves a lot to the interpretation of the PTE minister and to the resoluteness of Télécom management. The fact that Télécom began its operation under a socialist Quilés while Telekom emerged under a liberal Schwarz-Schilling may be more significant for the immediate future of these two organizations than the exact provisions of the respective legislation that established their charter.

The Legal Framework for the Reformed French Telecommunication System

The French telecommunication reform consists of a series of laws and decrees that were passed during July and December 1990. The laws provide broad guidelines for the desired reforms and the decrees supply the precise format for their administration. We shall briefly note their four main points, and then attempt to discuss and evaluate the entire body of the reform legislation in its context.

1. The law of July 2, 1990, established post and telecommunication as *service public* enterprises.[32] France Télécom, along with the postal service, became an auton-

omous profit-seeking enterprise, with a management board and its own budget and capital assets.[33] Broad objectives were specified. Several consultative commissions were established to provide broad participation in decision making.

2. The decree of December 18, 1990, restructured the ministry of post, telecommunication, and space (PTE) in order to accommodate the newly created public enterprises France Télécom and La Poste. It established within the ministry a supervisory board, the "Supervisory Directorate (DSP)," to assure that France Télécom met its objective.

3. The law on telecommunication regulation of December 29, 1990, redefined the scope of regulatory agencies for television and telecommunication within the PTE ministry. The DRG (Direction de la Réglementation Générale; which replaced Mission à la Réglementation in 1989) attained additional authority and was now responsible for authorization of leased lines, value-added service definition, and observation of standards, and granted network access to terminal equipment.[34]

4. The decree of December 29, 1990, established the general obligations, requirements, and goals of France Télécom. The decree of December 29 filled in the framework of the law of July 2, which established France Télécom as an autonomous *service public* enterprise.[35]

The body of legislation establishing a reformed French telecommunication system is opaque and complex; layers of consultative and supervisory bodies were created and both the PTE and the finance ministry explicitly and implicitly retained considerable influence. Figure 4.2 and table 4.2 show the relationship among the various institutions. In addition to the line and advising relations connecting France Télécom to various power centers, the new *service public* enterprise was also charged to develop three-year economic plans jointly with the ministries of PTE and finance to guide investment and tariff policies.

At the time these lines are written it is difficult to predict how autonomous the France Télécom management will be. We can, however, explore the changes in organizational structure, definition of monopoly and competitive services, and VAN authorization the reform has produced.

The total body of reform legislation consists of three components:

• The establishment of France Télécom and La Poste as autonomous, commercial public entreprises (*entreprise publique*)[36]

• The supervision of La Poste and Télécom through the PTE ministry and the government

• The revision of telecommunication regulation; establishment of clear demarcation between monopoly and competition

We shall discuss, briefly, each component and then attempt to assess the total reform effort.

Figure 4.2
Organization Chart, Regulatory and Advisory Bodies, Communication and PTE Ministries

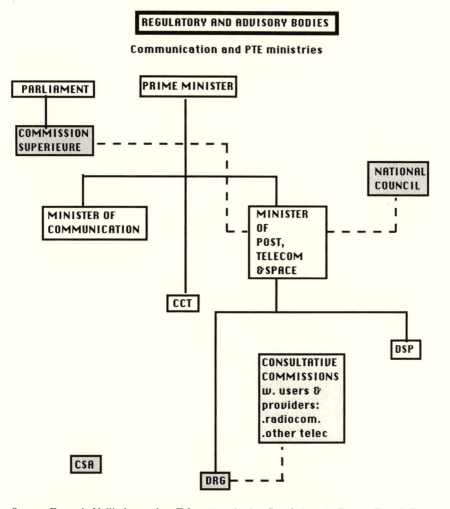

Source: Francois Vulliod, attache, *Telecommunication Regulations in France,* French Embassy to the United States, January 15, 1991.

Table 4.2
Regulatory and Advisory Bodies

Regulatory Bodies

CSA (Conseil Supérieur de l'Audiovisuel): Mass Media

- Spectrum management of the mass media bands
- Licensing of radio, television, and satellite broadcasters
- Licensing of cable operators (authorization of cable networks by municipalities)
- Independent body (nine commissioners appointed by the president of the Republic, the president of the House, and the president of the Senate [three each])

DRG (Direction de la Réglementation Générale): Telecommunication (including telecom services on cable networks); DRG is part of the ministry of post, telecommunication, and space

- Definition of technical specifications
- Spectrum management of telecommunication bands
- Licensing of radiocom providers
- Type approval of terminal equipment
- Granting of service authorizations, when required

CCT (Comité de coordination des télécommunications)

- Apportions spectrum among government and military uses, mass media, and telecommunication.

Advisory Bodies

Parliamentary Commission (Commission Supérieure)

- Gives advice and opinions on all regulatory issues (rules, authorization procedures, specifications)

National Council: members of parliament, local authorities, users, associations, unions

- Gives advice on general telecommunication policy, broad issues (such as universal service)
- Gives opinions on the activities of France Télécom

Technical Commissions: members of users and providers associations

- Two commissions: radiocom, nonradiocom services
- Give advice to the DRG on authorization procedures, technical specifications

Supervisory Body

DSP (Direction du service public)

- Oversees France Télécom's fulfillment of its objectives, as stated by its license or three-year plan

- Formulates government policy (other than regulatory) in the telecommunication sector

- DSP is not a supervisory body in the American sense; at best it could only call attention to flagrant deviations from France Télécom's official three-year plan. Currently (1991/92) DSP's role has been usurped by the prime minister's office.

The Management and Structure of France Télécom

France Télécom is a *service public* enterprise, but remains under the supervision of the PTE minister. Its charter requires it to provide all public telecommunication services, at home and abroad. La Poste has similar postal service assignments.

France Télécom (and also La Poste) is simultaneously managed and supervised by an administrative board, the *conseil d'administration*. Unlike Germany or the United States, France and, in particular, the *service public* enterprises do not separate management and supervision. Still we could say that, for American purposes, the *conseil d'administration* is primarily a supervisory and strategic forum whose chair (actually president) is also the chief executive officer. The CEO, currently M. Marcel Roulet, general manager (*dirècteur général*) of France Télécom since 1986, is appointed by the president of the Republic and nominated by the council from one of its members.[37] The composition of the twenty-one-member council is of some interest. It consists of seven state representatives (*représentants de l'État*), all senior civil servants, seven experts (*personnalités qualifieés*), and seven employee representatives (*représentants du personnel*)—three nominated by the communist-led CGT, three by the left-wing socialist CFDT, and one by the Social Democratic Force Ouvriére. None of the seven employee representatives are full-time union members; all of them are middle-level PTE employees.

The president of the council is the chief executive officer of France Télécom, represents the organization in all forums, and bears the financial responsibility. He also appoints France Télécom representatives in subsidiaries and joint ventures. Most important, he appoints the chief operations officer (*dirècteur général*).

The supervisory and advisory role of the *conseil d'administration* is specified in the decree of December 18, 1990; it will take several years before the actual role of this council will become clear. Since a representative of the PTE minister will attend all *council* meetings in an advisory role, it is generally assumed that the council will not make waves, especially since the ministry representative must assure the coordination of ministry and France Télécom policy.[38] The dominant role of the ministry is clearly recognized by Quilés, who stated that "I have always said that the autonomie [of France Télécom] does not include independence. There is no France Télécom industrial policy on one side, an industrial policy of the French State on the other. *France Télécom pursues an industrial policy in accordance with my directives.*"[39] The establishment of France Télécom and La Poste as two "autonomous" *service public* enterprises was accompanied by a reorganization of the PTT ministry, during December 1990, now called the Ministry for Post, Telecommunication, and Space (PTE).[40]

For our purposes, two nearly established departments or "directions" are worth mentioning: the regulatory department (*direction de la réglementation générale* or DRG) and the department for supervision of public enterprises (*direction service public* or DSP). The DRG does, more or less (nothing is clear-cut in the French bureaucracy), establish a regulatory telecommunication authority separate from France Télécom but within the PTE ministry. The DRG is now virtually the sole regulatory telecommunication authority (virtually, because the Conseil Supérieur de l'audiovisuel [CSA] still retains jurisdiction over interactive telecom transmission via cable television networks). Since for North American telcos the DRG may very well be the most important agency to contact, figure 4.3 presents the DRG table of organizations, with their managers as of January 15, 1991.

We shall see, when discussing the regulatory structure of French telecommunication, that the DRG seems to have considerable discretionary power, considerably more than its German equivalent in the Federal Ministry for Post and Telecommunication (BMPT).[41] It will take at least a year to determine how broadly or narrowly the DRG will interpret its mission.

The DSP is the second important department in the PTE that deserves our attention. Its task is to supervise the performance of France Télécom and La Poste, to verify if these two organizations live up to their obligations as stated in the decree and legislation of December 1990. While the *conseil d'administration* supervises, essentially, the performance of management in achieving strategic goals set by the *conseil* and the PTE ministry, the DSP seems to be especially concerned with the delivery of the mandatory services and employee relations; and just to complicate the regulatory picture further the DSP also observes the pricing of monopoly services.

If the Anglo-American reader begins to be impressed by the echelon of supervisory panels that monitor the "autonomous" France Télécom and La Poste management, we can cite additional advisory-supervisory agencies that must make France Télécom and La Poste the most intensively monitored enterprises west of the former Soviet Union. The price for the relatively easy passage of the telecom reform legislation was the establishment of three commissions or councils that grant parliament and trade unions advisory roles that may or may not be translated into a type of parliamentary-trade-union codetermination in the management of France Télécom and La Poste. Actually, however, most observers seem to believe

Figure 4.3
Direction de la Réglementation Générale

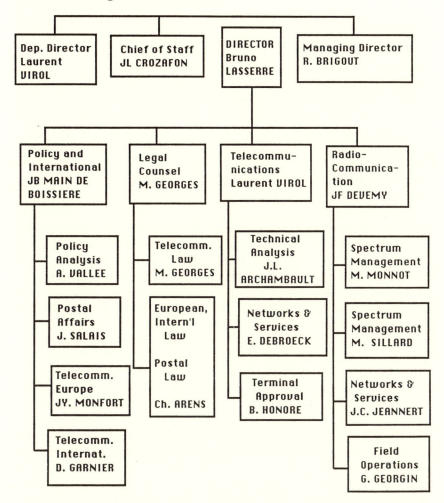

Source: Francois Vulliod, attache, *Telecommunication Regulations in France*, French Embassy to the United States, January 15, 1991.

that the three commissions/councils will have little if any impact on the actual decision processes. We shall only briefly describe the commissions.

The Commission for Post and Telecommunication is a parliamentary control organ that monitors the performance of the PTE minister as well as La Poste and France Télécom. The commission must be consulted in the preparation of the five-year plan and will, in turn, publicly comment on major ministry decisions. The commission consists of six members of parliament, four senators (the French senate is relatively unimportant), and three experts appointed by the PTE ministry.[42]

The National Council for Post and Telecommunication is supposed to represent the public and consists of a subcommittee from the parliamentary commission for post and telecommunication as well as government representatives, France Télécom managers, user group delegates, and trade union leaders. The council is chaired by the PTE minister and is supposed to serve as a forum that will discuss the economic, political, and social aspects of France Télécom and La Poste activities. The council has little impact on PTE policy.[43]

The Commission for Personal and Social Affairs is very similar to the German employee representation (*Personalvertretung*) and is a considerable step toward some form of employee codetermination in the French public sector. The commission consists of representatives from the trade unions, the ministry, and the management of the two *service public* enterprises and advises the minister on all social and personnel issues. The inclusion of the commission in the 1992 organization reform legislation played a significant role in the parliamentary passage of both the organization reform law (loi n° 90–568 du 2 juillet 1990) and the telecom regulation bill of December 28, 1990.

The echelon of supervisory agencies discussed above assures the conformance of the Télécom management to the guidelines of the ministry and to the provisions of the body of reform laws and decrees. Of greater importance has been or will be the establishment of various institutions and control groups that assure the continued effectiveness of the government's industrial policy in the telecommunication area. La Poste and particularly France Télécom are closely tied to the government's long-run economic planning efforts. The three- or five-year plans provide, in general, directives for government investment policies, objectives for state-controlled enterprise (supposedly tighter ones for the *service public* organizations than for the nationalized enterprises), and guidelines for public-private sector cooperation.[44]

In the case of France Télécom the planning process takes two forms. First, the government and Télécom (and La Poste) management negotiate a multiyear strategic plan (*contrat du plan*) that is in line with the government's overall industry and fiscal objectives. Second, the government uses the financial, technical, and managerial strength of Télécom to strengthen ailing nationalized enterprises such as Bull and Thompson that are important in terms of industrial policy or internal politics. The transformation of France Télécom from a government agency into a *service public* enterprise actually has made it easier to channel the profits generated by the telephone monopoly into areas outside the telecommunication field.

The point could be made that the association of a telco and a computer manufacturer is today desirable, as shown by British Telecom–IBM and IBM–Rolm– Siemens alliances and joint ventures. Bull, however, is hopelessly overstaffed and produces a very expensive, although technically proficient product. This situation has not changed since the mid–1960s, when GE bought Bull, and neither American, nor subsequently French-American, nor now the French state control has been able to change Bull's management culture. Continued state aid will not change Bull's performance. After reluctantly acquiring 17 percent of Bull shares, France Télécom as of April 1991 was trying to assert its independence by demanding that Bull turn over its internal telephone system group to France Télécom in exchange for further aid. However, IBM's acquisition of 10 percent of Bull's stock in February 1992 will probably make it difficult for France Telecom to obtain Bull's internal telecom system. In December 1991, Prime Minister Edith Cresson and her new industry minister Dominique Strauss-Kahn launched an even more serious attempt to channel France-Telecom's surplus into an ambitious scheme to rescue France's leading state-owned electronics enterprise. Under the Cresson plan, France-Telecom would have to purchase 14 percent of the electronics company Thompson S.A., reducing government ownership to 82 percent (4 percent is owned by several French banks). The purchase of 14 percent of Thompson for an as yet undisclosed amount reputed to exceed FFR 2.5 bn. has been bitterly opposed by Telecom management, the conservative-center opposition in parliament, and the European Commission, especially by Cresson's nemesis Sir Leon Brittan, the competition commissioner.[45]

The outcome of these examples of French *dirigisme* will tell us a lot about the independence of France Télécom, and about the ability of French industry minister Strauss-Kahn to flaunt EC objections to subsidize unprofitable enterprises.[46] Perhaps equally important it will clarify the ability of the *direction service public*, the new supervisory agency within the PTE ministry, to impose policy guidelines on the France Télécom management. The final outcome of the bailout of Bull and Thompson will illustrate how much autonomy its management really has.

The France Télécom Charter (*Cahier des Charges*)

The planning process sets the framework of national objectives France Télécom management has to achieve, and, supposedly, balances the interest of the PTE ministry with those of the ministries of industry, economics, finance, and budget.[47] In addition article 8 of the organization law also requires that the president of the Republic specifies by a decree the rights and duties (*cahier des charges*) of France Télécom and La Poste. In order to issue such a decree the president has to satisfy a bureaucratic ritual that includes consulting the cabinet as well as the commission for post and telecommunication and to obtain the approval of the Conseil d'État, France's highest administrative court.

In December 1990 the first *cahier des charges* for France Télécom and La Poste was decreed, and their competence and duties defined. This *cahier des charges* provides the outline for France Télécom monopoly and mandatory services that were subsequently restated in greater detail in the December 29 law on telecommunication regulation. We shall briefly enumerate the key points of this charter (*cahier des charges* can be literally translated as "responsibility notebook").[48]

1. France Télécom is authorized to operate, at home and abroad, every type of telecommunication service or network, and to supply every type of terminal equipment. Its performance should be guided by the needs of its customers and by state policy.

2. France Télécom retains its monopoly status for telephone and telex service and for the operations of the telecom network. The monopoly services are provided on a uniform and universal basis to all customers. The tariff system for monopoly services will be based, in general, on the actual cost of delivery, but can also consider the need for cross-subsidization.

3. France Télécom can compete in all areas in which it has no monopoly; it is required, however, to provide services in competition with private suppliers (*ouverts à la concurrence*) in the following areas:[49]
   • distribute the annual telephone directory
   • provide telephone information and switched data transmission
   • operate a public mobile telecommunication network (*radio téléphone publique*)

   The list of mandatory services can be extended, if necessary, if "general interest" requires.

4. France Télécom consults with the PTE ministry in determining its rates in the monopoly areas but is free in settling its rates in competitive markets. France Télécom may provide any service it wishes in competitive markets.

5. France Télécom is required to provide for its customers the highest quality service possible, and to inform its customers clearly about all conditions of service. To assure high-quality service, France Télécom has to report to the ministry its achievement as to universal service, penetration rate, product menu, and tariffs.

Telecommunication Regulation Law (December 1990)[50]

The key to the telecommunication reform, especially from the point of view of North American and European telcos, is the December 1990 telecommunication law, which goes beyond the charter to define carefully monopoly and competitive services and networks, leased-line usage, and previous ad hoc administrative rules that lifted particular regulations but could have been just as easily revoked received legal status.

During the 1980s, and especially during the 1986–88 period, existing rigid regulations concerning leased lines, value-added services, mobile telephones, and terminal equipment had been either liberalized or ignored. The new telecommunication regulations not only retained and in some cases extended the ad hoc liberalization of the 1980s, but attempted, in the best tradition of French devotion to logic, to define, first, clearly, every aspect of telecommunication service, transmission, or equipment and then apply each regulation to the appropriate telecommunication component. We shall consider the three usual areas—networks, services, and terminal equipment—and include in our discussion the telecom "definitions and principles."[51]

Telecommunication networks are defined as installations that transmit and switch telecommunication signals, including network terminations (*points de terminaison*). The legislation (Code de PTT) distinguishes between public networks and independent networks (the American term "private networks" is not quite the same because the *réseaux indépendants* also include railroad and utility company nets).[52] France Télécom has a public network monopoly. The network monopoly does not include mobile (cellular) telephone or satellite networks. Private mobile radio network operations require authorization from the PTE ministry. The authorization is not offered freely but must be in the public interest, compatible with France Télécom efforts to provide universal service (i.e., restrict "cream skimming"). Non-EC telcos may not own more than 20 percent of a private network operation. The private operator must also abide by a ministry charter (*cahier de charges*) that specifies quality, standards, and performance scope.

Telecommunication services are defind broadly and include all forms of transmission or switching of signals.[53] A distinction is made between signal transmission and signal enrichment (enhanced services) by adding information.

The telefon and telex services are monopoly services to be offered only by France Télécom.

Both analog and digital, individually and packet-switched transmission is a mandatory France Télécom service but also open to private competitors. Service authorization from the PTE ministry is received provided that private data transmission does not conflict with the public interest or the mandatory obligations of France Télécom. Private data transmission operators receive a *cahier de charges* that define their operation, including technical standards, compatibility, and scope.

Radiotelephone includes mobile-telephone and satellite communication.

Both are open to competition with France Télécom but require PTE authorization. Given the past neglect of the mobile telephone service by France Télécom, authorization for mobile operators or radio signal service has been granted freely. With the arrival of the digital European GSM mobile cellular telephone standards, radio telephone transmission will become a truly deregulated service in France.

The sale of *terminal or CPE equipment*, in particular the simple telephone, had been de facto deregulated during the 1980s; hence the telecommunication regulation law reaffirms the competitive nature of the CPE market. Enterprises offering terminal equipment still have to obtain permission from the PTE ministry. The conformance of all equipment to existing standards is required. Equipment that has not been granted network access cannot be manufactured in France or imported from abroad.

In spite of the bureaucratic formulation of the access requirements and their strict enforcement, the terminal equipment market in France, as in most EC countries by 1991, has been deregulated. There has been no indication that the access-granting process has been made difficult. There are signs, however, that the PTE ministry has been ambivalent, at times, about including PBXs in the competitive terminal equipment market. There is ample anecdotal evidence that during 1988–89 France lobbied the EC to exclude PBXs from its deregulation directives. In 1989 the French government challenged before the European Court of Justice the EC commission's rights to use article 90 of the Treaty of Rome to dismantle state monopolies. In particular, the 1988 EC directive to the twelve member states "to end special and exclusive rights—granted to state owned telephone companies—for the import, supply and use of telecommunication terminal equipment" seemed to limit the PTE's access-granting policy and prompted French resistance.[54] The court's 1991 landmark decision, upholding the EC, will enable telcos to protest unfavorable access conditions to Brussels.[55] The fact is, however, that the PTE has been quite liberal in granting access to terminal equipment imported from both EC and non-EC countries. At the same time the French government does not wish to be prevented from changing its currently liberal terminal equipment policy if it so desires.

A SUMMARY EVALUATION OF FRENCH TELECOMMUNICATION REFORM

The new French telecommunication reform is only a few months old. Nobody knows to what extent the potentially broad authority that still remains in the hands of the PTE minister and the French government will be used. There exist, however, objective accomplishments.

First, the reform legislation has confirmed the administrative deregulation efforts of the late 1980s in the areas of mobile communication, radio messaging, value-added networks, and leased lines. Recent EC directives on leased lines should further liberalize the PTE's private network policy, although France has been generally slow in accepting EC directives.

Second, competition in value-added services and terminal equipment both within the EC and globally is accepted. The German triage of the telecom market into monopoly, mandatory services in a competitive environment, and unrestricted competition has been adopted, although the PTE retains considerable authority in granting the necessary access to VANs, VAS, and equipment providers. (German legislation has attempted to narrow the criteria to be considered for access permission, thus enabling unsuccessful providers to challenge negative decisions before the courts.)

Third, the state's role in providing and improving the necessary telecommunication infrastructure is confirmed, as well as the state's unique responsibility to assure universal and uniform service throughout France, and to guarantee the equal treatment of all users by public and private service and equipment providers. Most important, perhaps, the state's role in coordinating telecommunication policy with national industrial policy remains assured.

Fourth, the ability of France Télécom management to adopt flexible, entrepreneurial policies, unfettered from hierarchical PTE control, remains to be established. The July 1990 organizational reform legislation enabled France Télécom to establish or purchase subsidiaries and control them through its COGECOM holding company; most of France Télécom's entrepreneurial activities have been channeled through its subsidiaries at home and abroad. Still, the law requires approval by the president in selecting CEOs for all subsidiaries; hence it is still possible that central authority may be reinvoked if France Télécom becomes too autonomous.

Finally, the numerous advisory or controlling councils and commissions threaten to obscure the decision-making process, especially if the authority of the president is undermined by another period of "cohabitation" (i.e., when president and prime minister belong to different parties).

In summary the telecommunication reform adapts the French regulation to the competitive reality of European and world markets without lessening, at least potentially, the commanding role of the state. It would be a mistake, however, to overemphasize the importance of organizational structure in assessing both the technical competence of the PTE technocrats and the entrepreneurial talent of the France Télécom management that has transformed the French telecommunication system during nearly two decades under various organizational formats and different governments. The success of subsidiaries such as Transpac and Minitel in offering sophisticated products both at home and abroad illustrates the importance of skilled cadres in achieving strategic goals.

NOTES

1. The totalitarian nature of the Jacobin regime, previously known only to specialists, has been exposed to public discussion in various scholarly books at the occasion of the 200th anniversary of the French Revolution in the late 1990s. For Americans Simon Schama's *Citizens* (New York: Alfred A. Knopf, 1989), is of particular interest because of its acute analysis of the left-wing Colbertism of the Jacobins.

2. See Alfred L. Thimm, *The False Promise of Codetermination* (Boston: Lexington, 1981).

3. Ministère des Postes, des Télécommunications et de l'Espace, *La Réforme des PTT*, dossier d'information, Paris, 1990.

4. Prior to the 1970s modernization efforts, France's telecommunication system was described as having one-half of the population waiting for a telephone, and the other half waiting for a dial tone. Every time President Pompidou would announce his goal to turn Paris into a world financial center, the traders in London and Frankfurt would laugh uproariously since Paris lacked the telecom infrastructure needed for a world-class finance center. For a brief history of the French PTT, see Patrice Alexandre Carré, "France Télécom culture d'entreprise et memoire," *France Télécom* (December 1990): 54–64.

5. For a colorful discussion of the various structures of French state enterprises, see Joël Carbajo, *Droit de services publics* (Paris: Havas, 1990).

6. Bull has been a money-losing manufacturer of large computers through all of its metamorphoses from a private sector French enterprise to one owned by American or American/French companies and ultimately to one owned by the French government. In spite of a shrinking European market share the government's deep pockets have kept it alive. Although a minor league mainframe computer manufacturer, Bull has been recently successful as a PC and peripheral producer. Among its recent successes are the "smart cards"—microchip-embedded plastic banking cards. France's success in dominating the "smart card" market can be considered a direct consequence of its industrial IT policy. See "Smart Cards: France Leads while the Rest Hang Back," *Financial Times* (November 7, 1990): 8.

7. An important but relatively unknown *grande école* is France Télécom's very own institution, the L'École Nationale des PTT. See F. Guillet, *L'École Nationale des PTT: Histoire de la naissance et de la formation d'un grand corps de l'État, 1888–1988* (Paris: Edition Hervus, 1988).

8. Patrice A. Carré, *France Télécom: Culture d'entreprise et mémoire*, *France Télécom* (December 1990): 60. See also M. Nouvion, *L'automatisation des télécommunications, la mutation d'une administration* (Lyon: Presse Universitaire de Lyon, 1982).

9. For a brief discussion of French trade union structure and ideology, see Thimm, "Codetermination in Western Europe: France," in *False Promise*, 243–53.

10. Carré, *France Télécom* (December 1990): 60–61.

11. See ibid., 62. For a more detailed discussion of the two cultures, see C. Giraud, *Généalogie d'une organisation: Rationalité et changement dans le service public des télécommunications* (Paris: Université Paris-Sorbonne, 1985).

12. Carré, *France Télécom*.

13. Ibid.

14. For a critical view of Chirac's policies, see Henri Bessières, "PTT, La réforme éntrouvable," *Télécom Magazine* (September 1989): 68–71.

15. J. P. Chamoux, "The State of the Reform Process in France," paper presented at the WIK Conference, The Future of Telecommunication, Bonn, 1988.

16. Ibid.

17. The French labor movement has been divided along ideological lines since World War I. After 1945 communist, socialist, and Catholic unions have emphasized primarily national (pro- and anti-NATO) and ideological objectives and have ordinarily neglected bread and butter issues. During the late 1980s, the CGT, France's largest trade union, opposed the transformation of Renault from a *regie* to a public enterprise. Similarly the CGT threatened to strike if Chirac proceeded with turning France Télécom into a public corporation. The FO supported in this case the CGT since its major strength lies in the public sector, including the PTE ministry. The socialist CFDT (Confederation Française Democratique du Travail) and the Christian Workers (CFIC) also opposed the so-called privatization of France Télécom, but neither of these unions was strongly represented in the PTE ministry.

18. Under the "basic" telecommunication law of 1837, "Code des Postes et Télécommunications," the PT minister has discretionary authority to permit additions to the public networks.

19. Actually France frequently lobbied in Brussels against liberal or antimonopoly policies. In 1988 France sued the commission before the European Court for overstepping its authority under article 90 of the Treaty of Rome in limiting monopolistic practices of government agencies in telecommunication and transportation. In March 1991 the court upheld the commission and ruled that it could force member-states to abandon public monopolies, especially in telecommunication. See "Court Boosts Brussels' Legal Power," *Financial Times* (March 20, 1981): 2.

20. See *Le Monde* (December 8, 1988): 35; and also *Le réforme des PTT* (Ministère des PTT, 1988), 9.

21. See *Financial Times* (July 20, 1988); and *Le Monde* (July 20, 1988).

22. Independent regulatory agencies have been unknown in France. In a first attempt to choose a quasi-FCC, the 1986 law had devised a Byzantine method to choose the ten-member commission from three administrative courts and the Academie Française. Since the CNCL only lasted until January 1989, we shall not discuss it further. Specialists interested in French bureaucratic ingenuity should see *CNCL: La Lettre d'Information*, Paris, November 2, 1987; and *CNCL: Rapport annuel*, 1986–87, Paris, 1988.

23. Loi n° 89–25 du 17 janvier 1989 modificant la loi n° 86–1067 du 30 septembre 1980 relative de la liberté de la communication.

24. Note again Quilés' already quoted article in *Le Record* of December 8, 1988, in which he announced "a fundamental reexamination of telecommunication reform" (p. 35).

25. The very impressive scope of the *débat public*, which included the use of video transmissions, Minitel, meetings, and publication, is recorded under "Le

Deroulement du Débat Public" (The Unfolding of the Public Debate) in *Hubert Prévot: Rapport de synthese*, 163–82.

26. H. Prévot, *Le Débat Public: Rapport de synthese, Ministere des Postes, des Telecommunications et de L'Espace*. (August 1989), 7.

27. Ibid.

28. *Rapport de synthese*, 75–158.

29. See Emmanuel Guillaume, "La réforme juridique de France", *Télécom Magazine* (July–August 1990): 512–518 for two different visions of the public discussion. The labor economist Henri Bessières, who seems to disparage the significance of the reorganization, describes carefully the different attitudes of the four major unions. "PTT, La réform éntrouvable," *Télécom Magazine* (Sept. 1989): 68–71.

30. Among the newspaper and journals that covered the liberal-conservative critique, *Les Echo* and *Le Figaro* should be noted, as well as the already quoted article by Emmanuel Guillaume. Two Figaro articles, dated November 11, 1990 and November 19, 1990, give a good survey of the public debate during July–December 1990.

31. See "France Grants Large Subsidies to Ailing Firms," *Wall Street Journal* (*WSJ*), April 2, 1991, p. 111; and "France Télécom Seeks Part of Bull in Return for Cash Help," *Financial Times* (April 2, 1991): 23.

32. Loi n° 90–568 du 2 juillet 1990 relatif à L'organisation du Service Public de la Poste et des Télécommunications.

33. Guillaume, "La réforme juridique de France," 512–518.

34. "Loi n° 90–1170 du 29 juin 1990," *Journal officiel de la Republique Française* 16439–16441.

35. "Décret n° 90–1213 du 29 décembre 1990 relatif au cahier des charges de France Télécom et au code des postes et télécommunications," *Journal officiel de la Republique Française* (December 30, 1990): 16568–16574.

36. Guillame, "La réforme juridique," 17.

37. *France Télécom* insert "Dernière Minute," January 1991. The same release gives the names and titles of the twenty-one members of the conseil d'administration de France Télécom. Quite typical, Marcel Roulet, a graduate of both l'École Polytechnique (1954) and l'École Nationale Supérieure des Telecommunications (1959), is a lifelong civil servant who has held important positions in France Télécom and is credited with having instituted management by objective in 1986.

38. Guillaume, "La réforme juridique," 19.

39. Quoted by Wolrad Rommel in *Die Reform des Post und Fernmeldewesen in Frankreich* (Bad Honnef: WIK, 1991), translated from the original quotation in *Le Monde* (November 23, 1990): 4. We have retrieved that particular *Le Monde* issue. My translation is from the original French, emphasis added.

40. Décret no 90–1121 du 18 décembre 1990.

41. For a very interesting comparison of the French and German telecommunication reform, see Rommel, *Die Reform,* 49–58.

42. The post and telecommunication commission was established in October 1990 (décret n° 9 90–25 du octobre 1990) prior to the government's submittal of the reform legislation in December 1990. The two other commissions had been included in the reform legislation.

43. Act 37 of the organization law does not specify how many will serve on the council nor their selection.

44. *Le Plan* attracted American attention in the 1950s and 1960s and spawned numerous articles and books. No significant new material seems to have appeared in English, as far as we know, during the past fifteen years. An excellent study has appeared in German, however, with an extensive bibliography. See Joachim Volz, "Länderbericht Frankreich," in *Industriepolitik im Westlichen Ausland* (Berlin: Deutsches Institut für Wirtschaftsforschung [DIW], 1987). The DIW is one of the five key economic research institutes in Germany and has had considerable influence on German fiscal policy discussion.

45. Ms. Cresson's industrial policy proposals have generated enormous comments in France, the U.K., and to a lesser extent, Germany. The single best discussion of this topic in English is William Dawkins, "Cresson's Champions," *Financial Times* (December 19, 1991): 16.

46. See "France Grants Large Subsidies to Ailing Firms," p. A11; "France Telecom seeks part of Bull." Note the *WSJ* editorial on French policy to bail out unproductive enterprises in "Syntax Error," *WSJ*, April 11, 1991, p. A14.

47. A plethora of financial control agencies from various ministries examine France Télécom investment and finance program and audit its budget. Articles 15 and 39 of the July 1990 "organization legislation" describe the details. When the victorious socialists hit upon the original idea of expanding the already heavily overstaffed French civil service in 1981, critics asked what the newly appointed servants of the state would do to keep busy. The answer was given in 1991. The new cadres are necessary to staff the legions of supervisors and control and co-ordinating committees that have been let loose on the "autonomous" enterprises La Poste and France Télécom.

48. "Décret n° 90–1213 du 29.12.1990 relatif au cahier des charges de France Télécom," *Journal officiel de la Republique Française* (December 30, 1990): 16568–78.

49. Ibid., art. 4, 16570.

50. Loi n° 90–1170 du décembre 1990 sur la régelementation des télécommunication.

51. Loi sur la réglementation, chap. 1.

52. Ibid., sec. 1, art. 33.

53. Ibid., sec. 2.

54. Cited from "Court Boosts Brussels' Legal Powers," 2.

55. Ibid. See also "EC Antitrust Efforts Boosted," *WSJ*, March 20, 1991, p. A17.

5

Teletel: An Industrial Policy Success

William L. Cats-Baril

INFORMATION TECHNOLOGY AND FRENCH INDUSTRIAL POLICY

In the mid–1960s, particularly after the American Congress denied a permit to export a large IBM mainframe computer to the French government, French political commentators started to voice concerns that France was falling behind the United States in information technology and that it would soon be in an intolerable situation of technological and cultural dependence. For example, President Giscard d'Estaing, in gathering support for moving France into the information age, stated that "for France, the American domination of telecommunications and computers is a threat to its independence in the crucially significant if not overriding area of technology and in the field of culture, where the American presence, through television and satellite, becomes an omnipresence." This line of thought continued to be voiced during the 1970s and became a central piece of the industrial policy of the country.[1]

In 1975, President Valery Giscard d'Estaing asked two researchers, Simon Nora and Alain Minc, to suggest a strategy to computerize French society. The Nora–Minc report delivered in 1978 and published in 1979 went on to be a best-seller (a first for this type of report). The report coined a new word, *télématique* (from telecommunication and informatique), and proposed it as the cornerstone of that strategy. Télématique was the merger of computers and communication technologies to create information-processing applications with broad societal impact.

Indeed, Nora and Minc predicted that eventually télématique would affect all aspects of society—education, business, media, leisure, and routine day-to-day activities. The way they saw it, télématique would, by increasing access to information, lead to decentralization of government and business decision making, and therefore lead to an increase in national productivity and competitiveness, and to an improvement in the ability to respond to an increasingly fast-changing environment (Nora and Minc 1979).

Nora and Minc's view, however, implied that a new national communication infrastructure was necessary for France to remain among the leading countries of the industrialized world. Their report also underlined that such a transformation would require a long-term strategy and cooperation between the government and business sectors.

One of the recommendations of the report was for the Direction Générale des Télécommunications (DGT), as France Télécom was named then, to encourage cooperation among computer services companies and hardware manufacturers to produce the technical components of the required infrastructure. Another recommendation was for the DGT to implement a research program to develop applications to leverage and take advantage of that infrastructure (Nora and Minc 1979).

These recommendations are typical of French industrial policy. The strategy of having the government orchestrate and subsidize large technological projects by creating alliances among companies and going as far as "rationalizing" an industrial sector by encouraging mergers—the computer and electronics sector being a prime example—had been used before (e.g., Ariane, Airbus, Concorde, TGV). As a senior official of the French government put it, "This type of large industrial projects, or as we (the French) called them 'les grandes aventures,' have always captured the imagination of French politicians."

THE FRENCH TELEPHONE SYSTEM IN THE 1970s

In 1974, when Valery Giscard d'Estaing became president of France, the French telecommunication system was very weak. There were less than 7 million telephone lines for a population of 47 million (one of the lower penetration rates in the industrialized world and equivalent to that of Czechoslovakia), a four-year wait to get a new line, and most rural areas in the country were still equipped with manual switches (Chamoux 1990; Mayer 1988).

President Giscard d'Estaing decided to make the reform of the telecommunication infrastructure a top priority. In April 1975, the Conseil des Ministres (a cabinet-level meeting among the secretaries of all agencies) approved the president's program under the banner "Le telephone pour tous" (a telephone for everyone).

Also in 1974, Gerard Thery took over as director of the DGT. At that time, the strategic direction of telecommunication technology was set by the Centre National d'Etudes des Télécommunications (CNET). The CNET was, and continues to be, the research and development arm of the

DGT. The CNET was dominated by engineers whose responsibility and vocation was the design of new products. They focused on technical prowess and innovation.

Once the design of a product was complete, the CNET negotiated directly with the telecommunication industry the development and commercialization of the product. Housel (1990) notes that because the CNET engineers were constantly trying new technologies without a clear technological migration plan, manufacturers were forced into short production runs, making manufacturing economies of scale impossible, driving prices up, and making network compatibility difficult to achieve.

They changed the orientation of the CNET. The CNET went from having an attitude of technological change for the sake of technological change to having a more commercial and pragmatic one. The change in culture was difficult at first: most of the engineers went on a long and bitter strike. Eventually, Thery's vision prevailed and not only did the internal focus of the CNET change but a new relationship between the DGT and the French telecommunication manufacturers was established (Housel 1990; Marchand 1987).

Thery's strategy to establish a more commercial orientation at the CNET was implemented by creating the Direction des Affaires Industrielles et Internationales (DAII) and by bringing in an outsider, Jean-Pierre Souviron, to serve as its director. One of the principal functions of the DAII was to insure standardization of equipment. The DAII invited bids not only from the traditional suppliers of the DGT (e.g., CIT-Alcatel, Thompson) but from others as well (e.g., Matra and Philips). To drive equipment prices down, the DAII announced that from then on an important criterion in choosing suppliers would be their ability to export and acquire larger markets.

The government push toward standardization and export was partially responsible for lowering subscription charges and more than doubling the number of telephone lines between 1974 and 1979. By the late 1980s, the penetration rate was at 95 percent, one of the higher telephone penetration rates among the industrialized nations (Chamoux 1990; Housel 1990).

The transformation of the French telephone network from the "joke of Europe" to the most modern of Europe ("from the ugly toad to the handsome prince," in the words of a government official) took some ten years and a tremendous amount of resources. Indeed, from 1976 to 1980, the DGT was the largest investor in France, averaging around 4 percent of the total national investment in the country (Hutin 1981). The total cost of the transformation has been estimated at around F 120 bn.

The magnitude of the investment in creating the telephone network raised questions as to how to maintain its expansion and how to leverage the modernization costs. In early 1978, with the telephone penetration rate growing very quickly, They realized that telephone traffic alone would not be enough to leverage the telephone network and the public packet-switched network (Transpac).

They asked the CNET to generate ideas for new services and established a list of requirements they had to fulfill. The services would have to (1) provide greater access for all citizens to government and commercial information; (2) benefit as many elements of society as possible; (3) demonstrate the value of merging computing and telecommunication; (4) be flexible enough to avoid quick technological obsolescence; and (5) be profitable (Housel 1990).

In November 1978, Thery prepared a report for the Conseil des Ministres detailing six projects: the electronic telephone directory, the videotex, the videophone, the wide distribution of telefax machines, the launching of a satellite for data transmission, and the voice-activated telephone. The background for his presentation was the Nora and Minc report and the need, as perceived by Thery, to counter the threat of IBM capturing critical strategic markets if left unchallenged. "Let us be the Japanese of Europe," he was constantly telling his entourage (Marchand 1987).

The Conseil des Ministres gave a green light only to the electronic telephone directory and the videotex. Three years after the successful launching of the "Le telephone pour tous" campaign, "la grande adventure du Teletel" was about to begin.

TELETEL: A BRIEF HISTORY

Work on Teletel began in the mid–1970s. The first Teletel prototype was shown at the 1977 Berlin Trade Fair. The British demonstrated at that show a very impressive operational system (CEEFAX, the precursor of Prestel). They realized he had to move fast and went on to persuade the government to allow the DGT to pursue the videotex project during the interministerial meeting of November 1978. The plan to test Teletel was set for 1979. Initially, there were plans for two applications: the development of an electronic telephone directory and classified ads.

With the installation of seven million telephone lines from 1974 to 1979, the telephone directory became obsolete as soon as it was printed (and it was printed twice a year). Also, the cost of printing the French telephone directory went up so rapidly that in 1979, the paper telephone directory lost F 120 mn. Between 1979 and 1984, seven million more lines were expected to be installed, and the cost of printing the directory alone was expected to double in the next five years. (The quantity of paper was expected to quintuple from 20,000 tons in 1979 to a projected 100,000 tons by 1985.) Directory assistance was hopelessly overloaded. It required 4,500 operators to provide a barely acceptable level of service. The number of operators needed in 1985 was forecasted to be 9,000 (Dondoux 1978; Marchand 1987).

Directory automation was proposed to address the directory assistance problem, which was becoming a serious public relations issue, and to bring about savings by avoiding the costs of printing telephone directories. The success of the electronic telephone directory assumed that a great majority of the subscribers would be able to use it. This notion in turn implied that subscribers would need to have access to an easy-to-use, inexpensive terminal.

At the DAII, planners developed the scenario of distributing terminals free of charge to subscribers. They reasoned that as long as a dedicated terminal could be produced for F 500, and with the cost of each paper telephone book being F 100 (and increasing), the cost of the terminal could be recovered in less than five years. The government agreed to try out the electronic telephone directory concept during the Conseil des Ministres of November 1978.

Another application that was discussed to help launch Teletel was for the DGT to offer classified ads. But after a vicious attack from the press and its powerful lobby, which saw their main source of income threatened, the DGT capitulated. The idea of making classified ads a videotex service offered by the DGT died on December 12, 1980. On that day, Pierre Ribes, secretary of the PTT, stated unequivocally that there would be no classified ads offered through Teletel in the videotex experiment to be started in Vélizy, a suburb of Paris, in June 1981. In a quid pro quo, the press dropped its resistance to the Teletel project (Marchand 1987).

The first tests of Teletel took place in the cities of Saint-Malo (1980) and Vélizy (1981), and later in the county of Ille-et-Villaine (1983).[2] The initial testing of the electronic directory began in July 15, 1980, in Saint-Malo. The actual videotex experiment started at Vélizy under the name Teletel 3V. The test began in June 1981 with a sample of 2,500 homes and 100 different services. After two years, the Vélizy experience showed that 25 percent of the users were responsible for 60 percent of all traffic, that a full one-third of the sample never used the device (this proportion of nonusers has remained constant throughout the dissemination of minitels), and that, overall, households had a positive experience with Teletel. The experiment was considered a success in both technical and sociological terms (Chamoux 1990; Marchand 1987).

On February 4, 1983, a full-scale implementation of the electronic directory was started in the county of Ille-et-Villaine. In the opening ceremony Louis Mexandeau, the new secretary of the PTT, exulted: "We are here today to celebrate the beginning of a 'grande aventure,' an experience which will mark our future." François Mitterrand had replaced Valery Giscard d'Estaing as president of France and the "left" was now in power, but the rhetoric on the importance of télématique to the future of the country and the underlying industrial policy remained the same.

Soon after the successes of Vélizy and Ille-et-Villaine, the voluntary and free distribution of minitel terminals was quickly implemented. There were 120,000 minitels in France by the end of 1983, 600,000 at the end of 1984, over 3 million by December 1987, and more than 5 million in 1990 (see Figure 5.1). Videotex services went from 145 in January of 1984 to 5,000 at the end of 1987 to 13,000 in 1990 (Figure 5.2). From 1983 to 1990, the Teletel and electronic directory systems have been expanded and improved continuously (Table 5.1). Teletel can now handle 60,000 different services and 50,000 simultaneous calls. In 1989, France Télécom created new organizational entities (e.g., Intelmatique) to export Teletel and its know-how.

Teletel had to overcome four serious challenges in the early years. First, there were vicious attacks by the newspaper owners, in particular François-Regis Hutin, owner of *Ouest-France*, who saw among many philosophical reasons to stop videotex, a very pragmatic one (Hutin 1981).[3] Videotex was a serious threat to their main source of revenue: advertising. After a long fight, a political compromise was reached that gave newspaper owners, in exchange for dropping their resistance to the videotex concept, a say in the development of Teletel services, subsidies and technical help from the DGT to develop their own services, and a virtual monopoly on services for the first couple of years.

A second challenge was the feeling by some politicians that the system could be abused by the state. The public declarations of these politicians stated that this new mode of information dissemination was a potential threat to the liberty of the citizenry and that Teletel was the latest attempt of the state to manipulate information (the Big Brother syndrome). Later, the rapid proliferation of "chat" (*messageries*) services, some of which were considered pornographic (*messageries roses*), brought criticism from both government and private groups who were concerned that the state was billing and indirectly subsidizing immorality.

A third challenge was the early battle to establish an international videotex standard. The most advanced videotex system in the 1970s was the British system Prestel. Prestel was based on the CEEFAX standard, which was different from the one being used by the French. The DGT, realizing that they were at a disadvantage, tried to have their own videotex standard recognized at several international forums. In a decision typical of the byzantine regulatory politics in Europe, the Conference Européene des Postes et Télécommunications (CEPT) established in 1980 a European videotex "standard" with 10 variations! One of these variations was the French standard. Notwithstanding the fact that this decision assured the incompatibility of the European videotex systems during the 1980s, the

Figure 5.1
Rate of Distribution and the Number of Minitels Distributed, 1989

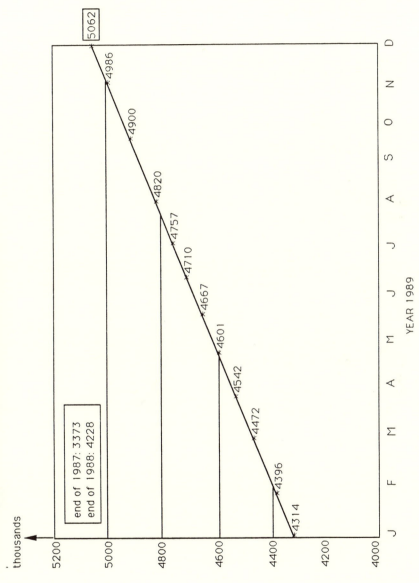

Source: France Télécom.

Figure 5.2
Growth of Teletel Services, 1985–90

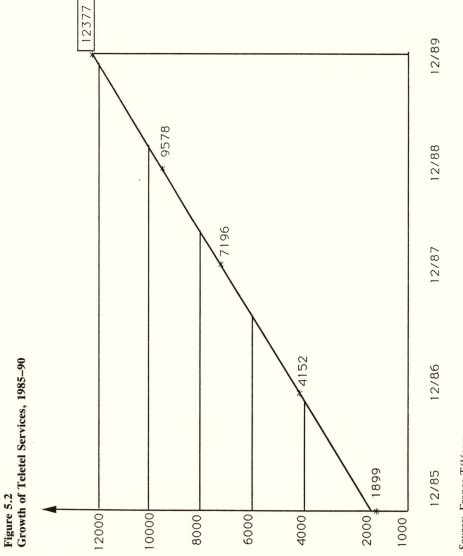

Source: France Télécom.

Table 5.1
Evolution of the Electronic Telephone Directory (ETD) and Videotex Networks

	Dec. 1987	Dec. 1988	Dec. 1989
Number of Access Points to the ETD	58	72	78
Number of ports to the ETD	14 220	17 280	19 020
Number of Information Centers	31	40	42
Number of Documentation Centers	15	18	22
Number of Videotex Access Points (VAPs)	43 160	49 611	50 500

Source: France Télécom.

decision allowed the DGT to continue the development of Teletel as planned.

The fourth challenge that Teletel had to survive was the negative publicity that surrounded the "crash of '85," the only system failure since its inception. The crash was the result of very heavy traffic of messageries services. The heavy traffic caused an overload of the Transpac switching system, and the network went down. The technical problem was easy to solve: the switching system was changed to handle higher volumes, and there has not been another crash since. The perceptual problem that Teletel was mostly about "sex," lingered much longer, slowed down teletel's development, and, paradoxically, increased its international visibility.

Overcoming these public controversies made Teletel stronger in the long run. Indeed, the political fury that Teletel generated in 1978–80, and later in 1985, led to a full and rich discussion on the issues of privacy rights, authority of the telecommunication agency, regulation of computer services, and the need to prevent the creation of a second class of citizens shut out of the information age. These discussions involved the president of France and the most notable political commentators and intellectuals in the country and eventually created a broad national consensus on the use and limitations of the technology.

Today, Teletel is an integral part of the French life-style. A survey conducted by France Télécom in October 1989 indicated that some 40 percent of the population had access to minitels at home or at work and that the system was used regularly by a broad cross-section of the population in a variety of ways (see Figures 5.3 and 5.4 and Table 5.2).

The success of Teletel as a sociological development and its positive impact on the technological literacy of the population are unquestionable. The primary concern about Teletel now is whether it is a profitable operation or not. But before exploring this concern, let us describe some of the technical choices and characteristics that made Teletel so far the only successful commercial videotex system in the world.

GENERAL CHARACTERISTICS OF TELETEL

A comparison between the technical characteristics and policies used in implementing Teletel and those of the other commercial videotex systems (e.g., American, British, and German) explains to a certain degree the great success of Teletel (more than 5 million subscribers) and the rather tepid development of the others (e.g., 250,000 subscribers for the German Bildschirmtext; 150,000 for all British videotex systems, including Prestel). The comparison among videotex systems can be made on four basic characteristics: (1) terminal design and strategy of terminal distribution; (2) system architecture and other aspects of service provision; (3) billing system; and (4) regulatory environment (see Schneider, et al. 1990).

Given the British experience, where the high price of the chosen TV-based videotex setup became a barrier to implementation, and the DGT argument that the Teletel investment would be paid back through increased telephone traffic and savings in the production of the telephone directory, it was clear that Teletel's success was critically dependent on the development of an easy-to-use, dedicated, and inexpensive terminal for mass distribution. The Vélizy experience had also established the need for a user-friendly terminal with an easy-to-use interface. The motto for Teletel became "make it simple"—simple to install, simple to use, simple to manufacture.

In an approach typical of French industrial policy, the government, rather than the consumer electronic industry, decided on the specifications of the videotex terminals. The DAII opened the procurement of terminals to multiple vendors, and the promise of a production run of some 20 million terminals encouraged low bids. The total cost of the original basic minitel terminal to the DGT was approximately F 1000.

Figure 5.3
Traffic Distribution per Age Group, 1988–89

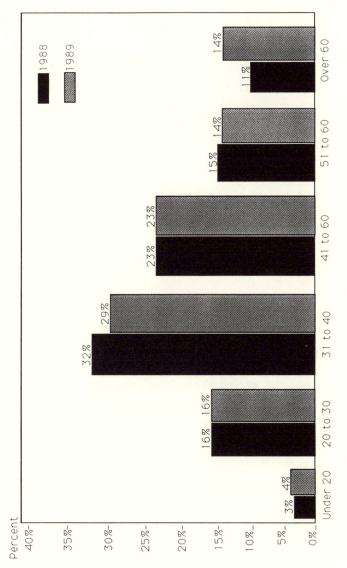

Source: France Télécom.

Figure 5.4
Partition of Teletel Traffic by Type, 1989

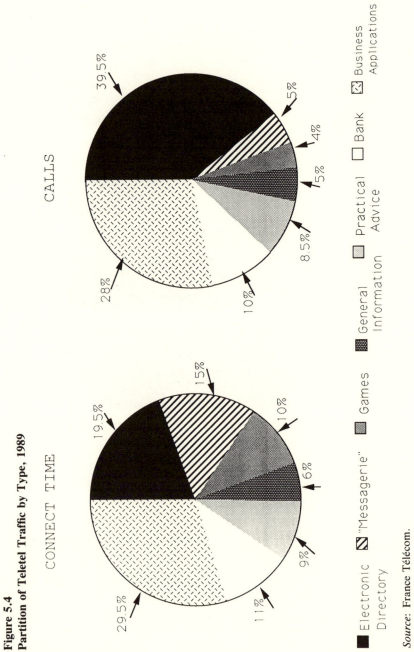

CONNECT TIME

CALLS

■ Electronic   ▨ "Messagerie"   ▥ Games   ▨ General   ▥ Practical   □ Bank   ▧ Business
   Directory   Information   Advice   Applications

Source: France Télécom.

Table 5.2
Minitel Traffic Statistics

	1986	1987	1988	1989
Total Number of calls	466 208 000	807 963 000	1 110 819 000	1 242 991 615
Total Number of connect hours	37 499 100	62 445 800	73 748 000	85 542 200
Average usage per month (in minutes)	105.9	111.3	97	93.2
Average number of calls per month	21.9	24	22.2	22.3
Average duration of all calls (in minutes)	4.8	4.6	4.4	4.2
Average duration of a call excluding the Electronic Directory (in minutes)	6.3	6.1	5.8	5.5

Source: France Télécom.

The key decision on whether or not to distribute minitel terminals free of charge generated intense controversy within the DGT. On the one hand, to distribute minitels on a free and voluntary basis had at least two advantages. Politically, it gave it an aura of democracy. Those who wished to have a minitel would not be impeded by its cost. Second, it made it easier for the mass public to try out the device and the services it offered.

On the other hand, some senior officers at the DGT thought that a nominal fee on a per-month basis was not only sound policy from a financial point of view to recover development costs, but that a fee would also send an appropriate message to the users to counteract the "if-it's-free-it-cannot-be-very-good" syndrome. They also reasoned that once the system was distributed for free, it would be practically impossible to charge for it later on without generating intense public resistance. In what turned out to be a critical decision in the success of Teletel, it was decided that minitel terminals would be distributed free of charge.

Another critical factor in the success of Teletel was the decision to implement the Teletel concept by interfacing the public switched telephone network with the Transpac packet-switching data network. The subscriber was to be linked to the electronic directory or any other database via his telephone through a gateway—called a videotex access point, or VAP—giving access to the Transpac network to which the servers and host computers were to be connected.

This design approach had three basic advantages. First, Transpac charges are based on traffic (i.e., minutes of connect-time) and not on distance, which means that any provider, independent of its geographical location, has equal access and costs to gain a national audience. Second, it established a common, standard protocol (i.e., the CCITT X.29), making connections to the system straightforward and relatively cheap (F 100,000), which was crucial to attract service providers. Third, the networks were already in place, consisted of the latest technology, and could support a rapid expansion in the number of subscribers and providers.

More importantly, the decision to use the Transpac network kept the DGT from becoming an information provider. With the exception of the electronic directory, the DGT acted as a common carrier and was responsible only for the transmission of information and administration of the network.[4] This is in contrast to the centralized solution offered by the British and German systems, where British Telecom and the Bundespost provided the storage and design of the databases. In Teletel, the storage and manipulation of information was left to the information providers.

The decision to build Teletel on a decentralized network and with an open architecture went a long way to alleviate the "Big Brother" concerns of the press and politicians, and encourage innovation in information services, since there was no government interference, clear standards, and the entry barrier to the information provider market was very low.

Another critical element in the success of Teletel is the billing system introduced by France Télécom in March 1984 and named the "kiosk." The billing is done by France Télécom and not by the service providers. The system was named after the newsstands where a variety of publications can be bought without leaving a record of what was bought or who bought it. The Teletel charges appear on the regular telephone bill as "minitel use" with no reference whatsoever as to what specific service was used.

The kiosk works as follows: when the connection to the desired service has been set up through the VAP, the VAP sends charging pulses to the subscriber's meter at a faster than usual rate to cover the cost of using the Transpac network and the cost of the service. The Transpac network keeps track of the connection time and pays each provider as a function of that time.

The kiosk is a very clever idea because it protects the anonymity of the users (important on both a financial and philosophical level), because it does not require passwords or payments in advance, because service providers do not have to worry about billing and its associated administrative costs, and because it allows differently priced services to be offered easily through a series of different numbers.

The monopoly that France Télécom had in the basic telecommunication services and the fact that it did not have the return on investment pressures of a commercial firm, provided Teletel with the necessary time to mature.[5] The type of infrastructure-based services like Teletel requires a longer time horizon to assess and determine profitability. There is no doubt that the regulatory umbrella that shielded Teletel in the early years is one of the critical factors in its success.

Another component of the French regulatory environment that was important to the development of Teletel was the ability of France Télécom to subsidize ventures from its subscribers' revenue. Such subsidies are forbidden by American and British regulations. The subsidies allowed France Télécom to take a long and patient view on Teletel and helped amortize the free distribution of minitel terminals, which cost F 6 billion over ten years.

One specific benefit of this protective regulatory environment is described by Housel (1990). He notes that the ability to implement changes of tariffs quickly, without going through a lengthy political process to justify them, allowed France Télécom to respond to changing market conditions. For example, there were many services that Teletel users could access and use without staying connected for very long. The user paid no fee because the tariff allowed free access. Because of the revenue-sharing arrangements with the service providers, however, France Télécom had to pay for each connection. France Télécom asked the regulatory bodies to charge subscribers a small access fee for every connection regardless of its duration. The request was barely scrutinized, and the charge was approved without debate.

Another advantage to the regulatory environment in France was the ability of France Télécom to run the kiosk billing system. The arrangement has come under fire on two fronts. First, a billing system that results in the state (in the form of France Télécom) collecting fees for the distribution of services that some deem pornographic has been argued to be unlawful. Second, it has been suggested that billing, which could be a very profitable stand-alone operation, should instead be carried out by a third party. These criticisms have not stopped France Télécom from performing the billing.

The regulatory environment in Europe, with its myriad standards and protocols, was good for Teletel initially because it served to protect the fledgling service from being battered by competition from abroad. However, that same environment has now become a barrier to Teletel's penetration of other European markets.

Finally, one must note that it is to France Télécom's credit that, in such a heavily regulated environment, it pursued an open network architecture and stayed out of the information services business, with the exception of the electronic telephone directory.[6]

This policy of decentralization and liberalization of services, contrary to the centralization policies in Britain and Germany, led to an explosion of services. Indeed, while in France the number of providers has grown steadily and the number of services today surpasses 13,500, in Britain the number has stagnated at 1,300 or so, and in Germany the number has not only stagnated but has actually declined to less than 3,000 (Schneider et al. 1990).

A comparison of the three videotex systems in France, Britain, and West Germany is shown in Table 5.3 and Figure 5.5.

TELETEL: A SOCIOLOGICAL SUCCESS

It would be a mistake to analyze Teletel exclusively in terms of its return on investment without taking into consideration its sociological impact. Though the nonfinancial (i.e., social, educational, and political) benefits brought by Teletel are difficult to measure, the increase in the technological awareness and literacy of society has to be factored into any cost-benefit analysis of the system.

Through its 13,500 services the Teletel system offers information about entertainment events, train schedules, television and radio programs, jobs and classified ads, interactive games, banking services, grocery and home shopping, home banking, comparative pricing, and many other consumer services (Housel 1990; Marchand 1987; Mayer, 1988; Sentilhes et al. 1989). Most services follow the same rules and command structures and the same multicriteria search process (e.g., a subscriber deciding on whether to go to the movies or not can search what films are showing in a given area, on a given topic, or starring a particular actor or actress), making it easy for users to move from one application to another.

Table 5.3
**Implementation Strategies and Structures of the Videotex Systems in Britain,
France, and Germany**

	BRITAIN	FRANCE	GERMANY
Terminal configuration	Adapted TV set provided by TV industry and to be bought by subscriber	Simple dedicated compact terminal (Minitel); free distribution (until 1990)	Adapted TV set provided by TV industry and to be bought by subscribers (change in 1986: multitels)
Network Architecture	Several central databases; one update center; closed system	Primarily privately owned databases, service computers connected to Transpac	Hierarchical network one central database with regional sub-bases; interconnection to private computers
Information Provision	Only by private IP (common carrier) (change in 1983: BT becomes IP)	Trigger service "electronic phone book" by PTT; other services by private IPs	Only by private IP (common carrier)
Billing System	Subscription fees page-based charges phone call charges	No subscription fees time-based charges	Subscription fees page-based charges phone call charges
Regulation Political Control	No specific regulations, less politicized	Specific regulations liberal regime politicisized; promoted by industrial policy	Specific regulations very restrictive regime politicized.

Source: Schneider et al. 1990.

Figure 5.5
Technical Configuration of Videotex Systems in Britain, France, and Germany

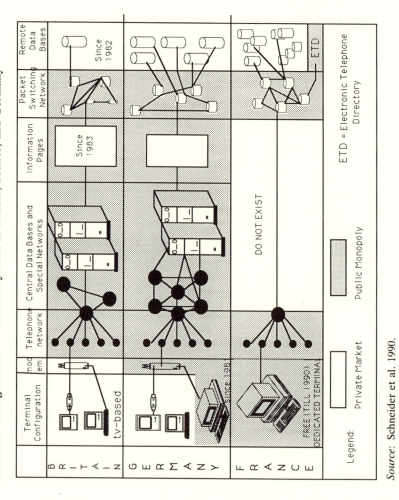

Source: Schneider et al. 1990.

It is hard to assess the impact of Teletel on business, since it varies by company size and industry sector. France Télécom estimated in 1990 that the overall penetration of the business sector is at least 30 percent and growing, and that the penetration for large companies (more than 500 employees) is 95 percent. Indeed, some industries have been profoundly affected by Teletel applications. For example, the Telerouting system has influenced the transportation industry in France. Transportation companies have minimized the number of return trips when their trucks and moving vans are empty by posting the schedules of these return trips on minitel and matching them to requests from customers (Marchand 1987; Sentilhes et al. 1989).

Almost every single bank has developed its own minitel-based home-banking system, allowing their customers to check the status of their accounts, order checks, pay utility bills, and trade stocks. Most retailers have also developed an electronic catalogue business, and although volumes are moderate at present they are expected to explode as soon as payment can be done directly with the minitel terminal. Television stations run minitel-based surveys every night. Travel agencies, insurance companies, and consumer products companies have developed Teletel services.

Whether it is to be in greater touch with clients, to increase efficiency in distribution, to gain market share, or to develop videotext products and services, minitel has become an important component of the business strategy of companies operating in France. Figure 5.6 shows the increase in business-related volume over the years, and Table 5.4 shows the main applications for business users in 1989.

From a social point of view, Teletel has had an impact in a wide variety of ways. For example, the success stories of the various Teletel chat services (*messageries*) range from relatives separated by World War II having found each other to faster matching between organ donors and people in need of a transplant. Although the chat services have been in steady decline since the mid–1980s and represented only 5 percent of all calls to Teletel in 1989, they are still one of the most popular services available, representing 15 percent of the total connect time (see Figure 5.6).[7]

The anonymity that the chat services provide has encouraged the sick and the troubled to discuss their more intimate problems with others. Teletel has also played a role in helping elderly and disabled individuals to shop, bank, and make reservations. Universities now use Teletel to coordinate student registration, course delivery, and examination results. Other services give students access to help from teachers at all times.

Teletel services have been used in the political arena in innovative ways. During the last presidential election, a service allowed minitel users to exchange letters with the candidates. Any voter accessing the service could view the open letters and the politicians' replies. Another example was how the student unrest in December 1986 could be followed by using minitel

Figure 5.6
Professional Traffic as a Percentage of All Teletel Traffic, 1986–89

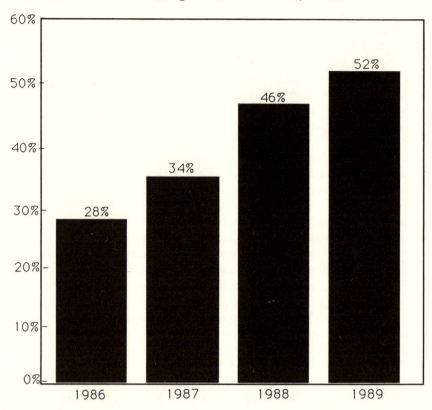

Source: France Télécom.

terminals. One service, sponsored by the newspaper *Liberation*, allowed organizers to issue instructions to any minitel user to participate in various political activities without the mediation of a third party.

These examples illustrate how broadly Teletel has been used as a decentralized, grass-roots vehicle for the discussion of a variety of societal issues. This utilization is very much in keeping with the original vision of télématique proposed by Messrs. Nora and Minc back in 1978.

TELETEL: IS IT A FINANCIAL SUCCESS?

With a project the scope and magnitude of Teletel, it is difficult to generate precise estimates of costs and revenues. There is a public perception, in part based on the free distribution of minitel terminals, that Teletel is another Concorde: a high-tech, money-losing proposition. A

Table 5.4
Most Popular Minitel Applications among Business Users

Electronic directory	95%
General information (newspapers)	42%
Electronic mail (and communication services)	39%
Professional data banks (legal, financial, commercial and sectorial data banks)	37%
Banking/Management (cash, accounting)	34%
Transport/Hotels (timetable, reservation)	27%
Business (orders, billing, after sales service)	13%

Source: France Télécom.

recent report from the state auditor general has stated that Teletel revenues have not covered its operating, depreciation, and capital costs. The secretary of the PTT, Mr. Quilés, disagrees with that assessment.

On the one hand, the total investment in Teletel consists of the cost of the minitel terminals plus the costs of the gateways to the Transpac network (VAPs) plus the costs of ports to the electronic directory network. A minitel terminal costs approximately F 1,000, including R&D. The typical VAP has costs of around F 5 million each. On the electronic directory network, one port costs approximately F 50,000. The following are approximate figures describing the investment of the France Télécom in Teletel:

Minitel terminals	F 5.4 bn
Electronic directory	F 1.0 bn
R&D directory	F 0.2 bn
VAPs	F 0.6 bn

R&D (Teletel)	F 0.3 bn
Transpac	F 0.3 bn
TOTAL	F 7.8 bn

On the other hand, the sources of revenue from Teletel include: (1) fees from revenue sharing with information providers (France Télécom takes in, on average, 30 percent of the revenue generated by information providers); (2) advertising; (3) electronic directory usage above and beyond the free allocation; and (4) rental of minitels (Housel 1990). Gross revenues from Teletel were approximately F 2 billion in 1989.

For cost-effectiveness analyses purposes, however, the savings from printing fewer telephone books and having fewer directory assistance operators must be taken into consideration. Also, the additional revenues based on value-added tax from products, services, and increased employment spawned by Teletel should be included but are difficult to calculate. Finally, the Transpac revenue generated by Teletel—almost 50 percent of all the Transpac revenue and close to F 1 billion—needs to be considered. Quilés estimated that the total value-added of Teletel amounted to approximately F 6 billion in 1988.

France Télécom's official version is that Teletel revenues and expenses were in balance at the end of 1989 and that the system is expected to start showing a significant return on investment in 1992. Unofficial estimates of Teletel's return on investment during the 1980–90 period are between 8 and 12 percent (Housel 1990). Moreover, in 1991 France Télécom started to charge a monthly fee for the new minitel terminals.

The view by senior officials of France Télécom is that this type of accounting may be a bit premature and potentially misleading, since Teletel is a major infrastructure project for which profitability needs to be measured on a long-term basis. Nevertheless, officials have been on record all along saying that the break-even point for Teletel would be ten years. Given France Télécom's numbers, those predictions seem to be right on target.

RECENT DEVELOPMENTS

From a hardware point of view, the line of minitel terminals has been expanded to include eight models with varying levels of intelligence and functionality (e.g., color screen, extended keyboards, compatibility with ASCII standards, service number memory). These second- and third-generation terminals are not distributed free any longer; they must be paid for or leased. More than 600,000 of these had been installed as of 1990.

The new generation of minitel terminals allows the user to prepare a message before placing a call, to monitor call setup, and to switch between voice and text transmission during a call. They also serve as an automatic answering device with protected access, and a portable minitel is available that can be used over the cellular telephone network. ISDN terminals have already been tested for the Teletel system.

From a software point of view, the kiosk now allows eight levels of pricing. A new routing capability allows information providers to use several host computers under a single minitel access code. This new routing capability also allows the caller to access another service within Teletel without making a new phone call.

France Télécom is also experimenting with natural language interfaces for Teletel services. The Minitel Service Guide came on-line in 1989 with an interface that allows users to access the guide to minitel services using French, without the need for special commands or the correct spelling.

With the internal market progressively being saturated and growth slowing down, France Télécom has made the international market a high priority. France Télécom has created Intelmatique—a division to sell videotex infrastructure and knowhow. Recent clients include the Italian and Irish telephone companies.

Intelmatique markets the Minitelnet service, which provides foreign users with access to the Teletel network. The new service utilizes a multitariff billing scheme corresponding to the same tariffs on Teletel and greets foreign users with a personalized welcome in their native language. The service generated 30,000 hours of traffic in 1989, a 300 percent increase over 1988. Belgium (45 percent of the traffic) and the United States and Canada (20 percent of the traffic) were the two major markets.

Major efforts are currently being made to export minitel services to the U.S. market. A number of companies (e.g., US West) have established gateways with the minitel system. The Minitel Service Company, another entity of Intelmatique, was set up for the sole purpose of selling videotex knowhow in the United States.

CONCLUSIONS

This chapter was written to document some of the major decisions—both technical and political—that went into making Teletel the only successful commercial videotex system in the world so far. The Teletel story is that of a successful government-directed technological push sustained by political will and technical vision. It is also, however, a story about how, even within an enlightened industrial policy framework, good people are needed to make decisions on the fly to adapt to changing social, political, and technological environments.

Teletel's development is a stereotypical case of the French industrial policy of "les grandes adventures." The uniqueness of the success of Teletel can only be understood by analyzing the industrial policy and political environment of France that nurtures high technology (*technologies de pointe*) projects. But are there any lessons that can be learned and applied to other products and services in other contexts? After all, the governments of Britain and Germany attempted to develop a similar product without success. To answer this question we need to look at the critical success factors in the implementation of Teletel.

On a political level, the will to see this project through was maintained through at least three administrations of different political persuasions, and several secretaries of the PTT. This unwavering commitment to "la grande aventure du Teletel" was crucial to accept the large start-up costs. The political discourse that addressed head on, and then combined, the need for a computer-literate society and the protection of personal liberties and privacy diffused all sources of resistance and led to the government staying out of the information provision business.

On a regulatory level, the monopoly of the basic services and networks allowed the DGT (now France Télécom) to subsidize start-up costs, to have a long-term perspective on videotex services as an investment, and to be able to create one standard and enforce it. All of these factors were critical to the success of Teletel. On a technical level the success factors include the ability to develop and implement a state-of-the-art telephone and data transmission networks, an easy-to-use interface, and a transparent billing system that insured anonymity.

Finally, a very important element in the success of Teletel was the keen understanding by the DGT of the dynamics involved in network externalities.[8] The DGT, by aggressively distributing an easy-to-use terminal at no cost to its subscribers and immediately making available a highly useful and useable application (i.e., the electronic telephone directory), by establishing clear and simple technical standards that allowed information providers quickly and cheaply to offer services with very few administrative headaches, generated a fast-feeding virtuous circle.

There are critics who argue that Teletel is still not profitable, and that it is mostly a French success since its penetration of international markets remains modest. However, there is no doubt that the impact that Teletel has had in the computerization of French society has been extremely positive. Teletel should be considered a success of French industrial policy.

NOTES

This chapter is based on a case study written while the author was a visiting professor in the Department of Technology Management at INSEAD. The study was funded in part by the INSEAD Research Committee, and its support is gratefully acknowledged.

1. Although the "enemy" has changed, and the main villain is now Japan, the policy is still very much in place today as illustrated by the French government's

decision in 1991 to save the consumer electronic companies Bull and Thompson from insolvency.

2. By comparison, the British television-based system Prestel had a field trial with 1,400 participants in 1978 and started commercial service in the fall of 1979. Full nationwide operation was established in March 1980. At the end of 1981, Prestel had only one-tenth of the users predicted for that time (Thomas and Miles 1989). The major reasons for this failure have been attributed to the late delivery and high prices of television monitors (Prestel was television-based and needed a connection between the telephone and the television set), uncoordinated marketing, and bad quality of the databases (Schneider et al. 1990).

3. Typical of the attacks is the "call to arms" by the political commentator George Suffert. He argued, in an article titled "The Fight of the Century: Teletex versus Paper," that it was dangerous to let the DGT have a monopoly on the videotex system. He wrote: "He who owns the wire is powerful. He who owns the wire and the screen is very powerful. He who owns the wire, the screen, and the computer has the power of God."

4. That has now changed. France Télécom decided in 1990 to enter the information provision business by offering what they called added-value services. Most of these services are being offered through joint ventures with privately owned companies.

5. France Télécom is directly accountable to the French government for all its ventures and is required to justify its fee structures. France Télécom, more so than other state agencies, is asked to demonstrate the viability of its investments and therefore is under some profitability pressures, mild as they may be.

6. Whether France Télécom would have taken such an enlightened position without the ferocious criticism of the press lobbies and consumer watchdog groups is debatable. Still, when it comes to Teletel, the executives of the DGT and France Télécom have consistently exhibited excellent judgment.

7. The chat services are very lucrative since both individuals "talking" pay for the "conversation" unlike a telephone conversation where only one party gets charged for it.

8. The value of a network for any member of the network increases with the number of members on the network. Also, as the number of uses of the network increases, so does the perceived value of the network. Finally, the more members there are on a network, the more likely it is that uses will be offered on that network. Reducing the entry barriers (usually cost) to service providers and to users (usually ease of use and cost) starts a virtuous circle.

REFERENCES

Chamoux, J. P. 1990. "The French Telematique Experience." Paper presented at the Conference on IT/Telecommunications, Budapest, Hungary, November 5–6.

Dondoux, J. 1978. "Problemes Poses par la Presentation de l'Annuaire Telephonique." Unpublished paper, Inspection Generale des PTT.

France Télécom annual reports and special documents on Minitel. 1985–90.

Housel, T. J. 1990. "Videotex in France." Unpublished manuscript.

Hutin, F. R. 1981. "Telematique et Democratie." *Etudes* (February): 179–190.

Marchand, M. 1987. *La Grande Aventure du Minitel*. Paris: Larousse.

———. 1987. *Les Paradis Informationnels*. Paris: Masson.

Mayer, R. N. 1988. "The Growth of the French Videotex System and Its Implications for Consumers." *Journal of Consumer Policy* 11:55–83.

Nora, S., and A. Minc. 1979. *L'Informatisation de la Societe*. Paris: Documentation Francaise.

Prevot, H. 1989. "Report on the Future of the PTT." September.

Schneider, V., et al. 1990. "The Dynamics of Videotex Development in Britain, France and Germany." Paper presented at the 8th Conference of the International Telecommunication Society, Venice, Italy, March 18–21.

Sentilhes, G., et al. 1989. *La Minitel Strategie*. Paris: Businessman/First.

Thomas, G., and I. Miles. 1989. *Telematics in Transition*. London: Longman.

6

The Deregulation and Privatization of British Telecommunication

Great Britain was the first country in Europe to deregulate and subsequently privatize its telecommunication system. Although drawing on the American experience the deregulation-privatization policy was based on the ideology of the Thatcher administration, and applied to a broad range of government enterprises that were considered both inefficient and undesirable—inefficient because, a priori, government-owned and -managed enterprises were inferior to privately owned companies, and undesirable because government ownership represented an unnecessary intrusion into the economy.

It was the reduction of an overextended, ever-growing government role in the economic and political sphere of British society that the Thatcher administration intended to reverse across a broad spectrum that included enterprises nationalized during various Labor governments in the postwar periods and supposedly natural monopolies such as railroad, telecommunication, electricity, and water supply, which had been operated by the state since before World War I.

The contention of the 1980s that technological innovation had eliminated a natural monopoly in telecommunication and other areas merely strengthened the privatization argument but was not necessary for its approval. The disappearance of a natural monopoly, of course, could then generate the benefits of competition and assure that price or profit regulations of privatized, formally monopolistic, enterprises became unnecessary. Broad liberalization of existing regulations would permit market forces to play their important role. Market forces and liberalization, however, were merely welcome supporting forces for the primary strategy to privatize government operations.[1] This did not mean, of course, that the Thatcher administration and subsequently its regulatory agency, the Office of Telecommunication (OFTEL), did not have a strong commitment to the concepts of both competition as a discovery path and self-regulatory market forces as a superior form of resource allocation. It did mean, however, that privatization might occur in monopolistic markets before market forces could be introduced. In the latter case, regulatory agencies such as OFTEL had to prevent the potentially predatory behavior of privatized monopolies or duopolies until additional competition could be introduced. "Merely to replace state monopolies by private ones would be to waste an historic opportunity. So we (the Thatcher administration) will take steps to ensure that these new firms do not exploit their powerful position to the detriment of consumers or their competitors."[2]

Implicit in the Thatcher privatization deregulation seemed to have been the conviction that technology in many areas had, at least potentially, eliminated the existence of a natural monopoly. Since the critics on the left considered nationalization of the important enterprises—we could say the commanding heights of the economy—inherently proper and just, and the Thatcher conservatives considered government ownership inherently wasteful and dangerous, the proper role of natural monopolies in a market economy never entered the public debate. At the same time, and for the same reasons, the use of regulatory agencies as a transitory device to monitor a privatized, deregulated former monopoly until market forces could be strengthened was not made explicit by the Tories nor recognized as an issue by the left. The self-regulation effectiveness of market forces was not accepted as an alternative to nationalization until Neil Kinnock moved Labor in the late 1980s and early 1990s closer to the German-Swedish Social Democratic model.

Telecommunication deregulation in Great Britain developed in an entirely different context than in either Germany or France. First and foremost, given the adversarial nature of British politics and the Westminster parliament's "first past the post" election process, there was no need to search for consensus, as the postwar history of enterprise nationalization, denationalization, renationalization, and derenationalization clearly demonstrates. Supported by even a small but firm majority in parliament—which most often represented a minority in the population at large—the government can make important decisions that may be overturned by the next parliament; hence there is no need to search for a consensus. During the 1980s—and during much of the post-World War II history—a consensus on the proper role of market forces would have been difficult to attain, since Labor, or at least its dominant left wing, held on tenaciously to a nineteenth-century Marxism that was distrustful of "chaotic market forces." The Tories, during the same period, discovered the limitations of state intervention in the economy and affirmed the superiority of private over state enterprises.

The post-World War II German public has accepted fully the concept of a social market and merely discussed its demarcation, while the French body politic has accepted, in principle, the notion of both *service public* and industrial policy as guides to economic activity. The British, however, had few if any common principles in the area of political economy that were accepted by the left and the right. The absence of a consensus and the ability of a strong government to push through its legislation gave the British deregulation experience an entirely different flavor. Privatization, deregulation, and telecom liberalization became topics for politicians and affected interest groups but left the broad public disinterested. In Germany (and to a lesser extent in France during the 1970s) it was the demand for deregulation, advanced by elite groups, that found little resonance in public because of the very positive historical image of its PTT, the DBP, and its quality universal and uniform service, widely appreciated by rural and lower income residential users. In Great Britain the poor, bureaucratic service and low technical quality of the telecommunication system made the post office a very unpopular institution. While the public at large had little interest in seeing the status quo maintained, there was, at the same time, little faith in the improvement of the telephone service (assumed by connoisseurs of bad service in the 1960s to be not as bad as the French system) by such abstract concepts as deregulation or privatization.

Economists analyzing telecom deregulation in the United States and Europe have emphasized that both deregulation and industrial policy objectives could be the intended or unintended consequences of liberalization.[3] These statements do not apply to the British privatization-deregulation of the 1980s, unless the conviction that market forces will rejuvenate stale state monopolies is considered to serve as an industrial policy. The absence of an industrial policy designed to preserve or strengthen a national champion, however, is demonstrated by the acquiescence of the conservative administration in Fujitsu's purchase of 75 percent of ICL, Britain's leading computer information technology firm in 1990. By comparison France has continued to bail out Machine Bull explicitly to avoid its acquisition by a Japanese enterprise and the EC has, in vain, attempted to create a European champion by encouraging mergers among Philips, Siemens, ICL, and Bull.[4] Attempts during the early 1980s to foster cooperation among Bull, ICL, Philips, and Siemens failed badly, leaving behind a good deal of resentment, especially among the Siemens management involved. The EC information-technology directorate under its director Michel Carpentier, considered a bastion of *dirigism* by *The Economist*, has, however, not given up on creating a European champion and submitted another proposal in February 1991.[5]

Unlike protectionist French and EC policies, the British government welcomed Japanese capital and technology infusion. Information-technology products, produced on British soil, which would be competitive with world-class products would be a blessing for British and European users, regardless of the nationality of the manufacturer's shareholders.[6]

Given such an emphatic commitment to laissez faire, British deregulation lacks the intricacies of German or French telecommunication reform, and can be analyzed forthrightly, in terms of ideological conflict and self-serving vested interests. The winners and losers of telecom deregulation were the same in the United Kingdom as in France or Germany, but the ideological nature of the deregulation-privatization debate and the strong position of the government seemed to prevent the potential losers from presenting effectively their position. A brief look at the pre- and postderegulation history of British telecommunication will further examine this point.

THE BRITISH TELECOMMUNICATION SYSTEM, 1869–1981

British Telecom, the current dominant network operator, can trace its history to 1869, when the then private and competitive telegram service was nationalized. It was henceforth administered as a monopoly by the post office until 1981. The post office, however, never reached the exalted state of an autonomous ministry, as its German and French counterparts did. With a very brief exception, the British PTT had been supervised by one or more ministries that had other, and from their point of view, more important assignments. The stepchild role of the post office had two consequences that determined its performance throughout this period, and especially during the post-World War II era. On the one hand the post office had considerable managerial autonomy, since the various ministries had little understanding of its operations and little interest in the technical or policy issues it faced. On the other hand the post office never received the investment authorization necessary to provide first-class service. Although the post office had not been able to buy up the private telephone network National Telephone Co. (NTC) until 1911, twenty years of uneasy coexistence between a predatory post office bent on obtaining the monopoly status of the continental PTS and a defensive private sector did not encourage an ambitious investment strategy to improve the British telecom system. There is little doubt that by 1914, Germany had the technically most advanced telephone system in Europe.

The 1911 acquisition of the NTC network did not change the relationship between the post office and its ministry, which happened to be the treasury at the time. The post office had to turn over its revenue to the treasury but in turn did not receive sufficient financial support to upgrade its operation. The lack of investment funds—reminiscent of the same predicament faced by France Télécom—had an especially adverse impact on the telecommunication sector, since the post office, especially during the pre-World War I and the interwar period, considered the telegraph system its major profit source and was not inclined to create competition for it through expansion of the telephone service, nor the trunk and international networks. The poor performance of the post office in its telephone and telegraph operations generated broad public criticism, inside and outside of parliament, particularly in the interwar period.

The high-cost, low-density service was not improved by the government's decision to assign the public works department responsibilities for building telephone exchanges and telegraph offices. This peculiar decision led to an overinvestment in bricks and mortar and to a further neglect of technical innovations. By the mid–1930s Great Britain's telephone system had one of the lowest penetration rates of any major country and both business and private users relied on telegraphy or express mail for quick communication. (It should be mentioned that the British mail was efficient, reliable, and popular with the public at large. It probably was also profitable, although the post office accounting system made the separation of its four undertakings—telephone, telegraph, mail, and postbank—difficult.)

In spite of a general unhappiness with the post office's performance, no significant administrative changes occurred until the 1960s. In 1961 the post office finally received permission to retain parts of its profits for reinvestments and in 1969 the Labor government transformed the post office from a government agency into a public corporation. Interestingly enough the Post Office Employees Union (POIU) supported this transformation, unlike its French counterpart, because privatization as an alternative was already a possibility.[7] Although still under the supervision of the treasury, which had to approve its investment (capital) budget, the post office was expected to make a profit equal to 8 percent on its capital. The government could and did impose restraints on its tariff, for macroeconomic objectives.

In spite of the greater managerial autonomy obtained through public corporation status, the post office did not improve its cautious, bureaucratic manner of coping with the increased demand for telephone service. By the mid–1970s the waiting list for telephones climbed to over 250,000.

Consistently underestimating the demand for telephone equipment, the post office had been equally slow in adopting new transmission systems and switching exchanges. The Bell System had adopted the electromechanical Strowger central office (CO) switch in 1916 and nearly ten years later the post office decided on the Strowger switch as the standard CO exchange for its entire system.[8] The post office remained faithful to the Strowger switch for the next twenty-five years. British telecom equipment manufacturers kept producing this reliable but old-fashioned switch until the early 1950s. By that time AT&T, Ericsson, and Siemens had developed automatic switching gear for large COs and Ericsson and Siemens had introduced electronic switches for rural and small town exchanges (Ericsson's LME 500 was licensed to Stromberg-Carlson in the 1930s, giving what is now Siemens-Stromberg-Carlson a foothold in smaller exchanges in the United States that has been maintained until today). AT&T developed its crossbar and crossbar switches during the 1940s and 1950s, leaving the

United Kingdom and France behind in transmission and switching technology.[9]

The British telecommunication equipment industry suffered not only from being associated with an overly cautious, bureaucratic network operator, but also by being unusually fragmented. At a time when the United States, Germany, Canada, and France had no more than two major telecom equipment manufacturers, Great Britain prior to the 1960s could count on five—General Electric Company of Great Britain (GEC, no relation to the American GE), Associated Electrical Industries (AEI), English Electric, Plessey, and ITT's Standard Telephone Cable (STC). Dominated by the Strowger switch during the inter- and immediate postwar period, British equipment manufacturers failed to develop electronic switches.

During the 1960s a Labor government-induced concentration encouraged GEC's acquisition of AEI and English Electric. A grand concentration of GEC and Plessey did not take hold, supposedly due to personal rivalry between GEC and Plessey management. (The hostile GEC-Siemens takeover of Plessey in the late 1980s, a rare event in the clubby European telecom equipment fraternity, was the last act in the GEC-Plessey rivalry.)

The 1960s merger did encourage greater R&D efforts and Plessey in particular was able to compete with Ericsson in developing small electronic exchanges for export. During the same period AT&T installed its first computerized "stored program-controlled" switch in a New Jersey CO exchange while ITT's German and Belgium units (SEL and BMT) began the research program that would ultimately produce ITT's S–12 switch (now Alcatel's major export switch). Future business historians should examine why ITT's German research and development project did not influence ITT's British and French operations.

Monopolies are justly accused of delaying the introduction of technological innovations in order to exploit fully their installed capital investments. Even AT&T lagged behind France and perhaps even Germany in installing digital switches and fiberglass networks prior to its divestiture. It took a strong government commitment in France to force the PTT to change and invest heavily in digital switching and transmission systems. The policy commitment to ISDN had a similar effect in Germany during the 1980s. The British post office's extreme reluctance to abandon its prewar Strowger technology is, however, unique in the history of the PTTs. Pushed by parliamentary criticism and the government, the post office supported British equipment manufacturers' R&D projects that produced the modern System X switch in the 1970s (a digital System X version appeared in the 1980s). In spite of the R&D success the post office introduced the System X only slowly—depriving its manufacturers of economies of scale—and 75 percent of its network still relied on Strowger equipment during the late 1970s. The balance was made up by Ericsson LM500 switches, System X, and even a few manual exchanges.[10]

The post office's reluctance to replace its obsolete Strowger equipment and the slow installation of System X made it difficult for the British telecom equipment industry to maintain technological competitiveness in both the switching-transmission and the CPE market, at home and abroad. The decline in the technical reputation of the British manufacturers even gave the System X an unwarranted inferior reputation. In its particular class—medium-sized and small exchanges—it compared well with the international competition including Ericsson's AXE switch, and was attractive to less developed countries because of its simple maintainability. When Siemens Corporation (U.S. subsidiary), which had gained managerial control of Stromberg-Carlson and GPT (a former joint GEC-Plessey venture) began an effort in 1990 to combine the best features of Siemens– Stromberg–Carlson and GPT switches, it became apparent that System X still had a good number of satisfied customers who wanted the best elements of System X retained.

In addition to a cautious investment policy that kept network growth consistently below demand, the post office gave all indications of falling even farther behind other European countries by its reluctance to go beyond trial projects in digital and ISDN installations. The post office was equally slow in adapting to the growing demand for data transmissions, propelled especially by the needs of the London financial markets, and the concomitant growth in new financial services. There was no indication that the post office was impressed by France Télécom's Transpac success nor the DBP's Integrated Data Network (IDN). Clearly, the post office had become an obstacle to Britain's industrial competitiveness.

The Thatcher government, elected in 1979, had set itself the task to reinvigorate the stagnant British private sector, to introduce competition in the regulated public sector, and to roll back the scope of government by privatizing public sector enterprises. It became immediately clear that the telecommunication industry and its prime customer, the post office, met every criterion of the quasi-corporate industrial regime Thatcher wanted to change. Although the British telecom industry certainly carried part of the blame for its competitive weakness, the strong monopoly position of the post office, further strengthened by the Labor government to include all possible future services, seemed to offer the starting point for bringing the quality and technical sophistication of the British telecom system up to global standards. (It is fair to say that Thatcher started in 1979 from roughly the same position as Giscard d'Estaing in 1971. If in 1991 Britain has caught up with France and Germany, as seems to be the case, then on this one important criterion the Thatcher policy has been a smashing success. We shall return to this point.)

LIBERALIZATION AND PRIVATIZATION: THE REFORM OF THE BRITISH TELECOM SYSTEM

There seems to have been strong agreement within the Thatcher administration that quick deregulation and administrative reorganization of the telephone system were necessary. There seems to have been less agreement that far-reaching privatization was desirable. The success of the France Télécom modernization under government direction presented an alternative model, especially since the scope and sequence of the necessary liberalization-deregulation steps were not known. The American model seemed inappropriate, although the deregulation of CPE equipment was considered a great success in stimulating competition and innovation in the American market.[11] In spite of the fact that the Thatcher administration did not have a precise deregulation model at its disposal—other than its faith in monetarism, competition, and privatization—it moved quickly to change the post office structure.[12] Between 1979 and 1984, drastic changes were introduced.

The 1969 reorganization carried out by the Labor government had already established the post office as a public corporation that had shed various responsibilities not related to its main tasks, such as the administration of radio and television frequencies and the management of the national savings banks. The post office personnel also had lost civil service status and become public employees. Interestingly enough this change was readily accepted by staff and unions—it would have caused their French and German counterparts to mount the barricades—since the status difference was not large to begin with and the Labor government had made the new arrangement attractive by increasing management flexibility in setting wage rates and working conditions (note that exactly the same reform had been opposed by the French and German unions).

The Thatcher administration built essentially on the Labor reform by separating completely the telecom operation from the mail service, and by instructing the economics ministry to set precise profit objectives for the separated units, thus removing cross-subsidization opportunities. The 1979 structural reforms were again accepted by employees, their union, and the post office bureaucracy without much struggle. Although these reforms did not appear earth-shaking we must remember that they had become the burning political issue in the restructuring of the French and German PTTs. Apparently no one was willing to mount the barricades in the United Kingdom to maintain the post office's status.[13]

The separation of telecommunication from postal service seemed to have benefited both operations. In 1980, an experienced private sector (aerospace) manager Sir George Jefferson was appointed as CEO of British Telecom; and he imposed an entrepreneurial, customer-oriented management philosophy on top management even before the summer 1981 telecommunication legislation further strengthened the autonomy of British Telecom.

The Telecommunication Act of 1981 had a two-year gestation period but was quite simple and straightforward in the end. The Thatcher deregulators—primarily Kenneth Baker, minister of telecommunication technology—both influenced and anticipated the EC Green Paper and the restructuring of the DBP.

Telecommunication was completely separated from postal services. Telecommunication and data transmission services were administered by an, initially, public enterprise, British Telecom (BT), while postal services and post banking remained with the post office.

British Telecom lost its network monopoly. In addition to liberalized leased lines and VAN regulations, the government granted a network transmission license to a new operator, Mercury. Mercury, initially a joint venture of the telecommunication company Cable and Wireless, British Petroleum, and Barclays Bank (the last two sold their shares to Cable and Wireless subsequently), was intended to compete with British Telecom by building a new fiberglass network, connecting at least twenty-six major British cities. By not only permitting but encouraging "cream skimming," it was hoped that the smaller but technologically advanced duopolist Mercury could compete with British Telecom, force it to improve its service, and encourage investment in R&D. Actually, the act merely authorized the establishment of network competition. Mercury did not obtain a license until 1982 and began operating only in 1984–85.

British Telecom lost its licensing authority over value-added services and terminal equipment. An independent agency, the British Standard Institute, was to establish and monitor licensing standards, to assure network integrity and equipment safety. The ministry established a general license for VANs in 1982.

British Telecom was charged with the mandatory services of maintaining and servicing of the customer premises loops for the "first connections." It was also required to set up a profit-center subsidiary if it intended to participate in the "free competitive" sector, that is, in the voluntary supply of VAS, equipment, and maintenance provision.

The 1981 Telecommunication Act was recognized as an immediate first step in introducing competition into the equipment area and in creating the preconditions for an entrepreneurial telecommunication administration. (By comparison, the post office administration remained unchanged; apparently the government did not believe that the British mail needed a new management regime.)[14] There was much maneuvering by British Telecom to limit the potential competition from Mercury and also retain, de facto, equipment type approval authority. (The information technology ministry could and did at first cede equipment certification to British Telecom, and did not manage to obtain full control of that process again until early 1982.)

Some European and American economists doubted that a duopoly with a dominant carrier would generate competitive market conditions. In spite of a slow start, network competition did begin to flourish by the mid- and late 1980s. Critics of British liberalization have emphasized that within the next six to twelve months after the passage of the 1981 legislation few if any new products appeared on the market and that the British Telecom management sabotaged the deregulation efforts of the information technology ministry.[15] With the benefits of ten years' hindsight we can say that it was entirely unrealistic to expect immediate changes; the well-established relationship between British equipment manufacturers and the old post office had not encouraged quick adaptation to market conditions; nor should it have been surprising that mostly non-British telephone suppliers requested certification approval from the ministry during early 1982. Lastly, the attempts of a new management, faced with ambitious profit targets, to retain as much of its monopoly position for as long as possible was entirely natural, and, by and large, was countered effectively by the information technology ministry.

The unchallenged decision of British Telecom during November 1981 to manufacture its own telephones was perhaps surprising because it represented a form of vertical integration other European PTTs had avoided even during their unchallenged monopoly heydays. It has been pointed out, however, that British Telecom and the ministry were much more influenced by North American developments than by the traditions of the European PTTs; and, of course, AT&T and the Canadian Bell System have a long and successful tradition of vertical integration. (It is not widely known that Northern Telecom—called Northern Electric seventy years ago—Canada's entrepreneurial telco, is a Bell Canada subsidiary.) British Telecom's vertical integration efforts did not last very long; in the late fall of 1990 British Telecom sold its last manufacturing unit.

There can be no doubt, however, that the six- to twelve-month period that followed the passage of the July 1981 Telecommunication Act was a time of confusion. The fact that the information and technology ministry had the responsibility to draft the act, while the department of industry and trade was responsible for the British Telecom restructuring did not make this process more transparent.[16] There seem to be good indications that by 1982 the government was pleased with the consequences of the 1981 liberalization and British Telecom restructuring. British Telecom did upgrade its business services, made special efforts to improve its radio network for the financial community in London, and increased its profitability beyond the ministry's targets.[17] The government's basic strategy, however, had always considered liberalization and privatization as reinforcing measures to achieve competitive markets, entrepreneurial industries, and a withdrawal of the state from economic activity. Rather than considering the increased efforts during 1982 to privatize British Telecom as a consequence of some dissatisfaction with the results of the 1981 liberalization, plans for further British Telecom "divestiture" seem to have been merely the necessary and expected steps in implementing the Thatcher–Joseph strategy to restructure British society.[18] The British Telecom management seemed to have been on the right track and had displayed satisfying entrepreneurial activities in the transition period (July 1981–July 1982).[19]

The Thatcher administration had consistently drawn on right-wing think-tank academics for intellectual support and strategy recommendations. The 1981 telecommunication liberalization gained arguments and ideas from the so-called Beesley Report.[20] Beesley had recommended liberalizing VAS and VANs, including permitting the resale of leased-line capacity since deregulating leased lines would lead to network competition for British Telecom without having to license alternate network operators. The 1981 Telecommunication Act reflected most of Beesley's suggestions, but did not permit leased-line resale, thus reducing the potential network competition for British Telecom. Advocates of increased competition in the telecommunication sector could agree, therefore, that while the 1981 liberalization improved the managerial behavior of British Telecom, it was the threat of competition rather than actual market pressures that had created these changes. Hence, further steps including providing network competition became necessary if a revitalized telephone industry were to emerge. Another academician, Stephen Littlechild, expressed these sentiments most effectively and advocated the establishment of various forms of network competition.[21]

The long-run goal of privatizing government enterprises, including British Telecom, had remained an important ideological part of the Thatcher administration agenda, although little attention had been paid to its operational execution. Reorganization within the administration, as well as changing assignments to key players such as Kenneth Baker and Keith Joseph, probably played a major role in propelling privatization of British Telecom to the top of the Thatcher administration agenda. It is important to note that by 1982 British Telecom privatization and the concomitant licensing of a competitor had four distinct and at times conflicting objectives:

- privatization as a further step to increase the entrepreneurial role of British Telecom management while reducing the interventionist role of the state
- privatization as a means of encouraging long-run network competition beyond the licensing of the competitor Mercury
- privatization as a short-run device to raise capital for both British Telecom modernization and deficit reduction
- privatization as a means of turning middle-class Britons into shareholders

In order to achieve the third, and perhaps also the fourth objective—and incidentally keep the treasury happy—the British Telecom enterprise to be privatized had to retain, initially at least, a number of its monopolistic or market-dominating privileges. The need to keep the financial community and future shareholders happy did conflict with the objective to increase competition in all areas of telecommunication services. Privatization critics, both in the United Kingdom and abroad, overemphasized these short-run conflicts between successful privatization and competition. At any rate, by July 1982 the government through the industry ministry announced its intention to sell 51 percent of British Telecom to the public and also reaffirmed its licensing of the new private network operator Mercury.[22] By November 1982 the British Telecom privatization bill had been submitted to parliament. In addition to various provisions specifying British Telecom's remaining monopoly powers and its relationship to Mercury, the bill also established an office of telecommunication (OFTEL) to regulate the network duopoly and to maintain competition in the telecommunication system.

With 1991 hindsight we can say that the creation of OFTEL was probably the most important step in the liberalization of the British telecommunication system. As we shall see, it was OFTEL and not the shift to a duopoly from a network monopoly that gave Great Britain the most competitive, least-regulated telecommunication system in the world by 1990–91.

There was sufficient opposition to the privatization of British Telecom in and outside of parliament to slow the passage of the bill. Moreover, within the Conservative party and even within the government a new fifth objective of privatization emerged, namely, the transformation of British Telecom into a national telecommunication champion that could compete in a global market with AT&T, IBM, and NEC. Evidence for this reappearance of a pre-Thatcher, old-Tory predilection for industrial policy had been primarily anecdotal prior to 1984, but became noticeably evident when Cecil Parkinson and later Leon Brittan became minister for trade and industry in the second Thatcher administration.[23] Given the lack of a clear-cut privatization model—the Littlechild report emphasized desirability of network competition and supported privatization only indirectly—the government bill languished in parliamentary committees and died with the dissolution of parliament in 1983. Buoyed by the June 1983 election victory, the Thatcher administration immediately reintroduced the privatization bill in 1983 and succeeded finally in having the Telecommunication Act of 1984 enacted by parliament.

THE LIBERALIZATION OF THE BRITISH TELECOMMUNICATION SYSTEM, 1984–90: WINNERS AND LOSERS

The main provision of the 1984 Telecommunication Act was the privatization (actually, the sale of 51 percent of British Telecom shares) of British Telecom, the establishment of OFTEL, the requirement that British Telecom tariffs could not rise by more than the British retail price index (RPI) less 3 percent, and the commitment to reexamine the network duopoly by 1990. There were a number of other provisions specifying British Telecom–Mercury relations, British Telecom manufacturing activities, leased-line resale, VAS and VANs licenses, and access fees. We shall omit discussing the 1984 act in detail since OFTEL regulations, technology, and, above all, global competition modified the act considerably. Supposed major issues, such as British Telecom's equipment manufacturing, network dominance, and monopsonistic relationship with the British equipment manufacturers seemed to have become nonissues by 1990. Modal competition from mobile and private satellite systems, the economics of equipment manufacturing, and the exploding costs of research and development banished the parochial concerns of the mid–1980s. We shall, therefore, take a close look at the British Telecom regime of 1989–90 rather than discuss further the 1984 act.

The unexpected performance of OFTEL and the Thatcher government's (including monopoly commission) response to technological change had a significant impact on the telecommunication industry, telecom users, and British international competitiveness in the information technology area. In virtually every aspect the results, by 1990, were quite different from what had been expected in 1984. Before we examine the present regime and its socioeconomic environment, we shall take a brief look at the controversy that dominated the 1981–84 effort to liberalize the telecom system.

Deregulation and the dismantling of British Telecom as a monopolistic state enterprise generated very much the same opposition as had arisen in Germany and France. Since British Telecom did not have the broad public support of the DBP or France Télécom's technological achievement of the 1970s, opposition to liberalization and privatization seemed to have been weaker, more diffuse, and more narrowly confined to the potential losers than on the Continent. Moreover, the major opposition came from the left, the Labor party and its allies in the universities, who had just lost an election in 1979, and lost another in 1983, during the peak of the privatization controversy. The early 1980s were dominated by the Reagan–Thatcher revolution and advocates of government ownership and regulation had a difficult time in Great Britain, after decades of nationalization and government intervention in the economy had been blatantly unsuccessful.

The second source of opposition, the Post Office Employees Union (POEU), also could not bargain from a position of strength. The post office's performance, especially British Telecom's, had failed to gain friends for either British Telecom or its employees. Both Labor and the POEU emphasized the threat to universal service, but seemed unable to mobilize those who would have been threatened by a potential—but unlikely—policy to abandon unprofitable service in rural areas or small towns. The low penetration rate of British Telecom, which had made the telephone a luxury among lower income groups and border area residents, reduced the number of voters who felt threatened by a possible loss of phone service.

At any rate, the political representatives of the two above mentioned groups, the National Farmers Union, and conservative MPs from rural areas and Scottish and Welsh municipalities made their concerns known, and may have alerted the government and subsequent British Telecom and OFTEL managers to the importance of articulating their commitment to universal service. We can say in 1991 that universal service has not been undermined by liberalization or privatization. On the contrary, perhaps, telecommunication and gentrification have begun to prompt even secluded areas to demand sophisticated telecommunication products and services. What has happened in rural Maine and Vermont in the mid–1980s is now occurring in Scotland and Wales. It is doubtful whether an unreformed British Telecom and a noncompetitive British Telecom system could have provided these services.

Finally, the resistance to some of the proposed changes by British Telecom managers, and the opposition of the British Telecom equipment manufacturers to a deregulated, autonomous British Telecom should also be mentioned. British Telecom management did not have a Helmut Schön or a *Gemeinwirtschaftslehre* to elucidate its role as a protector of economically or geographically marginal groups, nor could they point to a costly infrastructure investment program that was designed to give the United Kingdom the best infrastructure for the year 2000. British Telecom management favored any legislation that would increase its autonomy and remove constraints on its decision-making freedom. At the same time British Telecom opposed the establishment of competitors, and resisted the elimination of monopolistic privileges. In other words, British Telecom acted wholly rational in order to maximize its profitability.

Given this eclectic opposition to liberalization and subsequently privatization British Telecom was able to hold on, for a while, to privileges such as licensing authority of VANs, and was also effective in changing the wording, here and there, in the final privatization bill. By 1985, and certainly by 1991, those issues had become lost in the competitive climate OFTEL and technology had created in the United Kingdom, and by the changes in management outlook and behavior market forces and global opportunities had created.

Very much the same can be said about the equipment manufacturers' opposition to deregulation. Every issue raised by the equipment manufacturers—and their able spokesman GEC's Lord Weinstock—had become irrelevant by the mid–1980s. The equipment manufacturers feared especially losing their privileged positions as British Telecom vendors. In the switching area, however, it had become clear that the United Kingdom could not continue to support a highly fragmented equipment industry. By the mid–1980s, the much maligned but actually sturdy and effective British switch System X had to be manufactured finally by a single firm GPT, then jointly owned by Plessey and GEC. By the late 1980s Siemens and GEC took over Plessey, and GPT is today an international firm, owned by GEC and Siemens, managed by Siemens and active in the United States, where Siemens-Stromberg-Carlson and GPT are jointly producing a new modular switch (a switch that could be upgraded by adding electronic "modules" or components) that is combining the best of Siemens, Stromberg, Carlson, and GPT. From the point of view of both the British Telecom system and the Thatcher/Major administrations, it is better for the U.K. economy to have a partially British enterprise operate in a global market than to have a number of small companies hold on to the production of obsolete equipment. Since the price of developing a new switch is about U.S. $ 1 bn, a fragmented British equipment industry would have been condemned to repeat the Strowger experience of the postwar period.

The same can be said about the opposition of the equipment industry to British Telecom's purchase of Ericsson's AXE switches. By the mid– 1980s virtually every major European or American network operator relied on at least two vendors for switching and transmission equipment (an exception is Canadian Bell, which purchases exclusively Northern Telecom equipment). Germany has always had at least two sources for switches, Siemens and the ITT (now Alcatel) subsidiary SEL. France has Alcatel and Ericsson; the Bell operating companies have three suppliers, AT&T, Northern Telecom, and either Siemens or Ericsson. Within the context of global competition and EC procurement directives any notion that British Telecom could have contrived to draw exclusively on British sources is wildly unrealistic.

The third major equipment manufacturer complaint about British Telecom's predatory behavior concerned the telephone apparatus market. Although terminal equipment had been liberalized in 1981, British Telecom still held 95 percent of the market. Like other European PTTs British Telecom had bought its telephones from predominantly British vendors, but had began to show an interest in manufacturing its own low-tech, low-priced telephones. Privatization could now enable British Telecom to manufacture terminal equipment and compete unfairly with its current vendors. Of all the industry's objections to British Telecom behavior, the threat of a vertical integration strategy by the dominant network was truly most threatening. Again, technology and global competition made any attempt by British Telecom to manufacture its own CPEs a losing proposition. British Telecom never had much success with even minor manufacturing operations, and by 1991 had given up on the entire idea, particularly since the low-priced end of the market is today dominated in both Europe and the United States by East Asian manufacturers. The British terminal equipment market is completely open today to international competition and British Telecom has returned to merely selling telephones obtained from various vendors.

In summary we can say that the opposition to British Telecom liberalization and privatization was diffuse and ineffective. The fact that there was sufficient misgivings in parliament to debate privatization for three years can be blamed more on indecisiveness in the government than on effective opposition from political and economic adversaries.

THE CONTEMPORARY BRITISH TELECOMMUNICATION REGIME

With the passage of the 1984 Telecommunication Act the British system experienced a most amazing transformation; over the next seven years it changed a slowly liberalizing telephone system into the world's most competitive market for diverse networks, value-added service products, and value-added networks. The three driving forces responsible for this metamorphosis were

- the creative destruction of existing equilibria through rapid technological change
- the inspired performances of the Office of Telecommunication, whose regulatory influence was committed to generate competition
- the fairly consistent commitment of the Thatcher/Major administrations to the rule of market forces in the telecommunication/information-technology industry.

The influence of the first and third forces will become clear in the next few pages. A few remarks about OFTEL are necessary, however, since under the skillful leadership of its director general W. P. B. Wigglesworth the originally ill-defined agency developed its own mission and authority. Omitting the various decisions OFTEL made in its first one or two years we shall look at its performance at the end of the decade.

Key Features of the U.K. Regulatory Structure

The 1984 telecommunication bill had given OFTEL a plethora of regulatory, advisory, and managerial assignments that were often conflicting; worst of all, OFTEL had little enforcement authority.[24] By the late 1980s, however, it had redefined its regulatory mission.

OFTEL excelled in expanding its mission to strengthen competition as the most effective tool to provide the best telecommunication services for Great Britain. The primacy of competition was especially important in the transition from monopoly to duopoly to a highly competitive environment (roughly 1984–88).[25] Competition was a means to an end, however, and in addition OFTEL had to perform the following regulatory duties:

1. Ensure that telecom services are provided to satisfy all reasonable demands and at affordable prices (a weaker version of Germany's uniform and universal service)

2. Promote the interests of users

3. Promote competition as a means of providing incentives for service providers but recognize that network competition is neither possible nor even desirable in all circumstances (i.e., marginal consumers may only be supplied by mandatory monopoly service)

OFTEL is an independent government agency. Its director general is appointed for a five-year term. The director general and his small staff (120 civil servants) enforce the requirements of telecom licenses issued and existing rules. If necessary OFTEL may amend existing licenses or rules by agreement with licensees or by referring amendment issues to the monopoly commission. OFTEL also approves terminal equipment for network access. Generally close cooperation with the Monopoly and Merger Commission (MMC) has given OFTEL additional clout and flexibility. If amendment to existing rules or license agreement seems necessary, a threat to refer this issue to the MMC has often been sufficient to attain cooperation.[26]

OFTEL's slim resources have promoted simple regulatory supervision practices that are easily observed or rely on incentives to obtain compliance. A typical example is OFTEL's price regulation of British Telecom that required a price reduction of 3 percent below the RPI (retail price index; the United Kingdom's inflation gauge) for a basket of domestic services from 1985 to 1988, and of 4.5 percent below inflation from July 1989 on.

OFTEL's decisions can be appealed to the courts, but can be overruled only if due process has not been followed. OFTEL's directives can be enforced with strong penalties if disregarded.

The Liberalization of Telecom Markets

The impact of OFTEL's support of competition and the concomitant appearance of new products had interesting consequences in different areas.

As mentioned above, the 1981 Telecommunication Act had already broken British Telecom's near monopoly in terminal equipment (or apparatus in British terminology), and objective CPE standards were prescribed by the British Standards Institution, while type approval was granted by another 1981 agency, the British Approval Board. In spite of some increased competition, in 1984 OFTEL was faced with a terminal equipment market in which British Telecom was still dominant and may even have extended its market share in large PBXs, where British Telecom had not been able to operate before 1981. During the 1981–84 period British Telecom had also been accused of various predatory actions and devious devices to maintain its well-entrenched position in violation of the intent of the liberalization act.

OFTEL, surprisingly to critics of the 1984 bill, dealt swiftly, fairly, and successfully with British Telecom. Making it clear to BT management that it was determined to establish effective competition in the telecom market, it convinced British Telecom that it had to adhere "scrupulously" to fair trade rulings and that it would be, furthermore, under active OFTEL surveillance.[27] OFTEL reports that it was successful in motivating British Telecom to adhere to sound competitive practices and that a 1987 user survey discovered general satisfaction with market conditions.[28] British Telecom's CPE market share had been decreasing while the variety of equipment had been consistently increasing throughout the 1985–90 period, by all accounts. Service and maintenance companies have been multiplying, and the demand for telecom products has been growing significantly.

The most pronounced growth, however, occurred in the supply and demand of VAS and VANs in the United Kingdom during the 1980s, especially during the end of the decade. We have mentioned that VAN licenses had become available in 1982 provided they added value to basic transmission. In 1987 provisions for licensing value-added and data services (VADS) were added, and opened all types of data transmission to competition. Only pure voice and telex service remained British Telecom and Mercury duopolies. Although simple resale of leased lines was still prohibited a "branch systems general license" (BSGL) was issued, also as of 1981, which permitted private network, leased-line systems on users' premises. A network code was established for requirements in order to maintain compatibility between private and public networks. Those requirements were further liberalized in the late 1980s, contributing to the growth of VAN and VAS suppliers, and giving the United Kingdom the largest telecom services market in Europe.[29] In February 1991 OFTEL finally announced that companies would be allowed to resell part of their private networks.[30]

The establishment of duopolistic network competition in the United Kingdom during the mid–1980s probably attracted more international attention than any other feature of the British liberalization process. Opponents of PTT network monopoly in basic services have demanded similar arrangements in their own countries. From Germany in 1987, when the liberals on the Witte commission proposed the licensing of a network competitor to the DBP, to Sweden in 1991 when a new network operator (Tele 2) was licensed, duopoly seemed to beckon as the harbinger of competition.[31] There is considerable doubt that the establishment of a second network will bring a net gain to the economy, especially the economy of a small country. There may even be a question whether the United States can afford three fiberglass networks; certainly neither Sprint/United

Telecommunication nor MCI have been spoiling their stockholders with rich dividends so far.

The U.K. network duopoly, however, seems to have encouraged competition because of the combined efforts of OFTEL intervention and technological breakthroughs in mobile and cable television communication that generated intermodal competition. Mercury, with OFTEL and ministry of trade and industry approval, followed essentially a cream-skimming strategy that would build new trunk networks to connect centers of high economic activity, and local fiber optic networks in London and in the business centers of key British cities. A relatively affordable investment of £ 500 insured a network that was about 20 percent of British Telecom's long-distance system but covered close to 100 percent of the most profitable intercity trunk lines.[32]

There is little indication that Mercury made a significant effort to enlarge its trunk network during the late 1980s and early 1990s. Instead it has been pushing its glass-fiber local networks in London—thus supporting Britain's "Big Bang" deregulation of its financial systems—and other major U.K. cities. Certainly by 1991, but already during 1988, the United Kingdom had more local area network and intermodal competitors than any country in the world. The emergence of modern broad-band cable television networks, licensed to provide a full range of telecommunication services, will further intensify local area competition.

Critics of both British Telecom and the government's privatization policy have complained that the flourishing network and VAS competition have primarily benefited the business community, and have left residential telephone users as frustrated as before. Even The Economist, a strong supporter of Thatcher policies, admitted that as late as the fall of 1989 residential customers had not benefited from liberalization.[33] Still the improvement in telecom service—including Mercury's provision of digital international service—to the business community began to spill over into residential services by 1990–91. At the very least we can say in 1991 that there have been few losers and many winners among the telecom users.

Much of the improved service has come from modal competition that was supplied with the encouragement of OFTEL. In 1988–89, for instance, Windsor (Cable) Television received OFTEL permission to provide switched voice telephony service in conjunction with Mercury, in Windsor's franchise area. Encouraged by the competitive, experimental climate created by OFTEL, Windsor has joined a consortium that has received the Birmingham cable franchise (four hundred thousand residential customers) that is now open to voice communication and could become an interactive television communication network, once a broad-band digital system has been completed.[34] Lastly, the already relatively low British tariffs for international telephone calls were further reduced during the late 1980s and early 1990s due to Mercury's vigorous price competition in this area. Both business and residential users have benefited from this competition.

The Revitalization of British Telecom during a Decade of Competition

There is a seeming conflict between two objectives of privatization: the establishment of network competition and the transformation of British Telecom into a national champion. Surprisingly both objectives seem to have been accomplished. British Telecom's entrepreneurial management was forced by the increasingly competitive environment and the threat of losing its last statutory monopolistic enclaves by 1991 to develop an aggressive global strategy to assure survival as a major player at home and abroad. Staffing reduction and operational rationalization increased productivity gains by 50 percent over the 1984–89 period.[35] Simultaneous tightening of financial controls enabled British Telecom to rebalance its tariffs from a usage-based to a primarily cost-based accounting system. Cross-subsidization still exists—OFTEL notes that connecting changes to British Telecom network still do not recover relevant fixed costs—but the reduction in tariffs for long-distance and international calls are economically justified and encourage greater use of the network.

Critics emphasize the transfer of telephone costs from the business user to the residential user who does not make long-distance calls. The same issue has been raised in the United States. To the extent that the significant gains of the relatively small number of businesses and residents making international calls is distributed over a very large number of local telephone users, there may be a net welfare gain, although no evidence has been cited so far. There is a good deal of anecdotal evidence that the liberal British telecom system has prompted multinationals to move corporate offices from Germany and France to the United Kingdom. The success of the "Big Bang" financial deregulation also has had a definite employment effect. The Big Bang would not have been possible without British Telecom's network modernization, which was, of course, prompted, at least in part, by Mercury's leased-line competition. We could say, therefore, that by 1989 there may have been few losers and many winners among telecom users.

The biggest winner in the long run may have been the British economy. Since privatization British Telecom has increased its range of services and rate of innovation. In 1984, 51 percent of British Telecom's revenue came from basic domestic telephone use; by 1988 the percentage had dropped to 48 percent and was estimated to be around 45 percent in 1990. No further significant decreases occurred after 1990 despite the continued expansion of BT's overseas activities. The decline in domestic basic telephone revenues occurred in spite of a substantial increase in telephone calls of 24 percent by 1988. The call volume has increased only moderately since 1988–89, a trend offset by BT's ability to hold on to 95 percent of the domestic market through 1991. BT's market share is somewhat misleading, however, since Mercury has been a strong and successful competitor in the profitable international and long-distance business markets.[36] Quite clearly British Telecom has had to increase its value-added services at home and abroad, and has had to reduce its dependence on the rate-regulated POTS.

Modal Competition: Cellular Mobile Telephones, PCNs, and Cable Systems

The strategy to develop network competition did not rely merely on establishing the fixed wire-based network duopoly of British Telecom and Mercury but relied upon the growing mobile telephone service to generate additional communication possibilities. By 1989, the two licensed mobile networks—Cellnet (owned by a consortium that includes British Telecom) and Vodafone (a consortium led by Racal)—had already attained seven-hundred thousand subscribers with a network investment of £ 200 to £ 300 m.[37] In addition the mobile telephone market had attracted about forty service providers that used the two existing networks to sell their value-added products. In 1987–88, the explosive growth of the mobile market had created congestion at several key points, and had prompted OFTEL to search for ways to license at least one additional mobile network. A third network was originally expected by late 1991, but by 1989 the two existing mobile network operators seem to have coped already with congestions by creating additional cells. (By splitting up large cells into smaller ones more calls can be accommodated. See Figure 6.1.)

Vigorous competition among different modes of mobile telecommunication—cellular, telepoint, and personal communication networks—along with the introduction of the European digital mobile standard GSM, have delayed the licensing of a third domestic mobile network operator. In early 1992 the government disclosed that it was ready to license a new international telecommunications operator in order to provide additional competition for BT and Mercury. The new operator, reputedly the American enterprise Sprint, would have to lease cable and satellite capacity from BT and Mercury rather than build its own system.[38]

The most amazing growth, however, is taking place in another mode of mobile telephone networks, the so-called personal communicator networks (PCNs). While standard mobile telephones require relatively heavy and expensive apparatuses designed originally for automobiles and trucks, the PCNs grew out of radio paging, in which British Telecom, Mercury, and two smaller competitors had already established a successful market. By 1989, however, technology had advanced considerably to make hand-held-

Figure 6.1
Cellular Network

portable radio telephones a versatile one-way communication device. At first the technology consisted of miniaturized handsets and a nationwide network of telepoints, each with a one hundred-meter range. These base stations could transmit radio signals from the fixed telephone nets. The telepoint industry was expected to repeat the spectacular financial success of the cellular telephones during the late 1980s and to provide serious competition for both mobile cellular and local fixed networks. By 1990, however, the telepoint industry was in dire straits, because it had sold its products without first establishing the proper infrastructure.[39] The telepoint industry is now experiencing a consolidation. Mercury Call Point and a smaller company, BYPS (a Barclay Bank, Philips, Shell consortium), are merging, but the future of telepoint is still dim, because by late 1992 the next stage of PCN technology, the technically superior two-way personal communication network, will appear. The rise and fall of telepoint illustrate the high rate of technological change in the telecommunication industry and the possibility of misallocation of investments in a free market. The two-way PCN is now the promising new technology. *The Economist* expected in 1989 that the market for handsets could be worth hundreds of millions of pounds, and the one for services, billions. In 1992, *The Economist's* estimates still appear very reasonable though the entire mobile telecommunication industry, especially the telepoint segment, has been overwhelmed by technological innovations, overly optimistic new market entries with shallow pockets, and deregulation uncertainties. Call volume increased slowly during 1991, and by 1992 tight cash flow at Cellnet and Vodafone—the two mobile carriers—discouraged applicants for a third cellular network, as well as the three winning consortia of PCN network licenses: Mercury PCN (a consortium of Mercury, Cable and Wireless, and Telefonica Española); Unitel (STC, US West, Deutsche Bundespost); and Microtel (British Aerospace, Matra of France, Millikom of the UK, Pacific Telesis of the US, and Sony).[40]

OFTEL had been fully aware of the importance of modal competition to eliminate gradually most vestiges of fixed network monopolies or duopolies. In early 1990 it awarded licenses for three new PCN networks that will give the United Kingdom four rival mobile telephone systems by 1992—with somewhat different standards, however. Somewhat earlier (late 1980s) OFTEL had announced six new licenses for the operation of point to multipoint specialized satellite services. This explosion in new, relatively inexpensive networks—inexpensive compared to fixed networks—was meant to make regulation of BT unnecessary before long. During the early 1990s PCN providers will still have to connect with the British Telecom network if they wish to reach British Telecom or for that matter Mercury subscribers. By 1995 the combination of new PCN and satellite-supported radio-based services will create for British Telecom and Mercury the threat of bypass. If such a development occurs, the market rather than OFTEL will regulate telephone rates during the late 1990s.

The PCNs are still in the very early stages of development and have to cope with different analog standards. The EC and ETSI, as a matter fact, have been disagreeing on how quickly to phase in the common European digital standard. The interim cordless standards CTI and CT2 are currently used in Europe, including the United Kingdom, but by 1993 the new cordless European telephone system (DECT) should be in operation, just in time for the United Kingdom's new PCNs to take off.[41] Uncertainty about standards delayed the quick development of PCNs and contributed to the collapse of the telepoint market.

The cellular mobile telephone systems are in much better shape, as far as standards are concerned. Although ETSI had been slow in approving the new digital mobile standard GSM (General systeme mobile) the specifications were already well known and the two U.K. mobile network operators, Vodafone and Cellnet, will begin offering full digital services in 1992. Each network operator had planned an initial investment of £ 150 m with the hope of providing digital service by July 1991; by August 1991 estimates of the investment necessary to build GSM digital networks had climbed to £ 500 m, and the starting date for full digital cellular service had been moved to 1992. Although a symbolic launch did take place in July, users of digital telephones are still expected to pay £ 400 a unit, though rapid market expansion could cut the cost quickly.[42] Subscribers to digital Vodafone or Cellnet service, however, will be able to travel throughout most of Europe and still use their mobile telephones, while current analog systems can be used only within one's country. Moreover, digital mobile central office (CO) and PBX switches will be able to supply ISDN subscribers call-forwarding, call-waiting, and message storage services.

There is a real possibility that the market-driven cellular, telepoint, and PCN network operators will offer more products than the public can either afford or are willing to use. Critics of "chaotic" competition, and even proponents of network competition, such as Christian von Weiszäcker, have warned about the dangers of competition. They point to the example of American railroads in the nineteenth century, when seven different rail systems connected Omaha, Nebraska, with Chicago, or when at least three sets of Wall Street barons competed for the New York City–Albany, New York rail traffic. The American railroad system never recovered from this wasteful competition that had been considered a natural monopoly throughout Europe.

There seems to be general agreement among the proponents of network competitors in the United Kingdom, including OFTEL, *The Economist*, and the *Financial Times*, that the estimated growth in demand for network services during the next decade will support a competitive market, even though inferior technologies such as one-way telepoint networks will be eliminated. The expensive investment in these short-lived systems could be considered a social waste, especially during a period when Europe seems to suffer from a lack of capital to rebuild the crumbling infrastructure of Central-Eastern Europe. The fact that the telepoint system was relatively cheap (£ 50 m to build a U.K. network) limits the misallocation. A careful government or PTT monopolist investment strategy, however, may be even more expensive in the long run. At a time when the development of a new narrow-band digital CO switch costs U.S. $1 bn, a U.S. $1.55 bn investment to build a PCN network in the United Kingdom does not seem outrageous. The initial entrepreneurial consortium may not be able to make its PCN network pay off, but, from a social investment point of view, its successors who purchase the system at bankruptcy prices will benefit, along with users in 2010 or 2020. The American passenger railroad system did not collapse because of overly sophisticated or intensive investment, but rather because of a reluctance to maintain technological standards. (Anyone doubting this statement ought to take the Montreal–New York City Amtrak train and then compare it with the Paris–Nice TGV or the Munich–Frankfurt "Inter City.") Given the current rate of growth in demand for telecom services and the macroeconomic costs of falling behind in the global technology race, we can assume that betting on market forces to allocate resources in the U.K. telecom market is a smaller risk than relying on a government industrial policy. After all a government-owned PTT was the last major West European network operator to use Strowger switches!

Equipment Manufacturers

The privatization and creation of a network duopoly had an immediate impact on the U.K. equipment market. The U.K. equipment industry lost its privileged position, and in the subsequent concentration the former Plessey-GEC joint venture GPT became a Siemens-GEC enterprise and the former ITT subsidiary STC (formerly Standard Telephone Cable) was acquired by Northern Telecom, the Canadian company that has become also a British as well as an American enterprise. GPT still provides its System X switches for British Telecom and Mercury, but AT&T and L. M. Ericsson have become alternate suppliers. In typical fashion Ericsson responded to the opening of the British market by establishing manufacturing locations in the United Kingdom to produce, among other products, its digital AXE 10 switch. By the late 1980s it had installed 2.5 million AXE 10 lines, and had about 4.25 million additional lines of AXE 10 switches on order from British Telecom. Ericsson's U.K. and U.S. operations are today an integral component of a nominally Swedish firm that has in fact become a global enterprise.

OFTEL concedes that the increase in competition in the transmission switching market "has not been favorable to the U.K. balance of telecommunications trade"[43] but emphasizes that the U.K. manufacturing industry had been responding vigorously, and that in the long run the country will benefit from both a more dynamic industry and a greater supply of modern products.[44] For example, STC's rental office switches and nontelecom business recorded big gains during 1990, the first year as a Northern Telecom subsidiary. The cellular equipment market is another good example of this globalization process. Rapid growth in a liberal market had given Japanese manufacturers an excellent opportunity, but British enterprises have gained valuable experience and are today in a position to benefit from Europe's exploding cordless and cellular market during the early 1990s.

The acquisition of 80 percent of the British information-technology enterprise ICL by Fujitsu is expected to have a similar effect on the British information technology-office communication market. There are signs that even the mercantilistic French are beginning to appreciate the value of the transfer of not-invented-here technology. As these lines are written Bull is negotiating with IBM and Hewlett-Packard to buy a 5 percent share in its company to avoid overdependence on NEC, the Japanese company that acquired 4.5 percent of France's failing computer company during 1991.[45]

A discussion of modal competition for fixed telecom networks must include the increasing role cable television operators may play in the United Kingdom during the 1990s. In addition to the thirty odd cable networks operating in the United Kingdom there exists an increasing interest among international telcos in establishing or acquiring broad-band cable television networks that can be licensed to supply a full range of telecommunication services. During the late 1980s Windsor Television received the first franchise to provide switched voice telephone service, originally on an experimental basis; by 1991 well over a dozen new cable franchises were licensed, or under consideration to be licensed, to various consortia. The regional Bell operating companies (RBOCs) were especially active in this field and by 1990 had received nearly 90 percent of the U.K. table franchises that comprised more than half of British fixed-linked lines![46]

The competitive threat—actual and potential—that broad-band cable networks represent to British Telecom and Mercury can be gauged by the increasing concern with which British network operators view the incursion of the "Baby Bells" in the U.K. market. Malcolm Argent, British Telecom's secretary and group director, complained, with considerable justification, that the RBOCs enjoying a protected monopoly market at home, are allowed freely to enter the U.K. telephone market to acquire British franchises with their monopoly profits.[47] Argent said he had no objection in principle to foreign network operators competing in the United Kingdom, but he was "disappointed by the U.K. government's apparent lack of determination to secure reciprocal agreements elsewhere."[48] Considering the vehemence with which the U.S. Trade Representative's Office and the Department of Commerce (DOC) had badgered the EC and Germany for market access during the MAFF (Market Access Fact Finding) campaign, a British request for a reciprocal market opening might perhaps cause some embarrassment in the DOC, although it probably would not have any result.

There is, of course, always the chance that deregulation in one market will generate deregulation in neighboring markets. Lord Sharp, former CEO of Cable and Wireless, the owners of Mercury, suggested in a Washington speech that the United States, Japan, and the United Kingdom "negotiate a charter for an open telecommunications market binding the Atlantic and Pacific enabling (network) operation already open to foreign competition to have national rights in each country."[49] Sharp's comments are a good indication of the operational commitment to a free market the liberalization of the British Telecom regime has generated. There is not a ghost of chance that the U.S. Congress or America's fragmented telecom decision-making centers (FCC, DOC's NITA, Judge Green, Trade Representatives' Office) would respond to Sharp's suggestions. Hence, the second part of Sharp's comments apply to the United States, as much as to France Télécom or DBP's Telekom: "(Such a charter) would force the protectionists in continental telecommunications to demand a place in the liberal sun or miss the boat taking all telecommunications into the 21st century."[50]

By 1990–91, OFTEL and modal competition combined had given the United Kingdom not only the world's freest telecom market, but had made the United Kingdom the moving force in global telecom deregulation.

THE BRITISH TELECOM REGIME, 1990s

Competition has proved to be a keen stimulus of entrepreneurial activity in the British telecom market. British Telecom, the initially recalcitrant bureaucracy, has developed a global strategy abroad and at least a moderate customer-oriented policy at home. In OFTEL's view British Telecom's quality of service has improved significantly.[51] Assured, at least initially, of strong regulations that kept the dominant network operator from abusing its market power, numerous service and transmission enterprises in addition to Mercury entered the market to provide British users the widest range of services and delivery systems at Europe's lowest rates. In spite of the flurry of competition that suddenly encompassed BT, its revenue position has remained firm, with a 1991 operating return on property, plant, and equipment of 22.6 percent compared to 16.6 percent for Ameritech, the most profitable RBOC, or 7.3 percent for NTT (Nippon Telephone and Telegraph). If there were any losers in the U.K. deregulation it must have been the British equipment manufacturers that were squeezed out, although the amount of telephone equipment manufactured in the United Kingdom may have actually increased. We can say, therefore, that telecom liberalization has produced more winners than losers in the United Kingdom.

A Glimpse into the Future

The 1984 Telecommunication Act had many aspects of an interim step toward the elusive goal of a fully competitive private telecommunication system. Critics of the act, as mentioned, frequently neglected to recognize the exploratory nature of the legislation and emphasized short-run contradictions between privatization and competition objectives.[52] A key aspect of the experimental nature of the legislation was the promise that OFTEL (and the government) would reexamine the state of fixed network competition in 1990. The deliberation lasted a bit longer but in March 1991 the government submitted a telecommunication White Paper that promised to open the U.K. market even further for new domestic and international telcos.[53] Proposed by the ministry of trade and industry (MTI) under the leadership of its secretary Peter Lilley, the White Paper set three objectives:

- End the British Telecom–Mercury communication fixed network duopoly
- Increase competition throughout the various segments of the telecom market, with major attention to removal of restrictions on leased lines, private networks, and the resale of excess leased-line capacity
- Reduce end-user costs[54]

To attain the three objectives the White Paper proposed the following steps:

1. Grant licenses to all future applicants for operating (fixed) wireline services, "unless there are specific reasons to the contrary"
2. "Subject to appropriate approval," the intermodal competition will be encouraged by
   - permitting mobile network operators to build fixed links
   - granting telepoint operators the opportunity to establish two-way neighborhood services
   - allow any corporation to build, own, and operate private networks; authorize resale of leased-line capacity; and let television network operators offer independent telecommunication services on their own franchise or jointly with other franchised operators
   - introduce, by 1994, telephone numbers that will be portable between different networks
   - provide immediate and equal access to the British Telecom–Mercury networks
3. Reduce end-user costs by compelling British Telecom to lower its national and international rates

The White Paper was accepted by parliament without any struggle. There had not been enough time for any opposition to further liberalization to emerge. British Telecom's criticism of the White Paper has been muted, partially because more radical proposals leaked previously had been removed. British Telecom's employees and unions were not happy, because to remain competitive British Telecom will have to cut its costs further and accelerate its strategy to expand its operation abroad. The Labor party has not come out with a new telecommunication policy that could be translated into specific measures. The fact that five Bell regional holding companies are already providing service in the United Kingdom has been noted by Labor, and, of course, by British Telecom management. The future of the White Paper is unpredictable, though over 20 companies have applied for licenses since the March 1991 policy review. In January 1992 the American telco Sprint emerged as the leading candidate to become the third international network operator.[55]

The White Paper has, of course, attracted considerable attention in the United Kingdom, but initially had been overshadowed in the popular press by other topics, such as the Gulf War and Kinnock's and Major's O level examination (roughly high school graduation) record. The expected delay in the White Paper's passage had also helped to soften discussion of the issues. The White Paper has encouraged the liberals in the EC bureaucracy, however, and has been noted with interest in the U.S. telecommunication community. OFTEL's review of BT prices, which began on January 1992, is very likely to result in lower telecom service prices and may therefore reduce the ability of competitors to gain market share through price competition. With OFTEL head Sir Bryant Carsbery leaving the Office of Telecommunications in June 1992, uncertainties have delayed the competitive impact of the White Paper.

Many observers in the United States, the EC, and even the United Kingdom seem to have overlooked a much less radical OFTEL proposal that will be implemented unless a Labor government takes over within the next few months. In line with its obligation under the provisions of the 1984 legislation OFTEL completed its study of the status of British telecommunication and proposed further liberalization in a recent paper "Further Deregulation for Business Users of Public Telecommunication Systems."[56] OFTEL intends to further increase competition by two measures:

- liberalize further Britain's £ 1 bn a year private telecommunication market
- increase competition for British Telecom in the fixed network market

OFTEL plans to accomplish both aims by

- abolishing restrictions on using private networks for ordinary conversation, thus encouraging new enterprises to offer additional VANs products to third parties
- permitting established companies such as IBM, Reuters (financial information

service), and the London Stock Exchange to offer rival voice services over their private network

It seems likely that OFTEL's further liberalization measures will be implemented over the next four months. The affected companies, primarily British Telecom, could appeal to the courts, but under British legal convention the courts can merely judge whether due process has been observed. There is virtually no chance that British Telecom could appeal. We can conclude, therefore, that the U.K. telecom market will be further deregulated regardless of the fate of the White Paper. Leading North American information-technology firms DEC, IBM, RBOCs, and Northern Telecom have already taken advantage of the United Kingdom's open telecommunication market. The role of OFTEL in the creation of a liberal telecom market in the United Kingdom cannot be overestimated.[57]

The National Champion in a Liberal Home Market

During the first stage of liberalization (1981–84), British Telecom did rather well, and if anything increased its dominance in the British telecom market. We have already mentioned that in the postprivatization phase (1984–90), aggressive entrepreneurial marketing tactics and tighter management control enabled British Telecom to maintain its position in spite of cream-skimming network competition. Very much like France Télécom and DBP Telekom, British Telecom began to sell its network management expertise in the global market. The strategy to look abroad for promising markets and to reduce its dependence on its domestic operation continued during the 1990–91 period. When the issues of further network liberalization became again prominent British Telecom's most recent venture, its so-called Pathfinder alliance with DBP Telekom and NTT (Nippon Telegraph and Telephone, Japan's dominant, semiprivate network operator), attracted the most attention, but was merely one more step in a series of foreign joint ventures.[58] Quite typically, the three national carriers (and national champions) would offer network management, value-added services, and one-stop shopping on a global basis. Interestingly British Telecom seems to have been the driving force in this alliance and was expected to own 48 percent of Pathfinder, while Telekom and NTT would have owned 26 percent each. IBM has been mentioned as an "arms-length partner," and all three carriers have had agreements with IBM during 1990 and 1991.[59] (In 1984 IBM and British Telecom wanted to operate a joint data network, Jove, initially only in the United Kingdom, but OFTEL prevented the licensing of Jove because it would have strengthened British Telecom's market dominance.) British Telecom has been discussing with IBM managing the latter's international telecom communication network, an international revival of the previous British Telecom-IBM network plans for the United Kingdom. The role of network managers of multinationals' large and growing private network is a natural strategy not only for British Telecom, but also for Telekom, NTT, and other former PTTs that are currently under severe attack in their home market as a consequence of both liberalization and new technological innovations that make the bypass of local networks imminent. So far the Pathfinder joint venture has not yet been realized, primarily because DBP Telekom, under pressure from France Telecom, has begun to waver. Regardless of the fate of Pathfinder, from 1986 to 1991 BT has been amazingly successful in its program of overseas acquisition and joint ventures. Neither France Telecom nor DBP Telekom have displayed similar entrepreneurial aggressiveness.[60]

British Telecom's Pathfinder alliance with Telekom and NTT is still on the drawing board, but is merely the last step in British Telecom's global strategy that has targeted the United States as the most promising market for its network management services and, incidentally, challenges AT&T on its home grounds. We shall merely mention two further British Telecom moves to convey the nature of British Telecom's international strategy. British Telecom negotiated with IBM during 1990 to offer jointly worldwide comprehensive communication services. British Telecom would take over managing IBM's internal communication system and link it with its international data network subsidiary Tymnet. Subsequently IBM and British Telecom plan to extend their cooperation to the international voice communication market, with IBM supplying information services and software for network management.[61] It is not quite clear how the British Telecom–IBM plans of December 1990 fit into the Pathfinder venture of March 1991. They may either be supplementary or competitive or they may be a grand design to take on AT&T as many managers in AT&T's New York City and New Jersey headquarters believe.

British Telecom is also making an effort to become a major player in the United States. Having purchased Tymnet from McDonnell Douglas, British Telecom did not make an effort, at first, to announce its ownership but continued to run America's largest specialized data network sucessfully during the late 1980s, while offering its network management services and VANs through its other U.S subsidiary, British Telecom Inc. In view of the current review of its duopoly network status in the United Kingdom, British Telecom demonstrated its non-U.K. emphasis and on March 31, 1991, merged Tymnet and British Telecom Inc. into British Telecom North America to display its commitment to the North American marketplace.[62] Business communication, especially global cross-border network management, has been a major and increasing source of profit for former or still existing telephone monopolies. In turn, information services, software, and office equipment are promising growth areas for computer companies that have not been able to penetrate this market alone, in spite of their early beliefs that a telecommunication network was merely a special case of information systems. Even in this new and growing market where each telco and each computer firm seem to have myriads of joint ventures and alliances there will be a shakeout during the next decade. British Telecom, however, seems well positioned to remain among the survivors. The British privatization legislation of 1984 seems to have succeeded in achieving its apparently contradictory goals: increase competition in the domestic network and VAS-VAN markets and strengthen British Telecom's position as a national champion.

NOTES

1. The role of the Thatcher administration's commitment to privatization as a separate force in the deregulation of British Telecom has been rarely recognized. An exception is Jill Hills, *Deregulating Telecoms* (Westport, Conn.: 1986), Quorum, chaps. 1, 3, and 7. Hills' book is a particularly perceptive study of forces promoting deregulation. We shall refer to issues raised by Hills on several occasions.

2. Conservative Party Manifest 1979, quoted by Hills, *Deregulating Telecoms*, 27.

3. J. Hills, Christian von Weizsäcker, Bernhard Wieland, and G. Knieps. See also Michael Beesley and Stephen Littlechild, "Privatization, Principles, Problems and Priorities," *Lloyds Bank Review* (July 1983).

4. In March 1991 Fujitsu acquired a 74.9 percent stake in the product division of Fulcrum Communication, British Telecom's last remaining U.K.-based manufacturing operation. See "Fujitsu Takes Stake in BT Unit," *Financial Times* (March 12, 1991): 21.

5. See "The Planners Strike Back," *The Economist* (February 16, 1991): 57.

6. The high prices charged for computers and office information equipment in Europe by Europe's fragmented IT industry have proven to be very profitable for American enterprises that have gained considerable market share in Europe, and have, at the same time, reduced the demand of European companies for IT products. See also "Steering The EC's Industry," *The Economist* (January 25, 1992): 14.

7. See House of Commons Selected Committee on the Nationalized Industries, *First Report on the Post Office* (London: HMSO, 1967); and Thomas Schnöring, "Die Änderung in der Regulierungs—und Organisations Struktur des Post Office," *Innovationen im Telekommunikations Sektor und Gesamtwirtschafliche Entwicklung* (Bad Honnef: WIK, 1985).

8. "History of Switching," *Telephony's Horizon of Technology Special* (February 1991): 5. See also *Telephony's All Fiber Network Series* (November 1991).

9. Ibid.

10. Hills, *Deregulating Telecoms*, 86–88; see also M. T. Hills, "System Development in Japan and the U.K.," in *Telecommunications Group Report*, Essex University, 1966.

11. *Report of the Post Office Review Committee* (Carter Report) (London: HMSO, 1977), 106–8.

12. See Schöring, *Innovationen*, 2, 3.

13. The post office had received precise profit targets since the 1969 reform—

and lesser ones even before—for both telecom and post service. After 1979 the profit targets were set by the economic minister's department for trade and industry and were in line with private sector profit expectations (ibid., 3–7). See also annual post office reports, 1964–84.

14. Schnöring points out, however, that the separation also invigorated the post office's mail service: "The identification with the objectives of its own enterprise, and the optimism about the future increases at least among the management. Productivity progress was achieved and a series of new services introduced" (*Innovationen*, 17; author's translation). See also *Post Office Review Committee*, 66, for the preconditions of the 1979 separation.

15. See Hills, *Deregulating Telecoms*, 93–97, for a critical view that represents the Labor party viewpoint.

16. Both the history of the July 1981–July 1982 period and the short-run evaluations of its consequences are not easily accessible since the rather small community of telecom analysts rarely bothered to define their terms. Much was made, for instance, of the distinction between behavioral and structural regulation. The first definition of these terms appeared in Schnöring's German analysis; "behavioral regulation" merely meant that performance indexes were established, and regulatory approval of capital investment was necessary (Schnöring, *Innovationen*, 9–10).

17. See the tabulated annual reports (1964–89) of British Telecom and the post office in ibid., 6. Also note *The Future of Telecommunication in Britain* (London: HMSO, 1982), especially 4–6.

18. Keith Joseph, minister of industry in the first Thatcher administration, was one of the outstanding intellects of the new right in the United Kingdom. An ardent and articulate libertarian (classical liberal), he was Thatcher's key advisor on domestic policy.

19. For a different viewpoint in line with the Labor party position, see Hills, *Deregulating Telecoms*, 89–98.

20. Michael Beesley, *Liberalization of the Use of British Telecom's Network* (London: HMSO, 1981). Beesley's report was published in April, but most of its main points had been known to the government for months.

21. Stephen Littlechild, *Regulation of British Telecommunication Profitability* (London: Department of Industry, 1983). The report was published in January 1983, but much of its findings had been known beforehand.

22. A letter of intent to license Mercury had already been issued in the fall of 1981.

23. Sir Leon Brittan has become EC commissioner subsequently and during the 1990–91 period has been on the forefront of preventing EC members, especially France and Italy, from distorting competitive markets by promoting national champions.

24. See Hills, *Deregulating Telecoms*, 130–32; and OFTEL, *First Report 5 August–31 December, 1984* (London: HMSO, 1985).

25. Bryan Carsberg, "OFTEL—the Challenge of the Next Five Years," *Information Technology and Public Policy* 4/1 (September 1985).

26. W. R. B. Wigglesworth, "The Experience with Competition and Regulation in Great Britain," paper presented at the WIK Conference on the Future of Telecommunication in Europe, Bonn, November 14–15, 1988.

27. Ibid., 4.

28. Ibid.

29. In 1988 OFTEL had a record two hundred companies operating under VAN licenses and forty-two VADS license service providers. VAS turnover was estimated at £ 100 m (*ibid.*, 5–6).

30. *Financial Times* (February 15, 1991): 18.

31. For a brief but concise description of the breakup of the Swedish monopoly system, see "Sweden Ushers in Competition," *Telephony* (April 22, 1991): 3. Interestingly Cable and Wireless, the owner of Mercury, is a member of the consortium that launched the new telephone compass Tele 2. Again, similar to Mercury's strategy Tele 2 will concentrate on building a new fiber optic network to provide data and other network services to the business community. Clearly the United Kingdom has been the model for Sweden's telecom reform.

32. Wigglesworth, "Competition and Regulation," 6. See also "Telephones That Get Up and Go," *The Economist* (September 16, 1989).

33. Ibid., 71.

34. Wigglesworth, "Competition and Regulation," 6; and Technology Survey, *Telephony*.

35. In a 1989 study for OFTEL James Foreman-Peck found that from 1964 to 1980 British Telecom's productivity grew at 2 percent per annum, and after 1984 grew at more than 3 percent (ibid., 7).

36. Hugh Dixon, "BT Makes Connections Overseas," *Financial Times* (November 29, 1991): 21, and Lawrence Hooper, "British Telecom Pretax Profit Rose," *Wall Street Journal* (August 9, 1991): A6.

37. "Telephones That Get Up and Go," *The Economist* (September 16, 1989): 71.

38. Paul Abrahams, "Sink or Swim at the Deep End," *Financial Times* (August 5, 1991): 13; Marcus Weinkopf, "Das White Paper zur künftigen britischen Telekommunikations Politik," *WIK Newsletter* (July 1991): 6–9; John Williamson, "UK, Greece kindle GSM Flame," *Telephony* (September 16, 1991): 12–14. See also Hugo Dixon, "UK to Grant New Telecoms License," *Financial Times* (January 21, 1992): 12.

39. See Paul Abraham, "Disarray as Industry Fails to Make the Point," *Financial Times* (December 9, 1990): 7. See also Paul Abraham, "Sink or Swim at the Deep End," *Financial Times* (August 15, 1991): 13.

40. Ibid.

41. "ETSI Rejects EC Cordless Ban," *Telephone* (March 11, 1991). The mobile network operator Racal took the most interesting approach to the absense of PCN standards during the crucial 1989–90 investment period. It promised to build an overlay PCN (on top of its digital cellular network) that would enable users to make and receive calls while sitting in cafes or wandering around the countryside. In order to make and receive calls while driving, the user's regular Racal mobile automobile phone would have to be used. Whether there will be enough yuppies or tycoons to require a cellular digital phone for their BMW and another for carrying on their person is not clear. *The Economist* doubts that all five PCN networks will survive but is still excited about PCN's future. In late December 1990 Europe seemed to come close to agreement on standards for an EC cordless telephone network and thus solve the bottleneck of overcrowded circuits. The EC council of

ministers underestimated the time necessary for developing the Dig'..al European Cordless Telephone (DECT) standards.

42. "Telephones That Get Up and Go," 7; "Sink or Swim at the Deep End," 13.

43. Wigglesworth, "Competition and Regulation," 9.

44. Ibid. Note in this context the statement of Northern Telecom's CEO, Paul Stern: "STC and Northern have been integrated to support our strategy of growth through globalization." The United Kingdom has gained a share of a major global telecompany even if its stockholders live in Canada.

45. "NEC in Talks on Group Bull Stake," *Financial Times* (April 24, 1991): 17. See also William Dawkins," Cresson's Champions," *Financial Times* (December 19, 1991): 14, and Hugo Dixon, "A Last Chance to Ring the Changes," *Financial Times* (January 20, 1992): 11.

46. Martin Dickson and Paul Abrahams, "British Telecom Attacks U.S. Telephone Monopolies," *Financial Times* (December 6, 1990): 16.

47. Ibid.

48. Ibid.

49. Ibid.

50. Ibid.

51. Wiggelesworth, "Competition and Regulation," 14.

52. Hills, *Deregulating Telecoms*, chap. 5, provides a valuable survey of Labor party criticism of British Telecom privatization and telecom liberalization. *The Economist*, on the other hand, strongly supported the view that the 1984 legislation was a "competitive experiment" ("Battle for Britain's Telephones," *The Economist* [October 27, 1990]: 16–17).

53. "U.K. Unleashed Competition," *Telephony* (March 11, 1991): 9–10. See also "Britain Urges Telecommunications Field Be Opened to Many Local, Foreign Firms," *Wall Street Journal*, November 14, 1990. The *WSJ* article referred to a November 1990 trial balloon by Peter Lilley, trade and industry secretary, who subsequently headed the task force proposing the March 1991 White Paper. Not surprisingly, the White Paper reflected Lilley's previous position, but leaves some regulation in place. See also "Competition in Telecoms," *Financial Times* (November 19, 1990): 16.

54. "U.K. Unleashed Competition," 9–10.

55. Hugo Dixon, "British Government to Allow More International Networks," *Financial Times* (January 27, 1992): 12.

56. OFTEL Atlantic House, London, 1991; see also Hugo Dixon, "Telecom Market Liberalization Planned by Industry Watchdog," *Financial Times* (January 31, 1991): 7.

57. Even OFTEL is not without its critics, however. William Leturin, professor at the London School of Economics and Center for Policy Studies, a right-wing think-tank, accuses OFTEL of not being sufficiently transparent in its price setting and in defining clearly its criteria for granting licenses. (*Freeing the Phones: The Case for More Liberalization*, Center for Policy Studies, London, April 1991.) Similar suggestions had been made by the *Financial Times* in its editorial "Clearer Rule for Telecoms" (December 17, 1990): 14. By January 1992 however, its approval of OFTEL was apparent. Dixon, "A Last Chance to Ring the Changes," *Financial Times* (January 20, 1992): 11.

58. "British Telecom Led Global Carrier Alliance," *Telephony*, (April 8, 1991): 3.

59. Ibid.

60. *Telephony* (December 24, 1990): 9. For an update on Pathfinder, see "Three Giant Phone Firms Plan Venture to offer Joint Service to Multinationals," *Wall Street Journal*, April 5, 1991, pp. A3–A6; "UK, Greece Kindle GSM Flame," *Telephony* (September 16, 1991); and Hugo Dixon, "BT Makes Connections Overseas," *Financial Times* (November 29, 1991): 21.

61. "IBM and British Telecom Plan Global Services for Companies," *Financial Times* (December 17, 1990): 1; and "Business Line in Telecom for British Telecom and IBM," *Financial Times* (December 8, 1990): 21. See also Alan Cane, "BT Revives Talks on Global Networks," *Financial Times* (January 27 1992): 12.

62. "British Telecom Gets New Look," *Telephony* (March 25, 1991).

7

The Telecommunication Policy of the European Community, Project 1992

The European Community has set itself the goal of achieving a U.S.-like "integrated economy" by 1992 in order to regain the economic and political momentum the Treaty of Rome created some thirty years ago. Although the goal of a United Europe has been overshadowed by constant parochial quarrels over specific agriculture, budget, environment, and steel policies, Europe in fact has been coalescing slowly but steadily over the past decades in various cultural, economic, and political forums, inside and outside the formal EC structure. More recently the success of the European Monetary System (EMS) and the subsequent emergence of the German Central Bank (Bundesbank) as the de facto architect of an anti-inflationary European monetary policy have been major factors in the creation of a coordinated European economic policy. In order to overcome the remaining but tenacious nationalistic-bureaucratic obstacles, the European council passed the Single Europe Act (SEA) in 1986, and, reaffirming the provisions of the Treaty of Rome (1958), renewed the commitment to a "Europe Sans Frontiéres" by 1992 (see table 7.1).

The SEA did succeed in invigorating the strategies of the major European countries to broaden their "European" activities. The intra-European mergers and joint ventures undertaken by companies whose managements decided to meet the opportunities of an integrated market as "European" enterprises have been a very important but (in the United States) little noticed consequence of the SEA. Particularly the efforts of EFTA (European Free Trade Association) country enterprises to gain a foothold in the EC through acquisitions, mergers, and joint ventures deserve close scrutiny by American management (see table 7.2).

The recent wave of mergers and participations established a favorable climate for the EC's industrial policy to encourage and coordinate joint research in the "high-tech" information technology (IT) area through

Table 7.1
All You Ought to Know about the EC but Never Asked

EC INSTITUTIONS

Legislative Body

European council: comprised of heads of state/governments. Meets twice a year.

Council of ministers: varies according to subject discussed; for example, topic of "tax harmonization" is considered by finance and economic ministers of member-states.

Committee of Permanent Representatives (COREPER): senior civil servants from member-states seconded to Brussels to prepare the agenda for the council of ministers.

Executive-Administrative Body

EC commission administers EC treaties, council policies. Seventeen commissioners head seventeen European quasi-ministries. Appointed by unanimous agreement among EC governments. President, Jacques Delors, four-year term.

European Parliament

Elected EC-wide; no real power so far although Single Europe Act extends its role in preparing and adopting budgets, recommending policies. Can dismiss EC commission through no-confidence vote.

TWO KEY EC TREATIES

Treaty of Rome, 1957

(i)   Elimination of customs duties, quotas

(ii)   Establishment of common customs duties and trade policies for nonmembers

       (i and ii constitute a customs union)

(iii) Elimination of obstacles to movement of persons, services, and capital among members

       (iii to become effective by 1992)

Single Europe Act (SEA), ratified 1987

(i)   Expands issues subject to majority vote (in lieu of unanimity) in the council

(ii)   Extends role of European parliament

(iii) Formalizes procedures for member cooperation in foreign policy

(iv)   Commits EC and members to integrate market (implement provision iii of Treaty of Rome) by 1992

Table 7.2
Recent Mergers

(i)   Bosch GMBA (Germany's second largest electronic enterprise) has pur-
        chased 20 percent of France's Jeumont-Schneider.

(ii)   Daimler-Benz acquired a similar share of the French defense telecom firm
        Matra.

(iii)   Assicurazioni Generali bought a controlling share of the insurance com-
        pany Cie du Midi.

(iv)   Carlo De Beneditti (Olivetti CEO) launched a hostile takeover of Société
        Générale de Belgique and amassed 48 percent of its stock but sold most
        of his holdings during 1990.

(v)   Asea, the Swedish electronics multinational, has merged with the Swiss
        Brown Boveri, to form ABB; however, in the new ABB, Brown Boveri's
        German subsidiary has become an equal partner with the original Swiss
        and Swedish owners. Clearly ABB hopes that its German component will
        establish Europe's second largest electronics companies as an EC enter-
        prise, come the revolution of 1992.

(vi)   Volvo acquired Leyland Bus division, gained an EC foothold, and re-
        placed Daimler-Benz as Europe's largest bus maker.

(vii)   Iveco (International Vehicle Cooperation), a joint venture of Fiat and
        KHD Germany, represents a successful attempt by a major European
        automobile manufacturer to establish a foothold in Germany.

(viii) VW's acquisition of 75 percent of Spain's SEAT has been a major step
        in broadening VW's European manufacturing base.

(ix)   U.K. and French computer service groups merged to form Semacar, now
        one of the top five firms in this industry (estimated 1988 sales $500 m).

(x)   Thompson S. A., France, merged its chip operation with Italy's SGS to
        form SGS-Thompson.

(xi)   Siemens-Philips joint megachip research and production venture MEGA.

(xii)   Ericsson (data division) and Nokia (Finland's largest EDP systems en-
        terprise) form Nokia Data GMBH with headquarters in Dusseldorf.

(xiii) Alcatel-AEG-Nokia form joint mobile telephone company.

(xiv)   Switzerland's Nestlé and Suchard attempt to acquire United Kingdom's
        Rowntree.

RACE, ESPRIT, and similar research projects. The collaboration among
EC scientists, universities, and key multinationals has been advanced by
the EC projects and, in turn, has contributed to the "Europeanization"
trend that has emerged during the past years.

   In addition to the slowly emerging long-run integrative consequences of
EC economic, industrial, and technological policies, the increasing protectionist and isolationist tendencies of the U.S. Congress and the Dem-

ocratic party, the very party with which cosmopolitan Europeans used to identify themselves, have convinced many European leaders that they can no longer rely unquestionably on the United States to provide the protection they may need if the former Soviet Union returns to Stalinism. Consequently the rediscovery of the EC as an economic and potential political power occurred, and has given the "1992" target strong emotional support.

Lastly, and perhaps most important, France, and within France the rising "new class" of young technocrats, entrepreneurs, and intellectuals, has rediscovered a united Europe as a worthy goal for both economic and noneconomic reasons.[1] In the immediate postwar era the (Catholic) Christian Democrats Konrad Adenauer, Alcide De Gasperi, Jean Monnet, Robert Schuman, and Paul-Henry Spaak created in the Treaty of Rome (1957) not only the structure for a European economic community but also a strong ideological movement to create a united Christian Europe from the ruins of World War II. The drive toward a united Europe was halted first by the French left that, under Mendes-France, rejected during the 1950s the creation of a European Defense Community, and subsequently by the French right under de Gaulle who opposed any surrender of French sovereignty and thus prevented the Common Market's metamorphosis into a supranational European confederation.

The disillusionment of French intellectuals with Marxism and the apparent rejection of Colbertism by the new generation of technocrats and entrepreneurs have not only made room, once more, for the concept of "Europe" to emerge as a worthy political-ideological objective but for the first time ever have gained broad support over the entire French political spectrum for the goal of achieving a fully integrated European market by 1992 as a necessary step for further political and economic integration. The importance of French leadership in creating a "European market" cannot be overestimated.

In spite of the various and formidable forces that reinvigorate the EC, the considerable parochial, bureaucratic, and nationalistic obstacles to integration must not be underestimated. We shall see in the telecommunication case that the very institutions that give lip-service to "1992" will strongly resist deregulation if their own narrow interests are at stake. There will be many instances during the next year, moreover, where Brussels will remain a forum for the antics and quarrels of national bureaucracies and industry associations, and it will be the parochial posturing of European politicians that will be chronicled by the press.[2] Still, the economic-political-technological requirements for integration are too strong, and the transformation of national into European firms too advanced to prevent the establishment of an integrated Europe.

"The simple expedient of setting a date to achieve [the integrated European economy] may ... be working wonders. The minds of European governments are increasingly concentrated on ensuring that their countries are ready to compete in the Community's open 'internal market.' "[3] The emergence of the EC as a key economic and political factor has provided special opportunities for those American firms that have established a strong manufacturing and R&D presence throughout Europe. Companies such as Apple, DEC, Ford, GM, and IBM can be considered, in many respects, truly European companies. For the past decades, moreover, most multinational firms have based their long-run strategies on establishing strong positions in the three major global markets of North America, Japan, and Europe. Access to the "Common Market" (the European Community) has been as necessary for non-European multinationals with global aspirations as the presence in the North American market has been to European firms. If, however, the EC succeeds in establishing a continental nonfragmented economy, the strategy of even well-established American MNCs will have to be revised significantly.[4]

The emergence of a truly continental market requires a continental information-telecommunication infrastructure. Both European and non-European multinationals, therefore, have a vital stake in the development of an integrated European telecommunication system, either as producers or users of equipment, networks, and services. Moreover, for economic and geopolitical reasons the EC has chosen the telecommunication sector as *the* "leading industry" of its integration strategy.[5] The role of the telecommunication industry in the EC integration process provides, therefore, an interesting case study for the interaction of technological change, EC industrial policy, and the enormous role technological standardization must and will play in the emergence of a European economy.

The pace of integration in the telecommunication field will be the index for the success and the nature of the new, post–1992 EC. Whether the new EC will be a mercantilistic confederation in which protectionism and state regulation have been merely moved from national capitals to Brussels, or whether the new market will be an open, free-access one will be demonstrated by the developments in the telecom area.

TECHNOLOGICAL CHANGE AND EC INDUSTRIAL POLICY, 1984–89

The European Community has been concerned consistently with maintaining Europe's technological competitiveness with North America and Japan. During the 1960s and 1970s the failure to transform European research successes into marketable products caused consternation among EC technocrats. Much of the "revolution" in biotechnology, for example, had originated in British laboratories but was exploited by American companies, and the technical excellence of British, French, and German computer scientists was not reflected in the computers produced by ICL, Machine-Bull, or Siemens. Attempts by the EC to create a European computer technology and, perhaps, a single European computer manufacturer failed miserably because the leading enterprises, Machine-Bull and Siemens, had global rather than European aspirations.

The rapid convergence of computer and telecommunication technologies during the last decade, and the threatening dominance of the new global market in information technology (IT) by a few North American and Japanese computer-telecom equipment manufacturers, prompted the EC commission to make a major effort to launch EC research projects in the IT area.[6] This time, however, the EC accompanied the joint research efforts with an industrial policy that was designed to create an integrated European information-technology market and a telecom manufacturing industry with common standards for products and services.[7]

In February 1984 the council of ministers approved the ESPRIT (European Strategic Program for Research and Development in Information Technology) and allocated ECU 750 m (at that time roughly $750 m) for a five-year period; in July 1985 it approved RACE (Research and Development in Advanced Communications Technologies in Europe) initially for a preliminary eighteen-month period.[8] To the surprise of many skeptics, who had lost faith in "European" projects, ESPRIT and RACE have been successful, in both actual new knowledge gained and the establishment of scientific cooperation among European universities. Most noticeable has been the establishment of closer university-industry ties in such areas as software technology development, computer-integrated manufacturing (both ESPRIT areas), and integrated broad-band communication (RACE).

The theoretical, practical, and institutional successes of ESPRIT and RACE encouraged the council to commit itself finally in 1987 to a focused long-run EC research program, with special attention to information technology; further funding for ESPRIT brought its budget to ECU 1.6 bn. RACE received ECU 550 m for the period 1985–90, with additional funding originally scheduled for 1991.[9] The early research successes of ESPRIT, RACE, and other EC efforts failed, however, to transform the competitiveness of the European electronics industry. By summer 1991, moreover, the EC research projects became the object of an increasingly strident controversy over industrial policy. No decision has been made on the long-run future of ESPRIT and RACE. In the meantime, the EC will encourage rapid application of knowledge gained by European companies and institutions to provide the roots for a sophisticated European telecom infrastructure after 1992. If the European Community's interventionists gain the upperhand, ESPRIT, RACE, and other EC sponsored projects will become a funnel for subsidizing the national champions in the electronics and information technology industries.[10]

The scope and commitment of the EC's research and policy efforts are based upon the EC commission's firm conviction that Europe's survival as an economic and scientific world power will depend upon its success in establishing a world-class telecommunication industry and research capability. "Strengthening the telecommunication sector in the (European) Community is one of the most important preconditions for the *promotion of an harmonic development of the economic activity* in the Community and for the completion of the EC-wide market for goods and services by 1992."[11] The commitment to develop a European telecommunication infrastructure and world-class information technology has been the driving force in the establishment of the EC's telecom policy. The precise nature of this policy must be understood before its chances for success and its impact upon North American telecommunication companies can be analyzed.

The EC Model for a European Telecommunication System

The June 1987 EC *Green Paper on the Development of a Common Market for Telecommunication Services and Equipment* provided a concise description of the EC's strategy to develop a common European telecom infrastructure and industry. In EC terminology, Green Papers "initiate debates to attract comments from a broad spectrum of opinion" while White Papers present directives for the implementation of policies.[12] In fact, however, Green Papers are rarely presented without extensive prior discussion and the assurance of support from the council of ministers. Green Papers, therefore, are taken very seriously by European politicians and governments. The telecom Green Paper had the immediate effect of providing support for the deregulation recommendations the German government (Witte) committee on telecommunication was to submit to the German government in September 1988. The similarities between the Green Paper and the Witte recommendations are striking;[13] in a similar vein, the Green Paper—and the subsequent Witte report—made it easier for the French government to overcome bureaucratic resistance and establish the government's proposal for telecom reform: its preliminary report had been compatible with both the EC and the Witte recommendations and, in spite of subsequent changes, helped shape the 1990 reform legislation.[14] Moreover, virtually every European government is currently making changes in its telecom system that follow Green Paper recommendations. Given the importance of the Green Paper a closer look at its provisions is advisable.

Green Paper Recommendations

Goals:

(i)   Establish an open, (more) competitive environment for new services and terminal equipment.

(ii)   Provide a wide range of competitive, value-added services (VAS) for consumers; encourage PTTs to enter competitive VAS markets.

(iii) Maintain PTT monopoly of basic telephone networks and infrastructure investment in order to achieve economic growth and maintain the "social contract" to provide universal basic service for low-income areas.

Recommendations:

(i)   Continue gradual establishment of a competitive, open-access terminal equipment market.

(ii)   Provide an open, competitive market for value-added telecommunication services.

(iii) Maintain PTT monopoly of basic telephone service, network operation, and ownership.

(iv)   Introduce competition into the satellite transmission market (at that time restricted to "official" channels) and establish a common European position on satellite communication.

(v)   Separate the regulatory and operational functions of the PTTs (of special relevance for the deregulation of the German and French PTTs).

(vi)   Comply fully with the telecommunication provisions of the Treaty of Rome that explicitly guarantee the free movement of people and services.

(vii) Establish and harmonize cost-based tariffs for services throughout the EC.

(viii) Establish uniform conditions for open-access service and network suppliers.

(ix)   Establish a common European position on international telecommunication issues.

(x)   Open government (PTT) procurement procedures to all EC members but delay extending these policies to non-EC countries.

(xi)   Postpone decisions on changing external EC tariffs on telecommunication equipment.

A Strategic Analysis of the EC's Telecommunication Policy

The convergence of computer and traditional telecommunication technology has already been recognized by all global players in the information-technology market. The future of the EC's global telecom role will depend, therefore, on its success in adapting and further developing recent technological developments, particularly digital and optical transmission of information.

Although the Europeans had been lagging behind the Americans in the rate of establishing digital networks, Europe's PTTs, particularly in Germany and France, have not only begun to catch up, but have been benefiting from their monopoly positions by developing standardized ISDN-capable networks, rather than the variety of systems U.S. deregulation has bequeathed upon its users. French, German, and EC commitments to ISDN, the integrated voice-data networks, have been more explicit and focused than North America's. "While nation-wide ISDNs are currently being built and tested by the regulated European telecommunication monopolies, attempts to introduce the Consultative Committee on International Telephony and Telegraph's standard telecommunications architecture into the U.S. are running into barriers. America's hyper competitive policy and its fragmented communications infra-structure may leave users stranded by creating incompatible implementations of ISDN."[15]

The rate of technological innovations, however, has made the ISDN copper cable 64 kbits networks obsolete almost before they have become operational. The quality of Europe's telecom infrastructure will, therefore, depend on its ability to overcome the remaining technological obstacles to the operation of fiber optic broad-band networks and the bureaucratic resistance to standardization and innovation. A SWOT (strength, weakness, opportunity, threat) analysis may provide an answer.

A SWOT Analysis of European Telecommunication

Strengths

The EC, most European countries, and especially the FRG (Federal Republic of Germany) have established a long-run strategy that has committed each country to develop its telecom systems from analog to digital to ISDN overlay to broad-band ISDN networks.

This strategy has two components: (1) development of common European technical standards, accompanied by harmonized liberal procurement policies; (2) coordination in the research and development of common information infrastructure programs (see table 7.3).

The EC and the European PTTs have committed themselves to accept the CCITT-ISO (Consultative Committee for International Telephony, Telegraph-International Standards Organization) standards for the digital-ISDN networks currently under construction; although there are still some minor difficulties with differing interpretation of the 150 standard protocols by the PTTs, Europe will have an operational ISDN-compatible network by 1992 (by 1990 France already had achieved ISDN service on 80 percent of its network, Germany on about 60 percent). The newly established ETSI (European Telecommunication Standards Institute) contributed to the unexpectedly rapid ISDN installations by establishing firm standards on July 1990.

Similarly, there has been considerable progress in the establishment of European standards for terminal equipment and mobile networks. In order to revive the efficiency and speed of developing standards for information-processing and telecommunication equipment the EC had suggested in the

Table 7.3
Introduction of the ISDN–64 kbits in Different Countries

1. Experimental Installation of Technology and Field Tests
2. Offering of ISDN-Services in Limited Pilot Projects
3. Commencement of Public ISDN-Services
4. Introduction of the CCITT-Sign-system No. 7

	1	2	3	4
Belgium	1984/85	1988	1989/90	1985
Denmark	-	-	-	1985
Finland	1987	/1/	/1/	1985
France	1986	-	1988	1986
FR Germany	-	1986	1988	1986
Greece	-	/1/	/1/	1987/88
Ireland	1986/87	1988	/1/	1986
Italy	1984	1987/88	1990	1986
Netherlands	1987	/2/	/2/	1987/88
Norway	-	-	1987/88	1987
Spain	1985	1987	1988	1986
Sweden	1984	1987/88	/3/	1985
Switzerland	-	1987/89	/1/	1987
UK	1983	1984/85	/4/	1984
USA	-	From 1986/87 first ISDN-Installation		1986/87

/1/ Hitherto no decision
/2/ The introduction of ISDN is theoretically possible from 1988 on
/3/ Time depends on demand development
/4/ ISDN-pilot services are considered a regular public service and have been expanded by BTAU Mercury during 1989-90

Source: Mittelfristiges Programm für den Ausbau der Technischen Kommunikationssysteme, DBP, 1985; revised 1990.

Green Paper establishing its own Institute for Telecommunication Standards. CEPT (Conference of European Post and Telecommunication Administration) supported this suggestion strongly and the formal establishment of this institute took place in the spring of 1988. Since December 1986 the EC has worked with the three European standards organizations— CEN (Comité Européen de Normalisation), CENELAC (Comité Européen de Normalisation), and CEPT's telecommunication standard's office—to accelerate the formulation of European standards. In accordance with a 1986 EC decision, member states are required to implement these European standards. The formation of a European Standards Institute will speed up this process and prevent foot dragging by the standards bureaucracies.[16]

Most important, the EC has succeeded in facilitating the access of new equipment to the European market. The EC directive for the first phase of the mutual recognition of equipment access to PTT networks became effective in July 1987 and applied to all equipment for which European telecommunication norms had been established. Foot dragging by the PTTs' access-granting bureaucracies had previously slowed the process of establishing European norms for already existing equipment and services. Although all PTTs agree with the goal of common access standards they had complained that the EC was moving too fast.

Particular progress has been made in the coordinated development of networks, services, and research. In addition to ESPRIT and RACE, the Euronet-DIANE provides a transborder European information network that connects six hundred databases and banks to computers and telephones, and charges a common, cost-based (usage-independent) rate.

The EC's APOLLO project will implement satellite transmission of high-volume digital information and has already institutionalized a European satellite research program. INSIS and CADDIA enable member-states and EC agencies to communicate over ISDN networks and transmit texts, electronic mail, data, video text, and video conferences. The information network for public institutions began to operate during 1990–91.

Altogether, the progress already made on integrating regulatory procedures and on adopting uniform standards, as well as the broad acceptance by users, manufacturers, and network administrators of the EC strategy to provide Europe with an integrated ISDN-capable network by 1992, gave Europe a unity of purpose that has been lacking in the increasingly heterogeneous North American market. A standardized open-access system will also provide economies of scale for manufacturers and increased competition for users of vendor-neutral products.

Weaknesses

In spite of the progress made and the ambitious projects launched, a common communication market does not yet exist. EC and CEPT efforts to harmonize standards made only glacial progress until ETSI succeeded in speeding up this process. The relatively quick CEPT acceptance of common standards for new services and equipment cannot hide the tenacious attachment of the PTTs' standards (access-granting) bureaucracies to established procedures. There was, furthermore, no strong popular demand for quick integration of the phone system. Households and small businesses in the key countries had been quite satisfied with the existing services, and the unions, particularly in Germany, had been violently opposed to any changes in the status quo. PTT deregulation has been essentially an agenda of the large transnational corporations, the EC technocrats in Brussels, and pockets of deregulation enthusiasts in Bonn, London, and Paris. The objective economic-technological forces will overcome, however, the obstacles to integrating the EC telecommunication system, if not by 1992, then by 1993 or 1994; the path will not be smooth, and some of the mercantilistic policies might, initially, only be transferred from the member states to the Community.

European universities played an important role in the basic research that laid the foundation for the integrated semiconductor development; however, subsequent development, applied research, and training have been lagging behind focused efforts in the United States and Japan. In the view of the Brussels Eurocrats, strategic-military objectives generated the national support for applied R&D, education, and capital investment in the United States while Japan's MITI targeted the integrated semiconductor technology as a key discipline.

As a consequence, the EC produces only, on a per capita basis, about one-fourth of the microelectronic output of the United States. Even Germany "produces less than 1/3 of the integrated silicon switching circuits" used in its microelectronic products[17] (Figures 7.1 and 7.2).

Although the market for semiconductor components amounts to, roughly, only 6 percent of total electronic sales, Europe's backwardness in this key sector constitutes a serious weakness that will put it at a significant competitive disadvantage with its North American and Japanese competitors. By 1990, after efforts and considerable subsidies EC semiconductor manufacturers produced merely 56 percent of Europe's needs, and that included the European plants of Texas Instrument and Motorola; not counting the production of transplants Europe's share shrinks to 38.2 percent. By early 1992 Europe's market share has improved only negligibly, and whatever advances in applied technology and production have been made seem entirely due to alliances with non-European enterprise, such as the IBM–Siemens joint mega-chip venture. Even the French have finally given up on a European bootstrap solution for the electronics industry and are accepting such previously unpalatable solutions as an IBM acquisition of a minority holding in Bull.[18]

Moreover among the Europeans only Siemens produces the basic com-

Figure 7.1
Production and Trade in Semiconductor Switching Circuits

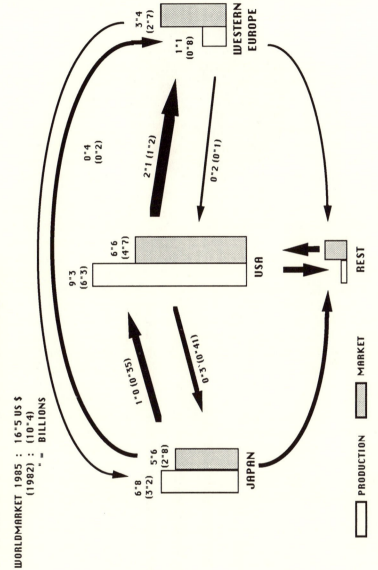

Source: E. Hofmeister, Siemens AG, Munich.

Figure 7.2
Semiconductors in Europe

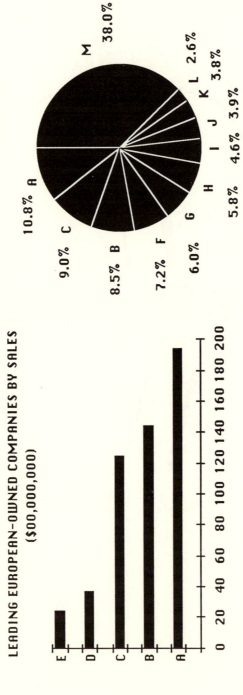

1990 EUROPEAN MARKET SHARE

38.0% M

10.8% A

9.0% C

8.5% B

7.2% F

6.0% G

5.8% H

4.6% I

3.9% J

3.8% K

2.6% L

LEADING EUROPEAN-OWNED COMPANIES BY SALES
($00,000,000)

0   20   40   60   80   100 120 140 160 180 200

E
D
C
B
A

A = PHILIPS, B = SGS-THOMSON, C = SIEMENS, D = GEC PLESSEY, E = TELEFUNKEN, F = MOTOROLA
G = TEXAS INSTRUMENTS, H = INTEL, I = TOSHIBA, J = NEC, K = NATIONAL SEMICONDUCTOR, L = AMD,
M = ALL OTHERS

Source: Dataquest, 1991.

modity chip d-rams, and Philips as well as SGS-Thompson have been losing money on their microchip and semiconductor operations. There is little chance that Europe will improve its performance in the microchip-semiconductor market in this century. The planned venture (1990) between Siemens and SGS-Thompson to build new manufacturing plants for 16 and 64-megabit d-rams failed because Siemens was reluctant to associate itself with a government (French and Italian) owned company beyond the already existing microprocessor joint venture. The French government is now frantically looking for an American ally for SGS-Thompson and is prepared to pour additional capital into the lossmaking operations. (The Italians are not.) Hewlett-Packard seems currently to be the choice of Mme. Cresson. Whether the alliance will take place is far from certain today.[19] There is very little time left, however, for a significant increase in Europe's semiconductor-microchip market share.[20]

Opportunities

There is almost unanimous agreement that the EC economy will obtain significant stimulation from a "Europe without frontiers." The elimination of the costly barriers to free trade, increasing competition, and enhanced economies of scale are the three factors that should rejuvenate Europe's industries. Estimates on exactly how large the economic benefits of a frontier-less market will be vary considerably. One of the most well-known EC studies, quoted in *The Economist*, estimated that market integration "could generate . . . $240 bn of extra wealth and provide up to 5 m new jobs."[21] One does not have to accept this optimistic but not untypical estimate to realize that a continental market will stimulate demand, and, especially, demand for additional telecommunication services and products.[22]

The increased telecom services demand will consist of three components:

1. Demand for the extension and technological improvement of existing telephone services in the poorer EC regions, especially the newcomers Portugal and Spain, but also Greece, Southern Italy, and Ireland. In this respect the ECO 780m STAR (Special Telecommunication Action for Regional Development) project for modernizing the telecom infrastructure of the Iberian peninsula and Greece is a good indication of the existing and potential demand for modern telecom equipment and networks that exists in the EC.

2. Increased demand for private (leased) lines and value-added transnational networks (VANs) from predominantly medium-sized firms, particularly in Germany, France, and the EFTA countries that are transforming themselves into "European" companies by establishing production-sales-research centers throughout the Community.

3. Increased demand in response to the economies of scale an integrated market will provide for the EC's telecommunication industry; moreover the increased competition of a continental market would force the medium-sized telecommunication companies to focus on specific areas (niches) in order to survive.

This trend can already be noted in the FRG. Germany's "second string" telecommunication companies (DeTeWe, Telenorma, ANT) benefited in the past from the DBP policy that paid above-market prices for telephone equipment and assured the smaller companies that they would receive subcontracts from Siemens and SEL for major DBP investment orders. The emerging DBP reorganization has prompted these companies to specialize in much narrower market segments.

Demand for office automation equipment, VAS, and VANs has been artificially depressed by PTT regulations within each country. A leading European telecom manager estimated that a deregulated telephone market would generate an annual 20 percent growth rate for terminal equipment, workstations, VAS, and VANs.[23] Particularly medium and small businesses have been prevented from utilizing fully the existing technology by bureaucratic PTT regulations and by, at least until 1990, excessively high fees for VAS, VANs, and leased lines. Since German telecommunication liberalization had been considered a test case for EC's telecommunication policy, it should be noticed that the deregulation process in the FRG corresponded fully to the Green Book recommendations and seems to be on schedule to reach the 1992 target. Significant changes in the FRG's telecommunication rate structure had been completed by 1991, according to DBP Minister Schwarz-Schilling.[24] Recent efforts by the German government to force DBP telecom to raise its tariffs in order to pay for the unexpectedly high unification costs upset the EC policy of lowering the telephone rates throughout Europe.

Altogether the EC standardization, deregulation, and tariff harmonization policy should, if not by 1992 then by 1995, give Europe the integrated telephone market that will give its leading telecommunication companies— Alcatel, Ericsson, Philips, and Siemens—an improved basis for international competition.[25] It is this aspect of integration that European planners value most.[26]

Threats

An integrated, liberalized European telecommunication market will provide a golden opportunity for the North American-Japanese IT giants (AT&T, Fujitsu, IBM, NEC, Northern Telecom) to expand their European market share aggressively. Except for AT&T all of these firms have already well-established production-research operations in Europe and AT&T's recent (1988, 1990) joint ventures with Telefonica Española and Italel may grow into viable manufacturing operations by the mid–1990s. IBM is particularly well established throughout Europe and only Alcatel, through its acquisitions of ITT's European telecommunication units, can rival IBM's ubiquitous European presence. It is feared, however, that IBM's greater experience in worldwide marketing, production, and research will enable it to capitalize on the economies of scale an integrated EC market would provide. The fear that non-European MNCs will, therefore, dominate the European telecommunication market pervades the EC and PTT bureaucracies and the second-line European IT manufacturing firms. This fear is, apparently, not shared by the leading EC enterprises Alcatel, Ericsson, Olivetti, Philips, and Siemens-Nixdorf, whose global aspirations prompt them to reject mercantilistic policies; however, influential groups within both the EC bureaucracy and various EC trade associations, trade unions, and ministries have been using the fear that foreign "multinationals" (primarily IBM) would replace the PTTs' domestic monopolies with a single international monopoly to advocate barriers to the free entry of non-European firms into the EC "until the European telecom industry can compete on a level playing field with the international multis."[27]

The mercantilistic EC tendencies that have emerged in the telecom case bring into the open two very distinct views of the nature of the integrated market that prevail in the Community: proponents of a liberal, deregulated Europe that will flourish as part of a free-trading East Asia–Europe–North America triad in which mutual open market access will generate growth through competition, and advocates of a mercantilistic Europe that would maintain tariffs and entry barriers until the integration of its market has been completed. There is, unfortunately, increasing evidence that France since 1988 has been attempting to forge a protectionist alliance with Italy and Belgium to force the EC to reverse its liberal telecom policy.

The very threat that non-EC telecommunication companies might derive the major benefit from an integrated European telecommunication market may have prompted the recent unprecedented cooperation among the major European IT-telecommunication enterprises. If the prevailing optimistic mood at Alcatel, Ericsson, Olivetti, and Siemens-Nixdorf is an indication, however, the threat of foreign domination of the EC telecom market may not materialize.

The reverse side of a possible foreign domination of the EC's IT market is the global aspirations of the major European telecommunication enterprises. Siemens' CEO K-H. Kaske has been particularly outspoken in explaining his global strategy, which seems to reflect the prevailing attitude among Europe's major IT concerns, and is worth noting. Kaske believes that the globalization of the telecommunication market and the increasing rate of technological innovation will require increasing economies of scale; a world-telecommunication market share of 15 percent will be necessary in order to remain a global competitor. The U.S. market, however, the most important telecommunication market in the world, is the playground where an enterprise's world-class qualification will be tested. The United States, according to Kaske, contains 40 to 50 percent of Siemens' accessible worldwide market, and intense effort, particularly during the six Kaske years, has increased Siemens' U.S. sales to $3 bn, 80 percent of it manufactured in America.[28]

Although the CEOs of Alcatel and the other major European telecom enterprises have been less outspoken than the prolific Kaske—a German Iacocca—their global aspirations are just as strong, and have in the past prevented serious cooperation among the major EC firms.

On the positive side, the global-minded telecommunication managers have opposed the mercantilistic tendencies in Japan and North America but especially in the EC. According to Kaske, "The European Community must remain open to the world market. Efforts to further liberalize trade . . . deserve our strong support. Such improvements are particularly important in preserving harmonious relations among the three biggest world trade partners—the EC, the USA and Japan."[29]

On the negative side, from the EC's point of view, the global aspiration and fierce competition among the major European telecom enterprises have threatened the EC strategy to overcome the fragmentation of the European IT industry by encouraging cooperation, joint ventures, and mergers among its leading enterprises (Brussels Eurocrats, for instance, have been dreaming of a Philips-Siemens merger for a long time). Although there has been a considerable increase in the cooperation on research and specialized production projects among European firms, especially during the last three years, the leading companies are still committed to a global strategy that conflicts with the EC's industrial policy:

Concerns like Siemens simply have to take an open-minded attitude toward the world markets, including the United States and Japan, not only because of the size of these markets, but also because important technological advances are being made there, just as in Europe. Cooperation between firms can therefore be hardly limited to the EC, nor can the relationship between the EC, on the one hand, and the United States and Japan, on the other, be an exclusive competitive one; it must also be marked by cooperation and partnership. My intention here is far from calling the significance of the EC into question. Indeed, the very fact that the U.S. and Japan will continue to be the European economy's chief industrial competitors . . . makes progress in the economic integration of Europe an imperative.[30]

Since Kaske defined the importance of the triad Siemens has been caught up in the momentum that "Europe 1992" has generated, and Siemens-Philips and Alcatel-ICL-Siemens projects have been flourishing. The EC moreover emphasizes that the rejuvenated post–1992 European Community with its 320 million citizens will become *the* most important market and encourages a shift in strategic priorities. Still, there is no indication that Alcatel, Philips, or Siemens are willing to sacrifice their global ambitions on the altar of an integrated European IT industry. "Siemens is primarily in the business of selling systems; and must (therefore) search the world market for the best solutions to his customer's (demands)."[31]

If the leading European firms are unable to reconcile the demands of the EC's industrial policy with their global aspirations the fragmentation of the European telecommunication–information-processing market will continue, and its domination by Japanese and North American enterprises will be prevented only by protectionist measures that will threaten the global economy and the European IT industry. There simply is no evidence that protection and subsidies have been able to revitalize an uncompetitive industry.

The EC's view of telecommunication as a Schumpeterian "leading industry" determined its policy to encourage concentration and merger within the EC and to discourage cooperation of European IT-telecommunication firms with non-European enterprises. European liberals (free market advocates) have distrusted the mercantilistic proclivities of the Brussels Eurocrats ever since de Gaulle changed the nature of the Community. Much of the opposition to the EC telecommunication policy has come from liberal German academic telecommunication specialists, including members of the government telecommunication (Witte) committee. Their objections to EC telecommunication policies are epitomized in a paper by Karl-Heinz Neumann, director of Germany's prestigious telecommunication policy institute, WIK. His main points are:

1. There is little justification for the EC view that (a) European telecommunication is not competitive in a global market; (b) European manufacturers cooperate little with each other and too much with non-Europeans.

2. It is wrong to assume that an integrated European market might provide greater advantages for the leading non-European concerns unless the EC follows a protectionist policy. A protectionist strategy would be a serious mistake since "greater competitiveness is not obtained through protectionism and less competition but only through more competition."

3. The effort of the EC to obtain uniform European policies for terminal equipment access, to create common open telecom network (ISDN) and transmission standards, and to achieve harmonization of lower, cost-based tariffs is a desirable goal but the hurried efforts of the EC to achieve a uniform European standard may be counter productive in view of the different national and institutional strategies that helped shape the structure of Europe's PTT policies.[32]

If points 1 and 2 of Neumann's critique of EC policies reflect the view of the liberal European telecommunication community, his point 3 reflects the thinking of the PTTs and CEPT during the mid–1980s (all concerned have changed their opinion in the meantime). Altogether, these views represent a threat to the creation of a European telecommunication infrastructure as the basis for the emergence of a "leading edge" European telecommunication industry.

SWOT Summary

Establishing the goal of an integrated EC by 1992 has created its own momentum that will overcome the obstacles identified in the SWOT analysis. Since the economic and technological trends of the time demand an integrated telecommunication infrastructure to assure Europe's continued competitiveness, the objective facts support the emotional momentum. The only question that remains is the openness of the telecommunication system that will emerge.

THE CONSEQUENCES OF EUROPEAN INTEGRATION FOR THE U.S. TELECOMMUNICATION INDUSTRY

An integrated European telecommunication network would enable the U.S. industry to sell terminal equipment, VAS, and VAN effectively throughout Europe. Although a standardized ISDN network might, in the short run, seem threatening to large American IT firms that have been selling effectively proprietary information systems, the anticipated increase in demand for all IT products would probably benefit even the major manufacturers of vendor-dependent systems. Europeans believe that their terminal-equipment VAS markets are already quite open and are citing as evidence the telecommunication trade deficit the EC had been incurring in its trade with the United States since 1986.[33]

Officially at least, EC commissioners and the CEOs of the leading European IT companies welcome American and Japanese competition, provided there is mutual market access. It may amaze American officials, but the Europeans do not believe that the U.S. market is as open as Americans imagine. We shall cite two examples:

Mr. Henri Froment-Meurice, former French ambassador in Bonn, calls for the Community to trade market-entry for American and Japanese against market-opening by them to European exporters: Since "reciprocity" is in vogue with many EEC and American trade experts, M. Froment-Meurice may be pushing at an open door.[34]

"With the United Kingdom now poised to fully open up its telecommunication market to foreign companies it is time for the United States to do the same," said Iain Valance, British Telecom Chairman . . . in Washington. "The United States has historically led the way in competition in telecommunication," Valance said. "This move (i.e., the government White Paper, *Competition and Choice: Telecommunication Policy for the 1990's*) takes the United Kingdom well out in front. . . . There is a worrying lack of reciprocity" Valance said of the U.S. refusal to allow foreign firms such as British Telecom to invest in telecommunications common carriers and broadcasters.[35]

Although a free market in terminal equipment, VAS, and VAN (including rapid extension in the availability of leased lines) is very likely to occur by and after 1992, with full participation by U.S. and Japanese firms, the PTT procurement policies for switches and network transmission equipment will be deregulated only slowly, although the EC commission has been moving quite decisively. It is doubtful that an intra-European competitive PTT equipment procurement market will truly emerge by 1992, because France and its allies Italy and Spain are not likely to change their purchasing practices in spite of EC directives and European Court decision;[36] it is in this area that the U.S. companies will have the greatest difficulty gaining significant access.

The EC commission originally believed that only a slow, gradual deregulation of the PTT procurement market was politically feasible and set the most conservative liberalization goals for 1992 (initially the EC had recommended that 10 percent of annual government procurement tenders be opened to other EC countries). The United States, on the other hand, had chosen precisely the network equipment market as a test case for its MAFF (Market Access Fact Finding) strategy. The basic premise for the MAFF strategy was the U.S. contention that it gave away market access through divestiture, and therefore had the right to restrict the U.S. market to foreign countries that had not changed their procurement policies in order to give American companies an opportunity to compete. The EC's decisive action on procurement took the United States by surprise.

The EC had been rejecting the U.S. demand to change its slowly evolving telecommunication policy because the American divestiture unexpectedly created access to the American market, and had turned a 1980 $1 bn surplus into a 1986 $1.7 bn deficit. Regardless of whether the U.S. telecommunication liberalization was responsible for the negative trade deficit, the EC could not be responsible for it, since it had been running a consistent deficit in telecommunication trade with the United States. The deficit was still ECU 0.6 bn in 1986, declined to ECU 0.5 bn in 1987, and shrank further to ECU 0.4 bn in 1988.[37]

The EC also strongly objected to the U.S. strategy to single out individual EC members, particularly Germany, for bilateral negotiations on telecom trade. Under current EC legislation, individual member states cannot negotiate bilateral agreements that conflict with EC regulations. U.S. disregard of the EC in this respect is reminiscent of the Soviet refusal to acknowledge the existence of the Community during the 1950s and 1960s. In particular, the American effort to pressure Germany to change its network standards in order to enable an American manufacturer without European subsidiaries to sell its equipment threatens the very heart of the EC policy. The fact that the United States has been running a substantial trade surplus over the past six years with the FRG in the telecommunication sector does not strengthen the U.S. case.[38]

The U.S. MAFF strategy had the potential for a first-class U.S.-EC row that could have had a negative impact not only on the evolving international aspect of the new EC telecommunication order but also on the entire U.S.-EC trade relations. There is little doubt that protectionists on both sides of the Atlantic reinforced each other's positions. The EC has been taking a much harder line on these issues than the Germans, who have been using American pressure to overcome domestic opposition to deregulation.[39]

The mutual irritation over MAFF talks, excessively rigorous standards, and heavy-handed trade negotiations on both sides cannot disguise the benefits the U.S. telecom industry will derive from an open, integrated European market. Similarly, it is just as much in the interest of the EC to maintain its position in the American market. It is my belief, therefore, that the economic benefits and opportunities of a strong U.S.-EC trade will overcome both current irritations and the myriads of difficulties Europe's "romp to 1992" will bring with it. The years that have followed the Green Paper have liberalized the European telecommunication system more than most Americans anticipated.

TELECOMMUNICATION IN EUROPE FOUR YEARS AFTER THE GREEN PAPER

Major changes have occurred in European telecommunication systems during the past four years as a result of the surprisingly swift implementation of the Green Paper recommendations and the concomitant establishment of an open network policy (ONP). Both the Green Paper and ONP attempted to limit the ability of public network operators (the former PTTs that had been liberalized in the United Kingdom and Germany) to retain monopoly power through bureaucratic practices. Since 1988, the EC has reemphasized its initial industrial telecom policy of replacing the fragmented European telecom network and telecom-information industries with a common, standardized infrastructure and a "harmonized" Europe-wide equipment market; only a harmonized market would enable the major European telecom enterprises to sell their products in all member nations and thus develop the economies of scale to compete globally with their Japanese and North American rivals. The EC uses the term "harmonization" to describe its efforts to coordinate the various national telecommunication regulations in order to facilitate the cross-border movements of goods and services, a necessary step to create a *European* telecommunication industry, market, and network. The term "harmonization," or more precisely, "harmonization of access conditions to the network," has a second, more specific meaning and refers to the 1990 EC directive establishing an open network provision (ONP), "a stable framework for the continuous process of . . . [establishing] access and usage conditions."[40]

The ONP concept has been interpreted in the United States as creating obstacles to market access. There is little justification for this interpretation. The term "open" means that "standards and interfaces offered for interconnection tariff principles and usage conditions, and provisions of frequencies" must be clearly and openly stated to enable all vendors who can meet EC access conditions, or the access conditions of a single member, to connect its equipment.[41] The ONP is, of course, incompatible with proprietary network standards but very similar to the open, vendor-neutral private networks of General Motors (MAP) and Boeing (TOP).

The Open Network Provision Directive

The ONP framework directive that facilitates access of private enterprises to the public networks, and the article 90 (Treaty of Rome) telecommunication service directive establishing the right for independent, private companies to offer new services on the telecommunication network, are closely related.[42] (An article 90 directive is issued by the EC under article 90 of the Treaty of Rome, establishing a common market. France and other member countries challenged the commission's right to use article 90 during 1989. The court upheld the EC in March 1991, as we have already noted.) The major features of the ONP directive are as follows:

1. Technical interfaces and service features will be subject to European standards to be adopted by ETSI. Service providers complying with those standards will be able to offer their services throughout the whole European Community.
2. The ONP directive is a "framework" directive to be followed by directives on specific issues. (In particular there were specific ONP directives for leased lines, voice telephony, ISDN, and packet switching by early 1991.) ONP directives intend to harmonize technical interfaces and end discriminatory tariff principles. Technical harmonization will be achieved in close collaboration with ETSI. In addition, in line with the article 90 telecom services directive, independent suppliers will have a guaranteed right of access to the national networks for new and developing services.

In February 1991, the EC recommended to the member governments that leased lines be leased to private companies in a "non-discriminatory transparent way."[43] The February 1991 recommendation is a further extension of the ONP and the services directive. The EC chose not to impose the leased-line liberalization through an article 90 directive in order to smooth over current tensions with member governments over excessive use of article 90 to bypass council of ministers approval.

The ONP directives do not affect the liberalized British and German systems, but would reduce the monopoly power of the public network operators in the rest of the EC. Although several EC countries may be slow in implementing every feature of the ONP directives, there can be little doubt that Europe will have come close to operating a telecommunication system that will generally conform to the ONP. The EC telecom policy will ultimately establish a European telecommunication network with the traditional PTTs, or their successors the public telecommunication operators (PTOs), reduced to the role of the BOCs in the predivestiture Bell system. This Europe-wide network may come earlier than expected— my guess is by 2010—but in the meantime the 1987 Green Paper *Toward a Dynamic European Economy* provided the initial short-run guidelines for this long-run development. By 1991 virtually the entire set of Green Paper recommendations already had been either approved by the council of ministers or implemented through EC commission directives.[44]

In order to assess the unusually quick rate of implementation we present in table 7.4 the EC commission's long-run policy objectives and the success in achieving implementation.

Table 7.4
EC Policy Objectives

Strategic Goals of EC Telecom Policy

1. Adapt national regulatory systems to new technological conditions and develop uniform, common European networks and regulations.
2. Reconcile public service objectives with broader consumer choice.
3. Create broad Europe-wide consensus on telecom reform (i.e., maintain national PTT monopoly on basic telephone service and network, within a broader, Europe-wide, harmonized system).

Status of Key Green Paper Provisions

Recommendations	Achievements (as of Dec. 1991)
1. Continued gradual establishment of a competitive terminal (CPE) equipment market by 1992	Virtually achieved by 1990. Only Italy and Spain still have restrictions on terminal equipment sales.
2. Provide an open, competitive market for value-added services	Great progress has been made toward establishing a fully reregulated VAS market in the EC. Continued controversy over the definition of "basic" or "value-added" service. France Télécom insists that ISDN is a "basic" service. Issue before the European Court of Justice.
3. Maintain government (PTT) monopoly of basic telephone service (POTS) and networks	This is the current status in much of the EC. Remaining questions: What is *basic* service, and will the definition change over time? Will ISDN become a basic service by 1995?
4. Liberalize satellite communication	
4a. Introduce competition into satellite transmission market	Prompted primarily by technological developments, a relaxation of restrictions on satellite communication has occurred. Need for satellite communication in East Germany, has prompted liberalization moves by DBP's Telecom. United Kingdom has liberalized satellite networks.

4b. Establish a common European position in satellite communication	Little progress so far. Latin Europeans (France, Italy, Spain) favor stronger regulations than Germanic countries (United Kingdom, Germany, Denmark, Holland)
5. Separate regulatory and operational functions of PTTs	Achieved in most EC countries, especially Germany, the United Kingdom, Holland, France (more or less); not yet in Italy, Spain
6. Guarantee free cross-border movement of (telecom) services in compliance with the Treaty of Rome	Will be achieved by December 1992. In effect already, on a bilateral basis. France's Minitel available in Germany, Germany's BTX in France.
7. Establish and harmonize *cost*-based tariffs	Slow but steady progress. France, Spain, and Italy slow to adapt leased-line tariffs but cost-based tariffs will be in force by December 1992 due to EC pressure and threat of bypass. German leased-line tariffs have decreased by 50 percent since 1988.
8. Establish common European position on international telecom issues	This recommendation has been more or less achieved by papering over the philosophical differences between the Latin and Germanic countries. The ITU conference WATTC '89 is a good example of an EC effort to reach a common position.
9. Liberalize government procurement in telecom sector, in particular open PTT procurement to all EC members. See Bulletin of the EC (Supplement 688).	Controversy within the EC Commission (DG XIV Telecommunication Directorate versus DG IV Competition Directorate) and among EC memberstates led to compromise: the EC procurement directive of January 1990 requires that as of December 1992 all procurement will be open to all member-states; a "buy Europe" provision opens telecom market to non-Europeans provided they underbid the lowest European offer by more than 3 percent (*Note*: The Buy American Act gives U.S. firms a 6 percent margin).
10. Postpone decisions on external EC tariff on telecom equipment until after 1992.	This recommendation is still in effect; it postpones the discussion over the nature of the EC, not only concerning telecommunication but for all aspects of international trade.

BEYOND THE GREEN PAPER: SIGNIFICANT
DEVELOPMENTS IN EUROPEAN TELECOMMUNICATION

The EC telecommunication policy has as its goal the creation of a truly European communication system that will include initially both the EC and EFTA countries (Austria, Finland, Iceland, Norway, Sweden, Switzerland) and ultimately all of Europe west of the Ural Mountains. Although the Green Paper spelled out specific liberalization requirements for its member-states to meet the goal of free movements of capital and services by 1992, it was always expected that the EFTA countries, and, after 1989, Eastern Europe would ultimately be included in the European telecom system. The means for extending EC telecom policy to all European countries has been the Conference of European Post and Telecommunication Administration (CEPT), which includes all European countries west of, what used to be, the Iron Curtain. Poland and Hungary have already applied for CEPT membership and we can safely assume that during 1991–92 the other East European countries will follow them.

Several EC initiatives have extended EC telecom policy to all of Europe.

CEPT has become the official lead agency in establishing the European Telecommunication Standards Institute (ETSI) and in adopting its provisions. ETSI consists of a small professional staff, located near Nice, and with a wide membership comprising all European public telecommunication operators (PTOs, previously PTTs), as well as equipment manufacturers and users. (U.S. telecom administrations have observer status at ETSI.) ETSI has surprised most observers by moving quickly to establish rigorous standards and by coming close to completing European standards for digital mobile (cellular) telephone transmission and cordless telephones.[45]

CEPT has been instrumental in transmitting EC policy on harmonization, ONP, and ISDN to all European PTOs. North American equipment and VAS/VAN sellers will find that one set of standards will by 1992 satisfy all European telecom administrations and users. Thus, services such as Minitel or BTX could be used throughout Europe without special gateways. (There is some doubt about Minitel living up to these criteria, since it does not really follow ETSI or even the broader CCITT standards.) American VAS providers that have adopted CCITT standards and have been thoroughly established in Europe, such as AT&T, American Express, and Dow-Jones, will benefit greatly from the EC-CEPT harmonization efforts, while providers of proprietary VAS/VANs that do not conform to ETSI or CCITT standards will encounter difficulties.

A major success of the "harmonization" drive has been the quick progress ETSI has made in developing a tight set of ISDN standards for Europe. In August 1990 the final ETSI standards had been established and sent to all ETSI members for approval. Standards for digital mobile networks

(ASM) were issued in July 1991. In the meantime France and Germany have been ahead of schedule in providing ISDN service on their national networks, and neither country has difficulties in adapting their current ISDN version to the final ETSI standards.

In spite of the progress made toward establishing a liberalized integrated European telecommunication system, however, several crucial issues have not been resolved, and may complicate post–1992 developments. These problem issues are political in nature and deserve a brief discussion.

The concept that the state provides an efficient infrastructure that is accessible to all is deeply ingrained in the value structure of Europeans. The European PTTs, especially those north of the Alps and the Pyrenees, have made the concept "uniform, universal" services a dogma that not only determined their strategies in developing their telecommunication systems but allowed them to oppose all alternatives to their service and network monopolies; private competition, they asserted, would lead to "cream-skimming" marketing in the most profitable segments of their operations, and thus leave the PTTs only in the undisturbed dominance of such money-losing services as bringing the same variety and quality of service to the peasant in Upper Bavaria and the banker in Frankfurt (uniform service) or the fisherman in the Bretagne or Friesland (universal service). Clearly, uniform, universal telephone service had to be subsidized in order to assure telephone access to subscribers in less accessible areas. The simultaneous emergence of competition in value-added services and the introduction of expensive new telecom products by the PTTs, such as videotex or ISDN, make adherence to the uniform and universal paradigm difficult, especially if the surpluses that financed cross-subsidization are reduced by competition. France, from President Mitterrand to the France Télécom managers, seems determined to abide by the uniform and universal service concept and, furthermore, wants to extend the notion of basic service to all new products that can be connected to private, non-business users, such as ISDN.[46]

The contrast between the economic nationalism of the Latin EC countries and the more liberal free market views of the Germanic countries has made it difficult for the EC to speak with one strong voice. The service components of the GATT negotiations, in particular, have suffered from the EC's inability to take a strong stand on liberalization of services. Hence the specter of continued EC-U.S controversies over telecom market access issues has reemerged. Such controversies tend to strengthen the protectionist elements on either side of the Atlantic and present a clear danger to further liberalization of the global telecom system.

Since 1987 the EC has had, on the average, annual trade deficits of ECU 1 bn and ECU .5 bn with Japan and the United States, respectively. These trade deficits are merely symptoms of the continued Japanese and American dominance of the information-technology sector. The post–1992 common telecom market may come too late to make the European telecom industry competitive with Japan and North America, or may even aid the non-European telecom giants in conquering a larger share of the European market. Although the fears of Euro-pessimists are, most likely, exaggerated, the continued inability of EC members to reconcile their ideological differences adds to Europe's perceived weakness in the telecommunication information sector.

The EC has made great strides in developing the technical standards and procedures that are necessary for establishing a common, integrated European telecommunication network by 1992. In spite of the retention of PTT monopolies in basic (voice) telephone services and networks, increased competition in terminal equipment and services will benefit the users, especially the larger business users. The emergence of a major European telecom equipment and service market will benefit both the large European champions (Alcatel, Ericcson, Siemens) and those non-European equipment and service providers that have had manufacturing and R&D locations in Europe for decades. The opening of Eastern Europe will provide business opportunities for the key players and may postpone the weeding out of the least efficient enterprises for another decade.

THE OPEN TELECOMMUNICATION MARKET COLLIDES WITH THE FORTRESS EUROPE

Since the EC was launched toward a single market in 1985, different visions of 1992 Europe have prevailed within the EC commission and its senior bureaucrats and among the member countries. Since telecommunication was included in the "Project Europe 1992" in 1987, the EC program for a European telecommunication system has been a major factor in building an open common market, free of monopolies, industry subsidies, and protectionist devices. One cannot dismantle well-entrenched monopolies in telecommunication and open up procurement to a pan-European and even international tender without affecting the ethos of the entire Community. There is no question that as far as telecommunication was concerned, the EC technocrats "were the good guys" (to quote a German EC observer); this term applies not only to the previously mentioned senior technocrats Ungerer and Schuringa, but above all to Competition Commissioner Leon Brittan, who in 1988 and 1989 used article 90 of the Treaty of Rome to push through directives liberalizing terminal equipment market value-added services, including electronic data interchange, and leased lines. Brittan had been supported by the German industry commissioner Martin Bangemann, the Italian telecommunication commissioner Filipo Pandolfi, and in the end by EC president Jacques Delors. During early 1992, however, the clash between interventionists and free marketeers became more intense, with Britain opposing Cresson's plans to subsidize state-owned industries. Under French pressure the Germans, including Bangemann, and Delors have begun to waffle. A dirigiste Fortress Europe is, in 1992, no longer as unlikely as it seemed in 1991.[47]

The position in the council of ministers and in the EC commission has been changing during the last eighteen months, however; the European electronics and computer industries have been demanding EC support to compete with the United States and Japan, and the automobile industry, supported by France and Italy, has been pushing for protection in a self-serving, unabashed manner that would make Iacocca blush. Brittan, however, has been able so far to continue at least the liberalization of the telecommunication industry and the deregulation in Britain, Germany, the Netherlands, Sweden, and France, so that in at least this field a competitive, deregulated market in a global environment is assured.[48] Can 1992 Europe be half-fortress and half-free? The answer lies with the computer and electronics industry where the crucial battle within the EC and the council of ministers will take place. (Forget about the auto industry. If the EC actually passes the protectionist anti-Japanese bill considered during May 1991, the demise of several protected key companies, such as Renault and Fiat, will be assured. We all know how similar legislation helped Detroit's Big Three.)

It is, at first glance, ironic that the highly competitive computer industry would spawn protectionist industrial policy pressures, while the traditionally monopolistic telecommunication industries and network operators have at least accepted, and in many cases now even support competitive policies. It seems that BT, DBP Telekom, and France Télécom have adopted the outlook and strategies of the regional Bell holding companies: keep up a rear guard fight to maintain the dwindling monopolistic position, but act aggressively in the global market to eliminate vestiges of (somebody else's) anticompetitive protection in order to share fully in the profitable, growing global market of network management, value-added services, and value-added networks.

The European computer and electronics industry, on the other hand, has been considered by the EC to be one of its most important leading industries—a leading industry, however, that by 1992 had not improved its competitive position vis-à-vis the American and Japanese industries, in spite of five to six years of EC-supported research projects, subsidies, and joint ventures. As late as November 1990, the EC was still committed to a "minimalist industrial policy" that rejected industrial subsidies and was considered a victory for the EC's free-marketers.[49] By February 1991, however, the EC commission's information-technology directorate under its *dirigiste* director Michel Carpentier produced a policy paper that asked for (more) help for the strategic computer and electronic industries.

The figures provided by Carpentier demonstrate that Europe's computer industry has not caught up with America's and is now threatened by Japan's. What the policy paper does not show is that in spite of EC-sponsored projects and joint-ventures such as JESSI (Joint European Semiconductor Selicon Institute; JESSI includes IBM Europe among its participants) the industry's market position has not changed. In the electrical component market the Japanese still hold about 41 percent of the world market, the Americans 31 percent, and European firms 17 percent. In computers Europe's trade deficit, primarily with the United States, is also still $10 bn; the European information-technology and electronics equipment industry provides 69 percent of Europe's demand.[50]

The policy paper proposes "more of the same" measures that have not helped before: more EC-sponsored research, more subsidies, more protection, greater efforts to obtain economies of scale by encouraging mergers or at least greater cooperation among European champions. The great faith of the information-technology directorate in the economies of scale is not supported by the American experience where relatively small companies such as Sun, Microsoft, and Apple have gained market share against larger rivals in a global market. A revealing statistic is provided by *The Economist* of April 1991 that ranks computer companies according to sales in Europe per employees. The top four are, in order, Apple, Compaq, Sun, and IBM followed by Siemens, Bull, ICL, and Olivetti. On the average, Americans sell more than twice the number of computers per employee than Europeans.[51]

This is not the place to consider the managerial shortcomings of the European computer industry. Its inability to produce a technically competent product at half the cost, with half the employees, is important only because it affects the future of the EC. "Computer firms everywhere are suffering from economic slow-down. But European companies have been the worst hit. Sheltered behind government contracts, trade protection, subsidies and other less overt forms of favoritism, they have been predictably slow to respond to what their private-sector customer wants."[52]

There are good indications that some computer companies such as ICL, Olivetti, and Siemens-Nixdorf are looking for alternatives to EC protectionism. The planners in directorate XIII supported by France's insistence on creating a world-class French, or at least French-European information-technology industry, have pushed the issue of a *dirigiste* EC industrial policy to the top of the agenda. The commitment of directorate XIII and France to an interventionist policy leads us back to the question raised before: Can Europe's economy be half-free and half-protectionist? Given the current lineup of forces in Brussels and in the EC council of ministers we can answer, probably yes. On many issues, including telecommunication, a liberal coalition within the commission led by Brittan and Frans Andriessen (foreign affairs) has so far prevailed, supported by the Germanic countries in the council of ministers. On issues of particular interest to France and

Mitterrand, such as computers and automobiles, we can expect the emergence of a protectionist Fortress Europe policy. Actually this half-free, half-protectionist policy is not very different from the U.S. policy, where protectionist reality and free-market vocabulary frequently clash.

We ought to add that the demarcation lines between "*dirigistes*" and "free-marketers" in the EC (and the United States) are not stable. A conservative coalition victory in France or a socialist one in the United Kingdom and Germany would change the lineup, at least in the council of ministers. Under these conditions, we shall see that in the global industries, especially telecommunication and computers, most major players will manufacture, carry on research, and service their customers in every major country in East Asia, Europe, and North America. As this process continues we may expect that IBM, Siemens, and Sony will lose some of their national identity and become increasingly global companies, just as IBM Europe and Siemens U.S. have already become virtually European or American companies, respectively.

The ability to plan and operate as a global information-technology company may become the decisive competitive advantage in both coping with managed trade and exploiting the advantages of free markets.

NOTES

1. "(The goal to integrate Europe by) '1992,' has been adopted by almost all politicians with evangelical enthusiasm." "A Survey of France," *The Economist* (March 12, 1988): 18.

2. A good example is provided by the initial opposition of some of the member-states and CEPT (the association of European PTTs) to the EC directive to give Europe-wide access to any telecom equipment that already has been cleared for network access by a European PTT. The disagreement seemed to reflect different interpretations of the EC commission's powers rather than principle. The commission claimed that article 90 of the Treaty of Rome gave it the right to impose deregulation by directive. The United Kingdom, Germany, and France opposed the EC interpretation, because they were afraid that it might set dangerous precedents. The American reporting of this issue had been entirely misleading (see "Europe's Phone-Deregulation Drive Slips," *Wall Street Journal*, March 31, 1988): 15.

3. "They Have Designed the Future and It Might Just Work," *The Economist* (February 13, 1988): 45.

4. The integration of the EC's economy required the adoption of about 300 laws, to be passed by the council of ministers. About 200 have been adapted so far. The rest will be submitted to the council over the next 12 months.

5. "Leading industries," according to Schumpeter, drive economic growth and change and determine a country's economic-strategic strength (*Business Cycles*, vol. 1 [New York: McGraw-Hill, 1939], chap. 4).

6. Subsequent activities of the EC that culminated in the Green Paper responded to the instructions of the council of (industry) ministers. See Karl-Heinz

Neumann, "Die Deutsche Bundespost vor der Herausforderung der Europäischen Telekommunikations-Politik," *Discussion Paper Wissenschaftliches Institut für Telekokmmunikationsforschung (WIK)* 23, November 1986. See also Herbert Ungerer, "The European Community Strategy," paper presented at the Communications Policy Research Conference, Windsor, United Kingdom, June 18–20, 1986.

7. Actually, European R&D efforts, if taken together, were comparable to the American performance in the mid–1980s. The German IFO-Institut für Wirtschaftsforschung measures R&D efficiency by percentage of patents obtained in IT, material science, and biotechnology and presents the following figures for 1984:

Country	Patents
United States	33%
Japan	26%
West Germany	17
United Kingdom	8
France	6
European Community	31%
Others	10%

Source: Statistische Anagaben: IFO, 1985 also quoted in *ZPF* (journal of the DBP) (January 1, 1988): 4.

8. The ESPRIT and RACE budgets allocate their funds as follows:

ESPRIT

Advanced information processing	22.2%
Software technology	18.7%
Microelectronics	24.5%
CIM	13.4%
Office equipment suppliers	21.2%

RACE

Integrated broad-band communications (IBC) technologies	66.0%
IBC development and implementation	12.2%
Integration of functions	21.8%

Source: German Review (January 1988): 7–8.

ESPRIT and RACE are the two most significant European research efforts. Others worth mentioning are EUREKA, sponsored by France in the early 1980s to launch "Europe's technological renaissance," and its spinoff EURECOM, devoted to the development of broad-band transmission; STAR, which will spend $1 b on up-grading Iberian and Greek telecom systems, is also worth noting.

9. The rapid fluctuations of the exchange rates make it difficult to convert European currencies into dollars. From a purchasing power viewpoint, it is safe to accept ECU 1 = U.S. $1 and DM2 = U.S. $1 rates. (Actually DM 2.30: U.S. $1 is closer to the real purchasing power parity.)

10. For a brief, perceptive analysis of the EC's industrial policy controversy, see "Europe's Industrial Tug-of-war," *The Economist* (January 25, 1992): 65–66.

11. Introductory sentence in Commission of the European Community, *Green Book Summary: The Development of the Common Market for Telecommunication Services and Equipment*, Brussels, April 1987, 1. The quotation is the author's translation from the German version of the EC *Green Book*.

12. Commission of the European Communities, "Towards a Competitive Community-Wide Telecommunications Market in 1992: Implementing the Green Paper on the Development of the Common Market for Telecommunication Services and Equipment," COM (88) 48 final, Brussels, February 9, 1988, 3.

13. Eberhard Witte, *Neuordnung der Telekommunikation* (Report of the Government Commission on Telecommunication) (Heidelberg: R v Decker-Schenck, 1987).

14. Jean-Pierre Chamoux, Chef de la Mission a Réglementation, *The Current French Telecommunication Policy*, Ministére des Postes et Télécommunications, 1988. See chap. 4 for a discussion of the Chirac–Longuet–Chamoux reform proposals.

15. "ISDN: Oceans Apart," *Network World* (August 4, 1986): 1. Although written over five years ago, these comments are as true today as they were then.

16. International Standards Organization (ISO) and CITT protocols are fully accepted by CEPT.

17. Hans-Joachim Queisser, "Der Sprung vom Komponierten zum Integrierten," *Zeitschrift fúr Post und Fernmeldewesen* (*ZPF*) (February 26, 1988): 10 (*ZPF* is published by the DBP).

18. See "Un plan Cresson pour sauver l'electronique, *Le Monde* (December 19, 1991): 1; Caroline Monnot, "Insuffisance de capitaux, contraintes europeennes," idem, p. 30.

19. Pierre Angel Gay, Caroline Monnot. "Le choix américain de Bull," *Le Monde,* January 15, 1992, pp 1, 18.

20. Ibid. Note also "National Champions Become Laggards," *Financial Times* (April 29, 1991): 17; and Mächtige Europa-Allianz, *Wirtschaftswoche* (June 1, 1990): 7.

21. "Single European Market," *The Economist* (April 23, 1988): 52–53.

22. Two ambitious forecasts of 1992 benefits are Paolo Cecchini, *The Economics of 1992* (London: Wildwood House, 1988); and the "Economics of 1992," *European Economy* 35 (March 1988) (Luxembourg).

23. Claus Kessler, senior vice president of Siemens, at the March 1986 CeBIT fair in Hanover, FRG. See also his "Market, Technik und Gesellschaft," *Frankfurter Allgemeine Zeitung* (March 15, 1988).

24. "The liberalization of telecommunication services must deal emphatically with the DBP's tariff structure. The proposed liberalization (i.e., Witte recommendations) will only lead to new services and competition if today's *usage-*

dependent rates for national (i.e., DBP) services are lowered, and replaced by a different system over a transition period. . . . *Usage-dependent* tariffs for data and voice transmission will be replaced in the near future by a cost-oriented flat rate structure" (C. Schwarz-Schilling, "1988: An Important Year for the DBP," *ZPF* (January 26, 1988): 1; author's translation, emphasis added.

25. Sweden's Ericsson has made great efforts to appear as a European and not as a Swedish (EFTA) firm. Especially its acquisition of 10 percent of France's state-owned CGCE has helped its "European" posture. EFTA-EC cooperation will intensify during the next four years. The second five-year ESPRIT research effort approved in April 1988 encourages explicitly cooperation with EFTA firms.

26. W. G. Berger, "Establishing the European Internal Market: Implications for Information Technology," *Siemens Review* (January 1988): 4.

27. A paraphrase of views frequently expressed by leading "fair trade" advocates in Europe. For a typical example of a European "level playing-field" speech, see M. Michael Carpentier, "The Future of European Telecommunication Policy: Moving Beyond the Green Paper," *U.S. Council on International Business* (March 1988): 3, 9–14.

28. The last figures are quotes from a Kaske interview in the *Welt Woche* (WW) (February 5, 1988): 42. The balance of the views ascribed to Kaske are gleaned from a number of speeches and articles by or about Kaske. Note especially "Siemens: Kultur-Revolution," *Wirschafts Woche* (February 5, 1988): 34–43; and Karl-Heinz Kaske, "Europe's Response to the World Economy," *Siemens Review* (January 1987): 4–8.

29. Ibid., 8.

30. Ibid., 4.

31. Kaske, interview; author's translation.

32. Karl-Heinz Neumann, "Die Deutsche Bundespost vor der Hearusforderung der Europäischen Telekommunikationspolitik," *Discussion Paper* 23, November 1986, WIK (WIK is the German acronym for Scientific Institute for Telecommunication Services). WIK is sponsored by the DBP and serves as its think-tank, but is completely free to publish research in accordance with the views of its staff.

33.

1986	exports to the United States	$368 m
1986	imports from the United States	$988 m
	EC deficit	$620 m

Quoted by M. M. Carpentier, director-general, EC Telecommunication, Information Industries, in *Future of European Telecommunication Policy,* 11.

34. "Single European Market," *The Economist* (April 23, 1988): 54.

35. "BT Chairman Calls for Open Market," *Telephone* (November 26, 1990): 8.

36. See Commission of the European Communities, *Proposal for a Council Directive on the Procurement Procedures of Entities Operating in the Telecommunication Sector*, Brussels, January 23, 1989. The directive was implemented in Jan-

uary 1990, and upheld by the European Court of Justice in March 1991. See "Court Boosts Brussels' Legal Powers," *Financial Times* (March 20, 1991): 2.

37. R. A. Cawley and P. Verbiergt, *Intra-EC and Extra-EC Trade Flows in Telecommunication Equipment in 1988*, Commission of the European Communities, June 1989.

38. See Thomas Schnöring, *Die Deutsche Informations und Kommunikationtechnische Industrye und Ihre Internationale Wettbewersbsposition*, WIK Discussion Paper 39, January 1988, 89.

39. Note, for instance, Schwarz-Schilling's kind words about the free trade policies of the Reagan administration: "The (Reagan) administration . . . worried about the continuation of free world trade, attempts with all its strength to prevent the progress of protectionist measures (in the U.S.) but does demand market-access (in Germany). . . . We (must), as quickly as possible, further liberalize equipment and services in the telecommunication area. There must not be any delay or it is possible that the U.S. will retaliate." (C. Schwarz-Schilling, "1988: An Important Year for the DBP," *ZPF* [January 26, 1988]: 6; author's translation).

40. Herbert Ungerer, *Telecommunication in Europe*, European Perspective series (Brussels: European Community, 1988), 202.

41. Ibid.

42. *Dawn of a New Era in European Telecommunication* (Brussels: European Community 1990), 2–3.

43. "EC Plans for Telecoms Leasing," *Financial Times* (February 21, 1991): 4.

44. Note especially the approval of the Green Paper objectives by the June 1988 council of ministers resolutions on the "Development of the Common Market for Telecommunication Services and Equipment up to 1992," the EC commission directive of 1988 on competition on terminal markets, and the June 1990 directive on telecom services.

45. Herbert Ungerer, *Current Status on Progress on Implementation of the EC Green Paper*, Telecommunication Policy Directorate, Commission of the European Communities, March 1989, 19–20.

46. Conclusions de l'avocat général M.G. Tesaure dans l'affaire C–202/88 REPUBLIQUE FRANCAISE contre COMMISSIONS DES COMMUNAUTÉS EUROPÉENNES, La Cour de Justice, 13 février 1990.

47. "European Telecommunicates: O What a Tangled Web we Weave," *The Economist* (October 28, 1989): 77. Note also "EC-Industry Politic: Sieg der Liberalen" (Victory of the Liberals), *Wirtschaftswoche* (November 23, 1990): 25–28 and "La Commission supérieure du service public demande une révision du contrat de plan entre l'État et La Poste," *Le Monde* (December 21, 1992): S1.

48. Note the profile of Brittan in the *New York Times* of May 8, 1991: "a European crusader for an open market" (p. D1).

49. "Europe's Computer Industry: The Planners Strike Back," *The Economist* (February 16, 1991): 57; and "EC-Industry Politic," 25–28.

50. "Planners Strike Back."

51. "Spare the Rod and Spoil the Child," *The Economist* (April 20, 1991): 64.

52. Ibid., 63.

8

The National and Corporate Strategies of International Standards: The Case of Telecommunication

Industry standards that control the quality and performance of a product have developed over half a millennium, but have attained strategic importance in the electronics and telecommunication industry only during the last forty years. In spite of the critical role standards have played in the penetration of new markets or in the defense of established ones, technical standards have remained an esoteric topic for specialists that, until recently, attracted little attention from most managers or senior government officials and none from the public at large. The worldwide deregulation of telecommunication and its convergence with computer technology created a new global information industry (telematics) that exhibited all the characteristics of a Schumpeterian "leading industry." Since, as Joseph A. Schumpeter recognized fifty years ago, leading industries not only dominate the economic growth of a nation but also determine its geopolitical significance, national governments have employed various aspects of industrial policies to help their national telematics champions obtain the global market share necessary for survival.[1]

In this new context international telecommunication standards have not only become a device to assure network interconnection, compatibility, and interoperability but a complex policy system to attain strategic enterprise objectives. As a consequence, the nature and role of government and corporate standards strategies have emerged as exciting topics that have drawn the attention of senior managers, politicians, and journalists.

It is the purpose of this chapter to demonstrate that common international standards, set by organizations in which carriers, manufacturers, and users are represented, can open telecommunication markets to the mutual advantage of customers and manufacturers, while nontariff trade barriers can be created by both proprietary standards and monopoly-driven national standards.[2] Moreover, we shall show that the continuing liberalization of national telecommunication systems will permit user interests to be reflected more effectively in international standards than in the proprietary standards set by dominant manufacturers.

Since the days of the medieval guilds, standards were supposed to protect the burgher against inferior products and, simultaneously, guard the producer against the "unfair" competition of low-priced, shoddy goods. If in the thirteenth and fourteenth centuries the size and consistency of bread and the purity of beer were clearly defined and these standards vigorously enforced by the guilds, the conformity of, say, automobile brakes or consumer electronics to safety standards are today tested by various national standard agencies. As a matter of fact the fourteenth-century German purity standards (*Reinheitsgebote*) for beer and sausages had become an EC trade issue in 1988. The requirement that beer could not contain any additives—organic impurities in the fourteenth century, chemicals in the twentieth century—had prevented foreign beer producers from penetrating the German market. The Dutch company Heineken perceived the German *Reinheitsgebot* as a nontariff trade barrier that violated the EC's basic constitution, the Treaty of Rome (1957). The European Court of Justice agreed with Heineken and ordered the FRG to cease excluding EC food imports (beer, sausages, cakes) that violated Germany's purity laws but met their home country's standards. This case illustrates perfectly the dual aspects of standards: on the one hand the *Reinheitsgebot* has provided the German consumer with excellent, unadulterated beer; on the other hand it has increased entry costs and protected local producers from foreign competition.

We shall explore below the protectionist and competition-enhancing aspects of standards, but shall merely mention now that libertarians, such as Milton Friedman, object to all forms of quality standards and professional licensing and claim that the free market would protect the consumer from inferior consumer goods, ill-trained physicians, and incompetent airline pilots. The proponents of standards assert that the market system would work too slowly to achieve these results.

Throughout the world, standard-setting organizations have been formed jointly by consumers and producers to determine and monitor industry-wide norms, while government procurement offices have, more or less, unilaterally, set minimum standards for acquiring goods and services. Standards have played a particularly important role in Germany, and the major German standards organizations DIN (Deutsches Institut für Normung) and TÜV (Technischer Überwachungsverein) have been perceived as guaranteeing the quality of German products. Especially in the electronics and machine tool industries, the high quality required by standards has helped German enterprises penetrate foreign markets, reduce the price elasticity of their products, and protect their own domestic position. German standards philosophy, therefore, has been playing a special role in the EC's standards harmonization effort, as can be seen by EC president Jacques Delors' remarks: "History has shown: the DIN-Norm stands for German quality and manufacture and is therefore, an asset in the export business. I hope that the statement 'made in the European Community' will attain a similar significance."[3]

Among products that conform to industrial standards, we must distinguish between those that, like automobile brakes, perform their mission independently, and those that are linked to each other in a "network," where the product's utility increases with the increase in the number of users. Modern telecommunication networks generate "network externalities" not only by linking users, but also by linking different user equipment. In order to gain positive network externalities telecommunication networks require, therefore, not only devices that do not impair network performance but also compatible equipment and subnetworks provided by different vendors. (We shall discuss the compatibility below, but define it provisionally as the *ex ante* design—linkage of two systems without further technological contrivance.)[4] National and international standards organizations have attempted to develop telecommunication standards that will provide positive network externalities for the consumer and increasing returns to the manufacturers. To the extent, however, that international consensus standards replace or are meant to replace in many cases de facto standards of a dominant manufacturer, the emergence of international (or industry consensus) standards reduce the competitive advantage for some manufacturers or countries.

The role of standards as a nontariff barrier to international trade and market entry was already recognized during the 1970s "Tokyo-round" negotiations that led to new GATT (General Agreement on Tariffs and Trade) standards codes; however, the convergence of the market-driven computer industry with its proprietary standards and the regulated monopolistic telecommunication industry with its mandatory national and international norms, turned the entire topic of national and international standards into a contentious issue during the 1980s and 1990s. Moreover, the U.S. government through its MAFF (Market Access Fact Finding) talks, and the EC through its infrastructure harmonization strategy for the 1992 single market, made telecom standards issues of national policy. Periodic meetings of international telecommunication union member countries and GATT conferences have elevated telecommunication standards into components of national trade policies that expose conflicting ideological and national interests. The recognition that telecommunication standards are one of the major nontariff trade barriers both within the EC and North America and also among the three major trading regions (the EC, East Asia, and North America), has given additional significance to the conflict between proprietary and international standards.

Our discussion of the role of international standards and the EC effort to "harmonize" telecommunication norms requires a familiarity with the international standards organizations in table 8.1.

Table 8.1
The Major Standards Organizations

International

CCITT	Comité Consultatif International Télégraphique et Téléphonique, Geneva. Standards organization of the ITU, the international organization of public network operators and post administrations. ITU is affiliated with the UN.
ISO	International Standards Organization, Geneva. Association of information technology industry manufacturers and users.
IEC	International Electronics Commission, Geneva. Association of global electronics industry.

European

CEN	Comité Européenne de Normalisation, Brussels. European standards organization comprised of representatives from national standards organizations.
CENELEC	Comité Européenne de Normalisation Electrotechnique, Brussels. Independent association of eighteen European electronic standards organizations; all EC and EFTA countries represented.
ECMA	European Computer Manufacturers Association, Geneva.
ETSI	European Telecommunication Standards Institute. Proposed by the EC (Green Paper, 1987), established July 1988 in Sophia Antipolis, France. Members comprise public network operators, national telecom administrations, manufacturers, users, research institutes in CEPT (Conférence Européenne des Administrations des Postes et Télécommunication) countries.
SPAG	Standard Promotion Application Group, Brussels. Association of European manufacturers.

National (Key Organizations)

ANSI	American National Standards Institute, New York
COS	Corporation for Open Systems. Association of about sixty North American enterprises to develop open, vendor-neutral standards in line with OSI - CCITT recommendations. Also includes leading European IT firms with American subsidiaries.
DIN	Deutsches Institut für Normung, Berlin. German standard-setting organization of manufacturers, users, and professional associations.

IEEE   Institute of Electrical and Electronic Engineers, Washington, D.C.

NBS/NIST   National Bureau of Standards, Washington, D.C. Government agency. Congress changed name of NBS to National Institute of Standards and Technology (NIST) in 1988.

During the days of AT&T Bell System monopoly, international telecommunication standards had no political or economic significance for the U.S. trade policy establishment although AT&T representatives were members of all important international standards agencies. American telecommunication deregulation during the 1970s and 1980s, however, had the consequence of opening U.S. markets to foreign competition while domestic manufacturers of network and terminal equipment continued to have difficulties selling telephone equipment in Canada, Europe, and Japan.[5] American efforts, spearheaded by the U.S. Department of Commerce (DOC), to improve the export opportunities for American telecommunication manufacturers took the form of pressuring our allies into imitating U.S. deregulation. American manufacturers objected particularly to tight European "access standards" that governed the connection of customer premises equipment (CPE) to the public network, and the United States demanded, therefore, the quick liberalization of the PTTs' procurement and performance standards.

The significant differences between the sociopolitical environment of U.S. and European telecommunication have been ignored by both DOC officials and American managers; both have viewed increasingly the continental telecommunication monopolies (the PTTs) and in particular the German Post and Telephone Administration (Deutsche Bundespost or DBP), as mercantilistic enemies of free trade. The European PTTs have undoubtedly exemplified a monopolistic-mercantilistic tradition that assigned to the state the administration of the infrastructure—post, telecom, public transportation—characterized by a natural monopoly and by monopsonistic carrier-supplier relationships. Over the past twenty years, however, key personalities in European industry, government, and universities have recognized the need for far-reaching liberalization in the telecom industry, in order to remain competitive with Japan and North America.

The popularity of the PTTs among the general public, as well as the powerful postal unions' vehement support for the status quo, forced liberalization advocates to move carefully and slowly in order to retain the support of key "liberal" union officials, Social Democratic politicians, and the handful of deregulation advocates in the PTT ministries. This process was managed most effectively in West Germany, where two sequential government-appointed telecom reform committees, under the skillful leadership of Eberhard Witte, steered the liberalization process over a fifteen-year period to its successful conclusion in 1990. The German reform advocates had to overcome both a popular five hundred-year-old PTT and the strong five hundred thousand-member European postal union; as a consequence, the significant liberalization moves that were made by the liberal post-minister Schwarz-Schilling over the past eight years were never recognized by Anglo-American observers. The perception of the "fortress on the Rhine" prevailed while in reality Europe has experienced, over the past fifteen years, a slow but steady liberalization. This process will be culminating in a continental market by or before 1995 in which only basic telephone services will continue to be regulated in each country, quite similar to the basic telephone monopoly retained by the Bell operating companies. This stage was already attained in Germany by July 1989 as a consequence of the German telecommunication reform legislation of April 1989 (see chapter 3).[6]

During 1989–90 EC directives implemented 1987 telecom proposals (the EC Green Paper) and deregulated leased-line, private networks and terminal equipment; even the PTT procurement procedures were exposed to greater competition, with additional liberalization planned originally for 1992, but implemented already in January 1990. The emergence, under European commission guidance, of a standardized, digital voice-data network plays a crucial role in the geopolitics of telecommunication and European integration.[7]

The EC strategy to "harmonize" European telecommunication standards has met with considerable misgivings in Washington and among those American manufacturers that have relied on proprietary network architecture, the de facto standards for global segments of the information-technology industry dominated by these enterprises. The American telecommunication industry, however, has not spoken with one voice on the harmonization issues, and especially AT&T has expressed on several occasions its support of international standardization efforts in general, and the ISO-CCITT efforts to develop common, open standards in particular.[8]

ISDN, THE EC'S COMMON INFRASTRUCTURE: FROM CONCEPT TO IMPLEMENTATION

The convergence of microprocessor-driven computer and telecommunication technologies has created a demand for networks that could simultaneously transmit voice and data traffic to multipurpose terminals in factories, homes, and offices. The communication needs of an international economy, and in particular the emergence of a global information society, require the adoption of worldwide standards and communication protocols for such voice-data networks. Accordingly, virtually every public carrier has been developing experimental digital networks that could transmit voice-data communication and integrate various special services, such as telex, teletex, datanets, telefax, and videotext, into one telecommunication system. The EC and the major European PTTs have agreed on a promising system for which international standards exist already: the Integrated Services Digital Network (ISDN). ISDN has been an important strategic concept that has attracted ardent advocates and vociferous critics in the United States and Europe. Not all critical and defending statements have been accurate, and some that were reasonable in 1985 or even 1988 are no longer valid in 1992. Moreover, many prestigious analyses of the monopolistic implications of ISDN turned out to be quite wrong by 1992, and were entirely unfounded even in 1985.[9] A brief history of the ISDN's metamorphosis from a concept (or a "vision," as Schumpeter might have put it) to an operating network is, therefore, in order.

The by now proverbial convergence of telecommunication and computer technology destroyed the stable, established telephone system and created an opportunity for the rapid implementation of already existing or just emerging technologies. The most significant consequences during the early 1980s were:

- Increasing digitization of the old analog networks, especially in Japan and France, to accommodate higher traffic at greater speed and lower cost.
- Merging of mainframe-centered local area networks with publicly switched telephone nets.
- Rapid emergence of value-added telecommunication services and networks.
- Increasing demand for open, vendor-neutral information systems. This led to the establishment of private networks by large manufacturers such as GM or Boeing; these corporate communication systems were to connect, ultimately, manufacturing plants, vendors, customers, and corporate headquarters throughout the world.
- Integration of the multiple public telephone networks that transmitted separately voice, data (circuit and pocket-switched), text (telex), and images.
- Adoption of telecommunication networks to the increasingly specialized and diverse demands of business users.

The growing importance of these six technological developments created the vision of a single digital network that could transmit all telecommunication services and could be connected to a host of terminal equipment at the user's office or home outlet with a single plug. The concept of a universal digital network, subsequently named ISDN, emerged in the Bell Labs during the 1970s, but almost immediately gained considerable attention in France, Great Britain, and Germany.[10] Especially two senior DBP civil servants, J. P. Arnold and Theodor Irmer (Arnold is today a telecom consultant and Irmer is managing director of CCITT), perceived the strategic implications of an integrated network that could deliver data and voice.

ISDN had developed from concept to strategy. The CEPT (European

Conference of Postal and Telecommunication Administrations) as well as the ITU adopted the objective of a global ISDN. In order to accomplish it, three steps had to be taken:

1. Digital networks had to replace or supplement the existing analog voice networks.
2. Digital switching equipment and software had to be developed.
3. International standards had to be developed to permit the emergence of a worldwide data-voice network that was needed especially by large corporate users.

Development and installation of digital transmission and digital switches proceeded slowly but relatively steadily during the 1975–85 period, although only France and Japan committed themselves to a full and rapid replacement of the old analog voice system with a digital network. The major difficulty comprised the necessary development of common standards for network interfaces and software that would permit voice, data, text, and fixed images to be delivered via a standardized plug to telephones, computers, fax machines, telex, and other customer premises equipment.

Most European network operators, AT&T, Northern Telecom, and various Bell operating companies introduced ISDNs during the mid- and late 1980s in the form of pilot projects, with full operations beginning in 1989–92.

The United Kingdom had been playing a leading role in digital-voice network research, and already introduced during 1984–85 a limited ISDN net on a pilot project basis. The Deutsche Bundespost had been testing an ISDN pilot project during 1986 and had the first phase of a narrowband overlay ISDN system in operation by late 1988.[11] (The ISDN "overlay net" consists of the existing telephone analog network's copper wire cables with software and electronic equipment added to permit delivery of digital services.) In the view of Anglo-American observers of European telecommunication policy, it has been Germany and its PTT, Deutsche Bundespost (DBP), that has aggressively promoted ISDN as a new telecommunication infrastructure for both Germany and Europe. Key executives in the DBP may have seen most clearly the strategic implication of an integrated digital network during the late 1970s, and they developed, therefore, an ambitious investment strategy that was to leap-frog the French lead in digital technology and provide Germany with a sophisticated telecommunication system second to none.[12] (See Figure 8.1.)

The DBP's modernization program was already by 1990 ahead of schedule. By early 1991 Germany had the most ISDN subscribers in Europe, with 10,000 connections in use out of 20,000 available basic-rate ISDN lines (basic-rate lines consist of two transmission and one signaling wire, or 2 B + D in ISDN lingo) and 800 primary rate (23B + D) ISDN connec-

Figure 8.1
DBP Strategy for Long-Run Network Integration

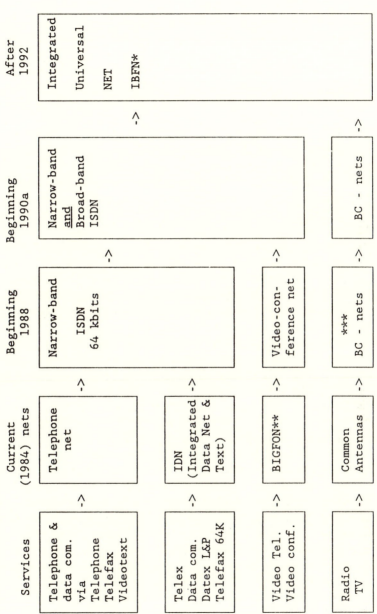

Services	Current (1984) nets	Beginning 1988	Beginning 1990a	After 1992
Telephone & data com. via Telephone Telefax Videotext →	Telephone net →	Narrow-band ISDN 64 kbits →	Narrow-band and Broad-band ISDN →	Integrated Universal NET IBFN*
Telex Data com. Datex L&P Telefax 64K →	IDN (Integrated Data Net & Text) →			
Video Tel. Video conf. →	BIGFON** →	Video-con-ference net →		
Radio TV →	Common Antennas →	*** BC - nets →	BC - nets →	

Figure 8.1 (continued)

Source: Siemens, *Telekommunikation für die BRD*, n.d.; and DBP, *Konzept der Deutschen Bundespost*, 1984.

*Integrated Broad-band Fernmelde (Telecom) Net

**German acronym for *Integrated Broad-band Glass-Fiber Fernmeldeortsnetz* (Local TeleComnet)

***Broad-band Coupling

[a]Broad-band ISDN nets were introduced on a preliminary basis in 1989.

tions in use out of 2,227, according to DBP Telekom. Telekom also states that it has been unable to keep up with demand for primary-rate connections, partly because its commitment to upgrade East Germany's telecom system has been an enormous drain on resources. The United Kingdom, however, is the country with the most primary-rate connections (over 50,000 channels by 1991). During the crucial 1980s, however, when ISDN had not yet gained full acceptance, it was France that made the greatest progress in establishing ISDN as a key component of its communication network. Thanks to heavy government investments in the 1970s, France has today the world's most modern telephone system, with over 80 percent of its entire network enjoying digital transmissions.[13] France Télécom, the telecommunication component of the French telecommunication administration, has been able, therefore, to introduce ISDN as an integral part of its digital telecommunication system, while the DBP and the other European network operators (NOs) had to install ISDN as a temporary overlay net. The French and German PTTs have been playing a leading role in both developing the ISDN concept as the basis for a European communication system and in promoting the necessary standardization of European telecom equipment and networks. France Télécom may not have emphasized the strategic significance of ISDN as much as the DBP but it exploited its advantage of possessing Europe's most modern telephone system and operated a nationwide ISDN service by early 1990, although it may have fallen behind the United Kingdom and Germany since.[14] France Télécom, moreover, holds a competitive edge in VANs (value-added networks) and has been especially successful with its Minitel videotex.[15]

According to surveys taken in 1985 and 1986 by the DBP, by ITT's former German subsidiary SEL (now part of Alcatel), and by France Télécom in 1987, Italy, Norway, and Spain were scheduled to have by the end of 1989 an ISDN network in operation, while NYNEX and Bellsouth began to introduce an ISDN system in 1987. Japan's NTT introduced the narrow-band ISDN in 1988, primarily for fax networks, and has been working on providing a broad-band glass-fiber network by 2000, while AT&T together with the Conference of European Post and Telecommunication Authorities (CEPT) has been building an ISDN-compatible optical digital glass-fiber network under the Atlantic Ocean.

The development of a sophisticated European telecommunication industry that can hold its own against Japanese and North American competition requires the full integration and standardization of vendor-neutral digital communication nets and services. The CCITT (Comité Consultatif International Télégraphique et Téléphonique), the international standardization forum of 161 telecommunication authorities, and the CEPT have adopted compatible ISDN standards, and the European Community has been striving to make the CCITT-CEPT standards mandatory for its members. The EC also had been urging *all* European countries to introduce

ISDN by 1988 at least on a limited basis, and was generally successful in attaining compliance. The EC established a European Telecommunication Standards Institute (ETSI) in April 1988 to promote the necessary standardization more aggressively. With the exception of Denmark and Greece, all European countries had declared their intention to implement, on a limited basis, an ISDN by the end of 1988–89 that was to conform to CCITT-CEPT standards. By 1991 several countries, such as France and Germany, were ahead of schedule, and had already begun to introduce broad-band ISDN (also called BISDN) "highways" among major cities; others were lagging behind, but the introduction of European ISDN standards in June 1990 and the appearance of sophisticated ISDN terminal equipment seem to have encouraged the stragglers to catch up; by December 1992 Europe (EC and EFTA) will have come close to achieving the common telecom infrastructure sought by the EC. In a memorandum of understanding, the members of the EC and EFTA agreed in April 1991 to begin the installation of a pan-European broadband net, METRAN (Managed European Transmission Network), that will establish glass-fiber based "electronic highways." The already existing broadband ISDN (B-ISDN) systems will be supplemented by the latest European network transmission technology, SDH (Synchronous Digital Hierarchy), to form the new, standardized network architecture METRAN that would bring about an almost revolutionary improvement in integrating various forms of data communication. (SDH offers the basis for the transport of data communications with different bitrates—a bit is a binary digit used to represent a signal or wave—and can transport asynchronous signals; asynchronous signals are not related to a specific frequency and provide a more flexible net usage than the existing plesichrome transmission mode in which all components must operate at the same frequency. Plesichrome transmission requires constant surveillance—add/drop multiplexing—and could not assure the compatibility between ISDN, B-ISDN, and METRAN systems the asychronous transmission technique (ATM) promises.)[16]

The establishment of global, or at least Europe-wide, digital voice-data systems would go far toward satisfying the North American multinationals' complaint over a fragmented European telecom network, and would simultaneously establish the necessary infrastructure for the purchase of sophisticated terminals (customer premises equipment) and value-added services the European and especially the German business community has wanted but has been prevented from purchasing by technological and regulatory obstacles.[17] Although the DBP has been lagging behind France Télécom in introducing digital network and switches, the German telecom industry, from the multinational Siemens to family-owned niche enterprises such as Hagennuck and ANT:, have committed themselves to the ISDN opportunities most enthusiastically and seem to be ahead of European and even global competitors in applied ISDN research and product introduction. Siemens' ISDN-capable PBX "High Com" is particularly noteworthy in this context and may have played a significant role in the joint Siemens-IBM operation of ROLM. The family-owned, medium-sized German telecom equipment companies have been successful during the past two years in bringing sophisticated ISDN telephones on the market, at reasonable prices, making ISDN an attractive service choice. Although many of the features of ISDN telephones, such as storage, call forwarding, call back, and programmed numbers, are available in North America without ISDN, these features have been associated with ISDN in Europe, especially Germany, and generated in 1991–92 an increased residential demand for ISDN equipment and service.

The enormous growth potential of a common telecom infrastructure has been emphasized by the EC.[18] The European information systems manufacturers, and also many North Americans, see in a European ISDN network an enormous opportunity to sell sophisticated terminal equipment and value-added services to a rapidly growing office equipment market. A telecommunication system that can connect equipment and software from many vendors will not only enable users to buy various services and CPEs from different manufacturers, it would also provide strong competition for IBM's proprietary SNA (systems network architecture) networks.[19] IBM holds today an approximately two-thirds share of the European mainframe and 20 percent of the PC market; the IBM-SNA network normally links IBM PCs and other office-terminal equipment to an IBM central computer. European and American telecommunication-computer manufacturers have found it difficult to sell specialized equipment or services to a potential customer who is already locked into a SNA net; moreover, as noted, political forces in Europe opposed to deregulation held up the specter of a private (i.e., IBM) monopoly replacing the national PTTs' monopoly as an argument for maintaining the status quo. Although IBM has lost some of its dominant European market position during the last five years, it has remained the strawman used by defenders of the status quo to oppose liberalization, even though IBM Europe has repeatedly acknowledged its commitment to open systems during 1991.

OPEN SYSTEMS AND COMMON STANDARDS

The competitive advantage of the proprietary SNA combined with IBM's market dominance during the early 1980s prompted the European Computer Manufacturers Association (ECMA) to adopt an "open convention" in 1984 that committed its members to "open communication" and "open standards." "Open communication" would enable everyone to communicate over equipment produced by diverse manufacturers, while "open standards" defined clearly the machine-network interfaces and described compliance with international norms. The EC's famous Green Paper on telecommunication (1987) formalized the rejection of proprietary networks by proposing adherence to "open network provisions" (ONP) of all European telecommunication systems. ONP requires that networks must be open to third parties, define technical interfaces and usage definitions clearly, and state principles that govern tariffs. The EC's ONP will be mandatory by December 1992 and is already operational in France and Germany. As a matter of fact, the French decree Resaux Télématiques Ouverts Aux tiers (1985) and Germany's Witte committee recommendation on open networks (1987) predated the EC's ONP recommendations. The ISDN is compatible with both the ECMA's open convention and the ONP and also conforms to the intricate international "Open Standard Interconnection" norms that clearly define the interfaces among different systems and have been developed by the International Standards Organization in accordance with CCITT and ECMA recommendations. ("Interfaces" connect two different communication systems. The simplest interface is a plug and cable that connect two devices.)

North American manufacturers also have been frustrated by incompatible equipment and the restrictive aspects of IBM's twelve-year-old SNA. When GM embarked on its visionary project to link all its terminals into a giant private telecommunication network, it developed first an "open standard" manufacturing automation protocol (MAP). General Motor's MAP and Boeing's private network TOP (technical and office protocol), were designed to conform to the ISO's open system convention standards (OSI) and to assure full compatibility among networks and terminal equipment supplied by different vendors.[20] GM demonstrated in its MAP/TOP Enterprise Network Event '88 how its automated production facility could be served by over two hundred computer and peripheral equipment vendors.

MAP was designed from its inception to take advantage of ISDN technology, once the OSI-CITT standards became operational. By early 1989, GM had decided that enough progress had been made in the adoption of compatible international CCITT-ISDN standards to speed up the installation of ISDN products in its own networks. Boeing and General Motors had demonstrated and displayed once more in 1989 the effectiveness of vendor-neutral networks conforming to OSI standards at international information-technology exhibitions in Baltimore and Hannover, Germany. Networks that consisted of components supplied by virtually every major computer-telecommunication equipment manufacturer operated smoothly in jointly directing simulated manufacturing operations. In spite of the criticism directed at the slow development of the universal seven-level OSI protocol, the key to common international standards, MAP and TOP proved that sufficient global standards already existed to accomplish well-defined tasks. (Protocols are the computer languages in which terminal and switches talk to each other to set up calls and prevent loss of information.)[21] MAP, TOP, and similar systems by AT&T, GE, McDonnell Douglas, and NTT are compatible with ISDN and represent full acceptance of the European standards concept in order to develop a common, global telecommunication infrastructure.

Clearly American manufacturers who are major users of telecommunication-computer services consider OSI-CCITT standards as the only practical alternative to proprietary networks, such as the restrictive IBM-SNA net. The increasing emergence of specialized niche equipment for office or manufacturing networks makes it very desirable for information-technology users to be free to choose among the products of numerous suppliers.[22] For these very same reasons the ECMA along with UNICE, the association of EEC-EFTA industries, have been strong supporters of both a universal ISDN protocol and of OSI standards in general. Although the ISDN network has had the strong support of European suppliers and carriers, the absence until recently of common, operational ISDN standards kept most telecom suppliers from introducing ISDN-capable terminal equipment, such as small PBXs, telefax, sophisticated telephones, and workstations; on the other hand even where suppliers offered ISDN-capable equipment such as the PBXs sold by Siemens, Philips, and Alcatel, users were reluctant to adopt them since they did not know what modifications would have to be introduced once the common European ISDN standards were defined by the European Telecommunication Standards Institute (ETSI). Although all European and Japanese carriers and most North Americans adopted the CCITT's ISDN standards, the existing standards options have permitted differences to develop that still require gateways for ISDN traffic between countries and between private and public networks within a country that makes use of differing options. Uncertainties, therefore, discourage users from acquiring existing ISDN terminal equipment, and consequently the absence of positive network externalities further reduces demand; the insufficient demand in turn discourages suppliers from offering the variety of cost-effectively priced equipment. The introduction of firm ISDN standards by ETSI in June 1990 has changed the situation not only for Europe but also the United States since representatives of American telecom industry and networks have participated in the ETSI decisions as observers. By early 1992 the prevalence of common standards affected the supply of residential and business ISDN equipment and stimulated a much more lively demand for these products. The growth in ISDN-capable computer-telecom nets, in both Europe and North America, will further support the ISDN equipment market.

The conditions in the mobile telephone market are somewhat different from the ISDN equipment sector. While the ISDN concept and subsequent investment strategy can be considered to have been an engineering-driven innovation, the mobile telephone market, and especially the cellular mobile telephone, was a market-driven innovation. Thus, the PTTs, especially the DBP, emphasized investments in ISDN network transmission systems and switches, and failed to encourage the equipment manufacturer to develop attractively priced business or residential terminal ISDN equipment until the physical network was almost completed. The mobile telephone manufacturers, however, competing in a relatively open market in Britain, France, and Scandinavia, and since 1989 Germany, produced the reasonably priced products the market wanted. The existence of firm European standards, and the EC's commitment to introducing these standards in 1992, removed the uncertainty that has delayed the acceptance of ISDN equipment by users and discouraged manufacturers from introducing tempting products promptly. The market-broadening impact of firm international standards, is clearly demonstrated by the rapid growth of mobile telephone network since 1989–90.

The Case of the C and D Nets

During the late 1980s, in spite of the growth of national markets, manufacturers and users of mobile telephones were frustrated by the existence of different national standards in Europe that made mobile telephones useless as automobiles passed national borders. Manufacturers in turn were prevented from realizing economies of scale by Europe's fragmented mobile telephone market. Europe's potentially most attractive market for mobile telephones, West Germany, developed a particularly forbidding set of standards that isolated the German market from non-German cellular telephone manufacturers, but may also have reduced incentives for German electronics firms to penetrate foreign markets. The ranking of leading enterprises in the global and German market in table 8.2 illustrates this point.

The reasons for the exacting German standards (the size of a Manhattan telephone book) were twofold. The first reason was the heavy concentration of NATO forces that required the assignment of well over 50 percent of radio frequencies to the military. The DBP emphasized that the civilian German digital mobile telephone net (C-net) had to operate with far fewer available channels than any other European country. The second reason for Germany's formidable C-net was the tendency of the prereform DBP to overengineer telecommunication standards. In 1989, the C-net transmitted the call numbers over a separate digital channel, and determined, in real time, automatically the distance to the nearest transmission tower in order to "optimize channel allocation." The production costs of satisfying C-net standards discouraged most, but not all, global telecommunication enterprises from entering the German market. The European

Table 8.2
1988 Market Share of Leading Mobile Telephone Manufacturers Worldwide

Firm	Market Share in Percent (Rounded Off)
1. Motorola	14%
2. Nokia	14
3. NEC	12
4. Panasonic	9
5. Toshiba	8
6. Mitsubishi	8
7. Oki	6
8. Novatel	6
9. Ericsson	4
10. Uniden	3
11. Philips	3
12. Siemens	2
13. Others	11
	100%

Federal Republic of Germany

1. Siemens	45%
2. Philips	25
3. AEG	10
4. Motorola	10
5. Bosch	10
	100%

Source: Wirtschaftswoche (September 15, 1989); Nokia.

commission, CEPT, and ETSI have, in the meantime, agreed on the standards for the European D-net, that is creating a common European digital mobile telephone network that will ultimately replace national networks. (The gradual elimination of national networks will increase the availability of channels throughout Europe, and especially in Germany.) To increase competition, Great Britain will add two additional mobile telephone network operators by 1992. Germany chose a second, private D-net operator consortium in December 1989. Numerous multinational coalitions of major enterprises, including American BOCs, had been competing for this profitable opportunity.

The new European digital D-net is expected to connect about 10 million users by 1993, thus creating not only significant network externalities for all customers, but also an entirely new and large market for equipment manufacturers. Motorola, Nokia, and Sony are all reputed to enter the European market with new custom-tailored equipment. Increasing competition, not only in Germany but throughout Europe, should improve equipment and service as well as lower tariffs. The European consumer will undoubtedly benefit from these developments. The European manufacturers, especially those who have relied on national standards-generated niches, will be faced with overwhelming competition unless they align themselves with one of the global telecom giants. Cooperation between Finland's Nokia and AT&T as well as Sweden's Ericsson with GE has been reported (note that the EFTA countries are included in all EC efforts to create a common European telecom market/infrastructure). Many other alliances can be expected. In this case, the common "harmonized" digital GSM (Groupe Speciale Mobile) standard that created the D-net generated vigorous competition. The benefits of competition, lower prices, and greater choice were already emerging in 1990.

The Case Against Mandatory Standards

Ever since *The Economist*'s 1985 telecommunication survey viewed the installation of ISDN systems as a ploy by the Deutsche Bundespost and other mercantilistic PTTs to maintain their monopoly position, an influential group of American policy analysts in the Department of Commerce and in the universities have opposed a European ISDN infrastructure. Most of the American objections have been conveyed directly to senior DBP and EC government officials. Eli Noam's "Integrated Digital Networks: Questions on Cost and Worth" in the *International Herald Tribune* of May 20, 1986, represents an effective summary of the anti-ISDN position that has not changed over the years, and still reflects the U.S.-DOC view. (In the meantime Noam has changed his views on ISDN. We shall quote him, however, since he conveyed perfectly the views of ISDN critics.) Noam's 1986 position is still popular in 1992, especially in the United States. We shall briefly summarize:

1. ISDN consolidates global telecommunication into one standardized network at a time when the concept of a unified and monopolistic network is increasingly being questioned on economic and political grounds. In the United States the politics of divestiture have sacrificed economies of large size in favor of competition.

2. A coalition of European bureaucrats and equipment manufacturers supports ISDN as a means of invigorating a profitable but mature market through replacements. The ISDN concept is "supply-driven" and does not reflect industry needs.[23]

The wide-reaching industrial and political support for the establishment of a compatible, standardized European ISDN demonstrated that the notion of ISDN as a product of a "bureaucrat-equipment manufacturers complex" is simply untenable. Moreover, rapid technological change has made the old analog networks obsolete. Digitalization of the telephone nets, with optical and broad-band transmissions becoming state-of-the-art networks, has turned a supposedly "mature market" into a rapidly changing infrastructure requiring massive investment. Although installation of narrowband ISDN systems will not be completed until the mid–1990s, broad-band digital networks are already emerging in Japan, Europe, and North America. German post-minister Christian Schwarz-Schilling introduced the first stages of the preliminary broad-band net (German acronym VBN) to the public in February 1989 and promised a million-kilometer fiber optic broadband net by 1990, with the objective of having by 1995 the Integrated Universal Broad-Band Net (IBFN) cover Germany. The IBFN will not only integrate cable television with the voice-data-text-image of narrowband ISDN transmission, but also offer many new services, including twoway communication between television audience and sender; the television set will become a two-way communication device. All previous transmission systems will become obsolete immediately.

All major investment projects contain externalities, which frequently become noticeable only after many years. The EC-DBP strategy to combine the establishment of a digital network with the introduction of a standardized system that can carry voice, data, text, and, ultimately, moving images on one line, is a rational effort to gain the benefits of connectability and universality externalities and simultaneously limit the capital investment required. We must, today, recognize the long-run EC strategy that already has produced Europe-wide liberalization in value-added services and terminal equipment markets and drives further deregulation as the necessary broad political consensus is established in each country. The necessity of such a consensus in support of deregulation cannot be overestimated, nor the role the EC has been playing in providing guidelines that strengthen the position of the deregulators throughout Europe.

Since publishing the Green Paper, the EC has recommended the liberalization of government procurement in telecommunication and, subsequently, in additional areas such as energy and transport. We have already mentioned in a different context the EC's effort to liberalize government procurement. We must recognize now that the EC's effort to open government procurement to all European telecom enterprises was an integral part of its strategy to create a *European* telecom infrastructure and industry. Europe-wide procurement, European ISDN standards, and "harmonized" European telecommunication networks are all parts of one strategy. Initially, the EC urged only that at least small proportions of government procurement be opened to all qualified suppliers regardless of nationality; the success of project 1992 prompted the EC commission suddenly to revise its gradual approach. The council of ministers decreed on February 22, 1990 that henceforth all community supplies must be procured on a com-petitive basis. A "Buy-Europe" clause requires non-EC members to underbid the lowest EC competitor by more than 3 percent in order to obtain a government contract. The EC quickly countered immediate American objections by emphasizing that the prevailing Buy-America Act gives U.S. companies a 6 percent advantage over their foreign competitors.[24]

France, in the American perception, is less strongly identified as choosing ISDN as a strategy to create a European telecommunication infrastructure. In fact, however, the French government, especially under the leadership of the former post and telecommunication minister Gérard Longuét, has made greater strides in providing ISDN services for its customers than any other country. It has been playing a significant role in the "group of four" (France, Germany, Great Britain, and Italy) ISDN working committee in generating a convergence of standards that laid the basis for further work by ETSI during 1989 and 1990.[25] (A Paris–Mulhouse–Karlsruhe–Bonn optical ISDN link was completed in 1989.[26]) The ETSI leadership has been confident that by 1992 digital mobile telephone standards will be ISDN-compatible.[27] France's success in installing ISDN services has further strengthened the pressure to establish quickly firm, optionless telecommunication standards for cordless telephones and give greater authority to the European standards organizations CEN/CENELEC (Comité Européen de Normalisation/Comité Européen de Normalisation Electro-Technique) and especially to the European Telecommunication Standards Institute (ETSI).

U.S. TRADE POLICY AND INTERNATIONAL STANDARDS

Official American trade policy views de facto international telecommunication standards as protectionist devices that bar American enterprises from access to foreign markets. The fact that OSI-CCITT standard recommendations have been developed with the participation of U.S. industry representatives has been widely ignored. In particular, EC efforts to harmonize telecommunication standards, and Japan's policy to adhere, in principle, to ISO-CCITT recommendations have been seen as a threat to American interests. One mini-case and one congressional bill will illustrate this point.

The IVAN Case

During 1987–88, IBM attempted to sell international value-added networks (IVANs) in Japan; its IVANs were governed by proprietary protocols that not only failed to conform to international norms but also precluded interconnection with networks that adhered to the CCITT's X.75 standards. Japan's post-ministry had committed itself to adhere to the ISO-CITT recommended open network architecture (ONA) whose nonproprietary interface standards promote third-party access and full use of underlying (public) network facilities. ONA is clearly designed to encourage service competition, and the Japanese ministry considered its policy of requiring IVAN providers to conform to CCITT standards as "establishing a level playing field."

IBM, however, considered the exclusion of proprietary networks as a discriminatory trade barrier. The Department of Commerce (DOC) accepted completely the IBM position and vigorously objected to Japan's implementation of the CCITT recommendations. Japan capitulated completely and adopted the U.S. position. Under Secretary for International Trade A. Moore's letter to Yusai Okuyama, vice minister of post and telecommunications (MPT), illustrates this point:

I am pleased that the Government of Japan has decided to allow firms' international value-added network services in Japan using *proprietary protocols*. It is important to note that decisions on interconnection will be made through negotiations *between private parties on the basis of commercial considerations*, which will be fully respected by MPT. This approach is consistent with the understanding reflected in the exchange of letters between Under Secretary Smart and Vice Minister Sawoda on March 10, 1987. (emphasis added)

In accordance with U.S. demands, Japan now requires merely that "International Special-Type Service providers who use proprietary protocols for network interconnection shall submit an operating agreement to the MPT which states their intention to have available *technical capabilities* to secure interconnection with other IVAN providers."[28] The technical capabilities can be satisfied by adopting CCITT recommended X.75 protocol or by an

Operating agreement between the two parties using proprietary protocols for interconnection with other IVAN providers. . . . detailed technical specifications required for interconnection will be *disclosed among negotiating parties*. . . . The operating agreement shall include a statement of intention to negotiate for network interconnection with other IVAN providers upon request. Details on specifications and functional information will be made available *only* to those service providers concerned. Decisions on interconnection will be based *on negotiations between private parties*. In these negotiations commercial considerations including but not limited to cost, confidentiality, security of the network, and points of interconnection, will be fully respected, while unreasonable discrimination will not be permitted.[29]

The above quotes provide an excellent presentation of the American position on mandatory international standards. This position is not as clearly revealed in U.S. negotiations with the EC, since the Brussels technocrats are much less malleable than their Japanese, or for that matter

German, colleagues. The fact that the EC, France, and Germany have been running trade deficits with the United States in the telecommunication sector has also deprived the United States of the leverage it has had vis-à-vis the Japanese. The IVAN case, however, has attracted considerable attention in Europe.

The "NIST" Act

U.S. standards policy, or perhaps more appropriately congressional standards strategy, is forcefully expressed in the National Institute of Standards and Technology (NIST) Authorization Act of 1988, an undisguised effort to inject industrial policy concerns into the standard-setting process.[30] The NIST legislation explicitly advocated providing public and private sector funds to countries that adopted standards that were compatible with those in use in the United States. Moreover the explicit purpose of this legislation that converted the old National Institute of Standards into a more policy-conscious instrument was the strengthening of U.S. enterprises' ability to penetrate foreign markets.

The U.S. position on standards has been clearly revealed by the IVAN case and NIST Act and must be considered when we discuss further U.S.-EC controversies on nontariff barriers. The trade policy considerations assigned to NIST make it very difficult to sympathize with U.S. efforts during the fall and winter of 1989 to become a member of the European standards organizations CEN-CENELEC and ETSI.

American telecommunication trade policy, as determined by the DOC, the U.S. Trade Representative's office (USTR), Congress, and the lobbies for the dominant information-technology enterprises can be epitomized by its "level playing field" rhetoric. In this view, free-trading America provides easy access to foreign manufacturers, while U.S. enterprises are prevented by protectionist devices such as standards to export their products. While the huge American trade deficit is a testimony to the accessibility of the American market, not all sectors of the American economy are easily accessible, nor is the trade deficit entirely, or even largely, due to trade barriers. Implicit in the American position is the belief that, if U.S.-style deregulation worked in America it ought to be successful in Europe as well. In particular, established national or emerging European standards that were not easily met by U.S. equipment manufacturers have been considered to be, ipso facto, protectionist devices that prevent American market access. There seems to be little realization in government and industry circles that decades of AT&T/Bell System dominance have helped to establish de facto American industry standards that have made foreign penetration of the U.S. telecom market difficult. The inability, for instance, of ITT to adapt its European-made central office (CO) switch SL12 to Bell requirements during the early 1980s is a testimony to the obstacles established Bell System standards create for the sale of non-American-made equipment in spite of deregulation and divestiture.

SUMMARY AND CONCLUSION: THE CONSEQUENCES OF THE ISDN STRATEGY

It is probably a good indication of the perseverance of the Europeans that they have not been willing to accept that the United States *is* the free trading country par excellence. Along with perceptions of American protectionism in various sectors, the fear of a possible IBM or AT&T (or NEC) dominance of the European information-telecommunication market was evident in the EC throughout the mid–1980s. The prospect of the multinationals' private telecommunication monopoly replacing the government monopoly may have been a specter created by the postal (telecom) unions in their drive to prevent liberalization. In Germany, between the submission of the recommendations of the telecom (Witte) commission in 1987 and the adoption of the government reform legislation in 1989, the postal union constantly presented the implementation of the DBP reform ("destruction of the DBP," in the postal workers' union rhetoric) as a means of establishing the monopoly of the foreign multinationals. Similar positions had been taken by the French unions, especially the CGT. There can be no doubt, however, that the DBP, France Télécom, and the EC technocrats had at one time viewed IBM's global dominance of the mainframe market, combined with its proprietary SNA standards, as an anticompetitive tool that could provide the infrastructure for a worldwide IBM dominance. Once an enterprise is committed to IBM's SNA system, the high investment costs make it difficult if not impossible to switch vendors.

European efforts to establish common (harmonized) standards and develop the vendor-neutral, open ISDN have been driven by both the fear of an IBM or IBM-NEC monopoly and the need to overcome the fragmentation of the European telecommunication industry. An ISDN-compatible open communication system, on the other hand, enables the user to buy equipment and systems from various manufacturers and combine them at will.[31] It should be added that IBM Europe—and especially IBM Germany—had committed itself to the open network architecture, and participated in the various open system forums in Europe. During the mid- and late 1980s, European public network operators (NOPs), as the former PTTs are currently called, and information-technology companies viewed IBM's commitment with skepticism, especially since the company continued to sell SNA-compatible services and products. By 1990–91, however, there was no doubt that IBM in both Europe and North America is not only committed to open system networking, but may be among the leaders selling open system networking equipment in the EC. IBM is still selling its proprietary systems, but so is Bull and many other European information-technology companies.[32] (This does not apply to telcos.)

Since 1989, AT&T and Northern Telecom have advertised aggressively their ISDN network capability in the *New York Times, Wall Street Journal,* and telecom journals such as *Telephony*. They have found that global ISDN standards provide new business opportunities in North America and Europe; as a matter of fact, North American companies with service and manufacturing capabilities in virtually every European country may benefit more from European standard harmonization than their leading European competitors such as Alcatel and Siemens, who are just overcoming their attachment to national versions of ISDN. (If ISDN is a common language, European and North American manufacturers spoke different ISDN dialects until ETSI merged these different dialects into a standardized language in 1990.)

Several early ISDN-compatible private systems that can adapt to an emerging European standard have been introduced in Central Europe since 1984, however, and Siemens alone had installed already by early 1980 one hundred thousand units of its PBX Hicom system in Germany; during 1988–91 Siemens Hicom sales in the United States were considerable. The installation of a common public European ISDN will enable private ISDN systems, such as Hicom, to communicate over the regular telephone line. There seems little doubt that a European, fully standardized ISDN will sharply reduce the competitiveness of proprietary networks and standards not only in Europe but also in the United States. This development should have the healthy result of laying to rest the specter of an IBM network monopoly in Europe. The fact that Alcatel, Ericcson, Siemens, AT&T, NT, NEC, and Fujitso are advertising their ISDN PBXs, CO switches, and networks worldwide should be ample evidence that global ISDN standards promote business opportunities and competition for both North American and European telecommunication enterprises. As a matter of fact while IBM in North America and Japan has still been fighting a rearguard action to protect proprietary networks, by 1990–92 IBM Europe had taken full advantage of the prevailing open system ISDN regime.

We have mentioned already in a previous chapter IBM's affiliation with BT and its support of the emerging BT-DBP Telekom-NTT joint venture. A new joint venture, TELECASH, between IBM Germany and DBP Telekom demonstrates again IBM's recent ability to establish close working relations with the entrepreneurial offsprings of the PTTs. TELECASH will build and operate an ISDN network to authorize electronic payments systems for all industries.[33] There are different attitudes between IBM Germany and IBM headquarters in Armonk, New York, concerning open systems. The role of subsidiaries with strong national identities, such as Honda U.S., Northern Telecom U.S., or IBM Germany will become a major management issue during the next decade.

Long-established relationships do not end overnight, especially not in Europe and Japan. It is to be expected that cozy relationships between Alcatel and France Télécom, and between Siemens and the DBP's new telecommunication organization Telekom will continue to linger on, particularly on lower management levels. Still the global strategies of Alcatel and Siemens require an end to protectionist requirements in Europe, East Asia, and the United States while IBM Europe adopts the characteristics of a European firm.[34]

The European telecom multinationals' opposition to mercantilistic regulations is certainly not always shared by smaller enterprises that have enjoyed privileged relations with their national PTTs for centuries, nor is there a lack of mercantilistic sentiments among senior PTT administrators in those countries that have retained their PTTs. Most important, the postal unions throughout Europe have been fighting any change that threatens to reduce their influence. Positions lost in Bonn, London, or Paris may be regained in Brussels. The irreversible movement toward a standardized, open European telecommunication market has begun, however, and the emerging national ISDN, B-ISDN, and METRAN networks should provide the vendor-neutral infrastructure that will make such a development possible. Since the BOCs, AT&T, GTE, DEC, and Northern Telecom will benefit from a vendor-neutral OSI network, North American interests are not threatened by ISDN or harmonized European standards. On the contrary American information-technology enterprises with manufacturing and R&D locations in Europe are the truly transborder European firms that stand to gain the most from a standardized European telecom infrastructure.

NOTES

1. Joseph A. Schumpeter, *Business Cycles*, vol. 1 (New York: McGraw-Hill, 1939). See also Richard R. Nelson's *High Technology Policies* (American Enterprise Institute, 1984) for an effective recent adaptation of Schumpeter's "leading industry" concept. Advocates of a *dirigiste* industrial trade policy have coined the term "strategic industry" to convey the same concept. Laura d'Andrea Tifson presents a thorough survey of the self-styled "New Trade Theory" in the *Siemens Review* (March–April 1988): 36–41.

2. "European telecommunication . . . is still dominated by a close relationship between very large usually state owned networks . . . and their respective national champion manufacturers. The relationship is generally protected and reinforced by *nationally based standards* set by the PTT and given political backing by the government." John Reissman, "A Business Agenda for the 1990's," paper delivered at The 2nd International Conference on Telecommunications Policy and Regulations, April 18–19, 1989, Amsterdam). One year later, however, surprising progress had been made in developing European standards and in loosening the relations between recognized PTTs and key suppliers.

3. Jacques Delors, quoted in *Binnenmarkt 1992* (Munich: Siemens, 1988), 2.

4. Paul A. David and Julie A. Bann, "The Economics of Gateway Technologies and Network Evolution," *Information Economics and Policy* 3/2 (1988).

5. The first significant deregulatory step that broke AT&T's dominance of the customer premises equipment (CPE) market was the Hush-A-Phone decision in 1956 (*Hush-A-Phone Corporation* v. *United States*, 238F. 2d 266, DC Cir. [1956]); we shall however arbitrarily declare the registration decision of 1975 as the beginning of the serious deregulation process in telecommunication (Proposals for New or Revised Classes of Interstate and Foreign MTS and WATS, 56, Fcc 2d 593, 1975; 75 FCC 2d 1316, 1976). This process had not yet been completed, as the recent attempts by the Bell regional holding companies to gain greater freedom demonstrate.

6. The deregulation trend in the EC has been epitomized by the German telecommunication reform process that began in 1975 and ended in April 1989.

7. A. L. Thimm, "Europe 1992. Opportunity or Threat for U.S. Business: The Case of Telecommunication," *California Management Review* (Winter 1989).

8. In this context note the speech of S. R. Willcoxon, president, Business Markets Group, AT&T, at the second International Conference on Telecommunication Policy and Regulations, Amsterdam, April 18–19, 1989: "Nations have realized that a common world-class telecommunication infrastructure is required; communications pathways carrying voice, data and images have become the coronary arteries of business all over the planet. When our businesses operated in more isolated markets, we all could tolerate isolated islands of communication. *Today, none of us can tolerate such isolation*" (*Proceedings*, 3; emphasis added). See also Scott W. Augerson, "ISDN's American Advance," *Siemens Comm* (March 1987): 7–9 on the global convergence of ISDN standards.

9. In a seminal survey, "The World on the Line," November 23, 1986, *The Economist* moved telecommunication policy from the technical journals to the front pages. Its otherwise excellent survey, however, completely misunderstood the subtle but effective liberalization strategy of DBP post-minister Schwarz-Schilling and painted him as an ardent monopolist. Based on this misjudgment, it also adopted the skeptical viewpoint on ISDN that OECD analyst Ann Hutcheson-Reid had been projecting in her famous but unpublished paper, "The Integrated Services Digital Network: A Presentation of Related Policy Issues." The Reid paper and *The Economist* "World on the Line" have, unfortunately, shaped Anglo-American policy makers' attitudes toward ISDN.

10. Although ISDN, or RNIS (réseau numérique a integration de service), was included in the long-run planning effort of the DGT, the effort to modernize the archaic French telecom system during the 1970s precluded any effort to popularize this concept in France. In spite of the actual progress made in introducing ISDN to France's digital network we find only during 1989 that this issue was presented to the public at large. See P. Gailhardis and J-P Termime, "Numéris: Le Réseau au Futur Simple," *France Telecom* (June 1989): 30.

11. By November 1991 the German ISDN net connected its twelve largest cities (including Berlin) with more than one-thousand connections in each location. By 1990, France, Germany, Italy, and the United Kingdom were able to connect their respective ISDN nets and open a European system. In February 1989, the DBP introduced its preliminary glass-fiber, broad-band network (VBN) to gain expe-

rience in establishing the network technologies for the twenty-first century. The VBN has been expanded to east Germany in 1991. (*ZPF* [April 21, 1989]). See Thomas Schnöring, and Une SZAFRAN," Telekommunikatives Aufschwung Ost," *WIK Newsletter* (December 1991): 5–8.

12. Note: *Konzept der Deutschen Bundes-Post zur weiteren Entwicklung der Fernmeldeinfrastruktur.* Bundesminister für das Post und Fernmeldewesen, Bonn 1984, and *Mittelfristiges Program für den Ausbau der technischen Kommunikationssysteme. Deutsche Bundespost, Bonn,* 1986.

13. *Selling Telecommunication Equipment and Services in France,* France Telecom International, December 1988. See also "Metran Challenges European ISDN," *Telephony* (May 13, 1991): 10, for comparison of European ISDN penetration. Metran-Managed European Transmission Network may become a special version of broad-band ISDN after 2000.

14. Gailhardis and Termime, "Numeris," 31. The authors emphasize that it took merely software modification to introduce ISDN to France's digital network. On the other hand, German Telekom officials believe that the special ISDN switches designed for Germany's ISDN network are superior to the older switches developed for France's pre-ISDN digital net.

15. France Télécom's most successful VAN innovation, the Minitel videotex, is currently sold in the United States, through Minitel USA to Bell Regional Holding Companies such as NYNEX and US West, as well as carriers like INFONET. Through an agreement with the DBP Minitel is also available to German telephone subscribers, although it does not meet CCITT videotex standards. In spite of having over 3 million users, it was still losing money until 1990.

16. *Green Book Summary: The Development of the Common Market for Telecommunication Services and Equipment,* (Brussels: Commission of the European Community, 1987), 1, and *passim.* See also Frank Stöckler, "Entwicklung der Nachrichtennetze," WIK, Bad Homef (November 1991).

17. *The Economist's* famous telecommunication survey, The World on the Line, provided the most detailed discussion of the multinationals' unhappiness with the fragmented European telecom system. Also note the speech of Siemens vice president Claus Kessler at the CeBIT Fair in Hannover, March 1986.

18. Note Herbert Ungerer, *Telecommunications in Europe* (Brussels: Commission of the European Communities, 1988).

19. General Motor's MAP and Boeing's TOP are the two best known vendor-neutral networks in the United States.

20. *International Standard 7498. Open Systems Interconnection-Basic Reference Model* (Geneva: ISO, 1984). An excellent nontechnical discussion of the ISO open system model is provided in W. Effelsberg and A. Fleishmann, *The ISO-Refernz Modell und Seine Sieben Schichten* (Heidelberg: IBM, European Center for Network Research, 1986).

21. "GM Proposes Demonstration of ISDN Interoperability," *Computerworld* (January 23, 1989): 10.

22. A good example of the role of niche suppliers is Toshiba's excellent advertising campaign to sell its telecopier in Europe. The Japanese already dominate the facsimile market in the United Kingdom, Germany, and Benelux countries and are now moving into related areas, stressing in each case the compatibility of their equipment with CCITT, CEPT, and national PTT standards.

23. See "New Lines for Old," *The Economist* (October 17, 1987): 34.

24. "E. C. Opens State Buying to Cross-Border Bidding," *Financial Times* (February 23, 1990); 1 and "E. C. Accuses U.S. over Telecoms Legislation," *Financial Times* (February 24, 1990), 26. See also H. Ungerer, *Current State of Progress on Implementation of the EC Green Paper* (Brussels: Commission of the European Communities, 1989), and *Proposal for a Council Directive on the Procurement Procedrues of Entities Operating in the Telecommunications Section* (Commission of the EC, 1989). These directives were implemented in January 1990.

25. Gérard Longuét, *Telecoms: La Conquête de Nouveaux Espaces*, 51–54; and "1' annexe 18: Le RMS dans les années, 90."

26. "France Opens Integrated Telecom Networks" *Financial Times* (November 30, 1988): 10; *France Telecom 1987* Annual Report, 17–19.

27. From an interview with D. Gagliardi, director of ETSI, June 1989. See also Jonathan Tarlin, "Beyond Technology: Market Forces Drive GSM," *Telephony* (Dec. 4, 1990): 22–24.

28. Appendix, p. 2, to Under Secretary Allen Moore's letter to Vice Minister of Post and Telecommunications Yusai Okuyama, November 21, 1988.

29. Ibid., 15; emphasis added.

30. "Bureau of Standards," *Congressional Quarterly Almanac 1988* (Washington, D.C.), 643.

31. R. R. Bruce, J. P. Arnold, and M. D. Director, "Telecommunications and Computer Standards: Interconnection, Compatibility, and Interoperability," ITC Telecommunication Forum, November 3–4, 1988, London, 14.

32. See "Spare the Rod and Spoil the Child," *The Economist* (April 20, 1991): 63.

33 .Gerhard von der Heyden and Volker Vosser, "TELECASH Communication Service GMBH," *Zeitschrift für Post und Telekommunikation* (March 27, 1991): 32–34.

34. In a July 1989 *Wirtschaftswoche* interview, Siemens CEO Kaske demanded that IBM Europe with its European manufacturing and R&D operation be recognized as a European company and included in EC-sponsored European R&D projects (e.g., JESSI). In return Kaske asked that the Siemens Corporation (U.S.) with its 80 percent national content in its products and large American R&D efforts also be recognized as an American enterprise and included in U.S. government-sponsored research. By 1990 IBM Europe had joined several European research projects, including JESSI.

Name Index

Subject Index

About the Author

ALFRED L. THIMM is a Professor of Management at the University of Vermont. Over the past twenty years he has frequently been affiliated as a visiting professor with the University of Munich, Institut fur Organization and the Wirtschaftsuniversitat, Institut fur Organization. An international consultant, he is the author of any scholarly articles and five books, including *Economists and Society* (with J. Finkelstein) 1973, ntscheidungstheorie (with E. witte) 1976, and *The False Promise of Codetermination* 1980.